FOLLOW A
WILD DOLPHIN

The Story of an
Extraordinary Friendship

HORACE DOBBS

SOUVENIR PRESS

To my own family of 'dolphins'

Contents

Parting day
Dies like the dolphin, whom each pang imbues
With a new colour as it gasps away
The last still loveliest, till — 'tis gone — and all is gray.

Byron: Childe Harold's Pilgrimage

1: A Frightening Experience

On 26 March 1972 Henry Crellin sat on the wall of his inflatable boat, put one hand on his facemask and rolled backwards into the water. He was an experienced diver, and dropping into the water in a harbour on the Isle of Man was no more alarming to him than the daily descent into a coalmine to a miner. As a diver he would of course be sensitive to his environment and alert to the hazards of working underwater. But when the blue-green waters closed over him that awareness was pushed to a subconscious level, and he bent his mind to the task in hand — laying a new mooring chain. He was deliberately over-weighted, and as he landed on the coarse sandy seabed clouds of silt stirred up by his arrival temporarily reduced the underwater visibility.

Henry Crellin was familiar with such conditions and immediately set about the task of joining the chain that was lowered down to him, to the ring in a block of concrete half-buried in the sand. He pulled the chain across the seabed. As it dragged across the sand more clouds of silt swirled into the water, giving it the eerie atmosphere of dense fog through which the weak spring sun glimmered as a deep orange disc. Henry Crellin knelt down and once again heaved on the end of the chain to bring it closer to the eye in the concrete block. As he did so he noticed that the light intensity was suddenly reduced. He looked up.

In a fraction of a second he registered a mental picture of a huge grey shape with a large dorsal fin moving silently past him just a few feet away. The open jaws were lined with sharp triangular teeth. At that instant his adrenal glands released a massive dose of adrenalin, his instinctive flight response took complete control of his body, and he hurtled to the surface as fast as his flailing fins could propel him. He came up alongside the inflatable and heaved himself, complete with aqualung and weightbelt, over the side, slithering into the bottom of the boat like a gigantic landed fish. His companions Dave Wood and Colin Bowen, who had been busy sorting out more chain and getting their diving gear ready, looked at him in amazement. Never before had they seen Henry make such a rapid, unexpected and acrobatic re-entry into the boat. His normal procedure was to hang on to the side in the water and hand in first his weightbelt, then his aqualung. Only when he had relieved himself of this 45 lbs of weight would he haul himself into the boat.

Before Henry could compose himself he blurted out "There's a bloody great shark down there."

Dave and Colin were incredulous. A big shark in the sheltered waters of Port St Mary was unheard of.

As men who had spent their working lives fishing and diving round the Isle of Man they knew of the huge basking sharks that were sometimes to be seen in the summer months trolling for plankton off shore. These large fish were usually seen just below the surface as they sieved the sea for the minute forms of animal and plant life that was their food. They had no teeth and were known to be harmless to divers. Other sharks were sometimes caught off the island, but these were invariably found well off shore in deep water.

"How big was it?" asked Dave as Henry slowly regained his composure.

"Bloody enormous," replied Henry.

Both of his companions knew that Henry was a quiet man, not given to exaggeration, and certainly not easily frightened. What could he have seen that had upset him so?

"Was it a seal?"

"No, it had a bloody great dorsal fin."

"Then it must have been a basking shark."

"But basking sharks never come into this harbour."

"They're not usually around at this time of the year either."

"Maybe not. But I'm telling you there's a bloody great shark down there."

They peered over the side into the water. As they did so a few yards away a large dark grey domed head broke the surface. On the top of the head was a hole about an inch in diameter.

There was a loud puff of exhaled air that sent a tiny cloud of spray into the air. The short puff was followed by the lower noise of air being sucked in. The two noises followed so closely one upon the other that there was no detectable pause between them, and in a fraction of a second the blowhole had closed and the head vanished once more. The entire sequence from the glistening dome breaking the surface to its disappearance took no more than three seconds.

As the head submerged the three divers caught a glimpse of a large black dorsal fin. It cut briefly and silently into the air before following the head back into the water. Although both head and the fin were large they left barely a ripple.

But that brief appearance on the surface of the sea resolved the question of the frightening creature's identity.

"It's a bloody dolphin."

"Well it looked like a shark down there."

As if to confirm their identification, the dolphin surfaced again a few moments later, made its characteristic puff, and descended once more.

Once he realised that the dark dorsal fin he had seen belonged to a dolphin, Henry Crellin's heart rate slowed down. He even managed to smile when his two partners burst into uncontrollable laughter. Well, it was an easy mistake to make in the underwater half-light. On the surface the dolphin looked large. Underwater it would appear even larger — as all underwater objects do to divers. However, he was the senior diver of the party and he decided to bring the merriment to an end.

"When you two have finished laughing you can get in the water and finish the job."

So after a serious debate on the prospects for their survival,

Colin Bowen and Dave Wood accordingly pulled their aqualung cylinders on to their backs and tightened the harnesses. Sitting on opposite sides of the inflatable they rolled backwards simultaneously, in spite of their recent laughter, a little apprehensive of what might happen in the next few seconds. The familiar swirl of bubbles hurried to the surface and the two divers hung in the green water looking at one another. They each turned to see what was behind them.

The mental state of the two divers was completely different from that of Henry when he had entered the water for the first time that day. Now all of their senses were alert and ready to register any strange happenings, and their nerves were geared to take considered defensive action — not uncontrolled flight. However, no such action was needed for there was no sign of the dolphin.

Colin and Dave exchanged the OK signal — the thumb and forefinger touching tip to tip and forming an "O" shape. Then they allowed themselves to drift slowly towards the seabed. The underwater visibility was good, about 30 feet, and the silt stirred up by Henry Crellin's earlier activities had settled. The two divers spotted the chain and the mooring block and, with their hearts still beating a little faster than normal, they peered into the limits of their horizons. They could not see anything unusual, so Dave picked up the end of the chain and started to pull it towards the block. Then he looked up and as he did so the dolphin appeared slowly out of the mists of the limit of visibility. Dave's heart rate increased.

The dolphin approached slowly and seemed to be taking a kindly interest in what was going on. Dave sensed no aggressive intent and watched as it slowly circled him. He could not help but admire the graceful and easy way the dolphin moved through the water. Very soon he relaxed completely and decided to get on with the job. He unscrewed the pin on the shackle and hooked it through the ring in the top of the concrete block. He pulled the length of new chain across the sandy seabed and attached the last link to the shackle before inserting the pin and screwing it tightly home with a marlin spike. As he did so the dolphin approached even closer and stopped with its curious smiling beak just a few inches away. When the shackle was fastened it swam off and was gone in a second, with two sharp upward beats of its tail fluke. Dave felt no turbulence from its flashing tail.

Dave continued with his job and pulled the chain over the bottom towards the next block. The dolphin seemed to become excited at this activity and appeared and disappeared from view several times. Colin helped Dave with the task and any thought of danger slipped from their minds. They were both after all seafaring men and to sailors through the ages the sight of dolphins round a ship has never been a threat, but, according to traditional belief, a sign of good fortune.

This belief indeed goes back at least as far as the ancient Greeks and Minoans, who seem not only to have held the dolphin in a benevolent relationship with man, but attributed to it a peculiarly sacred relationship with the Gods. Homer tells for instance how Apollo disguised himself as a dolphin and led a Minoan ship to found the Shrine at Delphi, to which it gave its name and which for a thousand years was one of the greatest religious and cultural centres in the world. And the history of the sea ever since has been rich in legends about the benevolence of these mysterious sea creatures.

Yet the incident off the Isle of Man was more extraordinary than perhaps even the three divers knew. For the traditional lore about dolphins almost always involves them accompanying ships at sea. A school of wild dolphins will not play around a stationary boat, as they will when it is on the move; and they keep well clear of submerged divers.

This the descendants of those ancient Greeks discovered, when in the early days of deep sea diving the sponge fishers in their copper helmets — 'coppernobs' as they were known — and lead-soled boots began to work in deeper and deeper water along the coasts of Greece. Trailing their hoses behind them, at the mercy of the dreaded 'bends', equipment failure and the unpredictable sharks, theirs was a hard and hazardous living.

Dolphins often frolicked around the fishing boats when they were on their way to the sponge grounds, and their presence invariably had an uplifting effect on the crew. It was a good omen — for one thing, the sponge gatherers knew that sharks and dolphins are seldom seen together, and that when dolphins appear sharks disappear, so a sponge boat in the company of dolphins was a happy boat. The crews were able to see the dolphins at very close quarters, when they surfaced alongside to breathe, and often a school would stay close to a vessel for a long journey. However, once the boats stopped and the divers prepared themselves for their work, the dolphins moved away. They would not come near the boats when they were stationary.

When working underwater a diver would sometimes hear the high pitched squeaks of the school of dolphins around him. But even when the water was extremely clear he seldom saw his guardians. On the rare occasions that he did observe them the dolphins would rush through the water at breakneck speed, darting here and there like a pack of playful dogs with boundless energy. Then in a few seconds they would disappear into the blue haze at the limit of underwater visibility.

Since those days men have captured dolphins and have developed close relationships with them in the confines of dolphinariums. To the spectators, the dolphins appear to be happy and enjoy the close proximity of humans. Yet in the wild their attitude towards divers has remained the same.

Thus the incident with Henry Crellin and his partners in Port St Mary on the Isle of Man was something special.

For a wild dolphin deliberately to approach divers and stay with them at close quarters for so long was a rare happening in the long annals of the sea.

2: The Dolphin Makes Friends

The Isle of Man has a comparatively small resident population, and as is common in small communities, lines of communication are direct and news travels fast. This is particularly true in the winter months when the tourists, who are a major source of income to many of the islanders, are not present to distract the locals from their gossip. Immediately before his encounter with the dolphin, however, Henry Crellin had been away in England, so he had not had time to catch up on local affairs. If he had been at home he would almost certainly have heard about the arrival of the dolphin, which had made itself known to a couple of divers just a few weeks previously. The two divers were Dr Joanna Jones and Michael Bates, both of whom worked at the Marine Biological Station. The incident took place in the bay at Port Erin, the very fishing village where Henry Crellin had his diving business and shop.

Port Erin, whose name is derived from the Manx words Purt Chiarn meaning Lord's Harbour, has a natural charm that is unspoilt by the commercial amenities of a modern seaside resort. Bradda Head to the north, almost a sheer cliff, rises 350 feet above sea level and is capped by a tower built in 1872. It was erected to the memory of a famous safe maker, William Milner, and the shape of the tower is said to resemble a safe key. Milner's Tower can be seen for miles from the sea and is a valuable reference point for boatmen when navigating around the south-west corner of the Isle of Man. In the summer Port Erin is noted for its clear water and smooth sheltered sandy beach, and that above all is what most holiday makers remember.

The local residents, however, know that Port Erin has

another very different face. For the mouth of the bay is open to the south-west and is subject to the full fury of the south-westerly gales that can lash the coast in the winter. In the middle of the nineteenth century work started on the building of a breakwater to dampen the energy of the mountainous waves that were often funnelled towards the shore. Huge concrete blocks, some weighing as much as seventeen tons, were spilled into the bay. But when work had reached an advanced stage in 1884, a mighty storm smashed the rampart with astonishing ease, and the project was abandoned. Today, the jagged line of rocks that jut from the south headland at Port Erin serve as a reminder, to any who might forget, of the awe-inspiring power of an unbridled sea. The jumbled underwater profusion of rocks now provides a sanctuary for fish and crustaceans.

Brilliantly coloured wrasse will often swarm round a diver there, if he makes unhurried movements. The fish are expecting to be fed, for just above the ruined breakwater, on the southern side of the bay, is the Marine Biological Station and fish hatchery, run by Liverpool University and the British Government, and staff from the Station, when setting off from the shore on underwater research projects, often take tit-bits with them to feed the wrasse. This is typical of the sympathy with which the researchers at Port Erin approach the creatures they study in the sea.

It was thus perhaps a happy accident that the dolphin first made its presence in the Isle of Man known to marine biologists, who would possibly have a greater understanding than laymen of its friendly character and benign behaviour when in the presence of man. Mike Bates certainly showed no fear of the dolphin when he first encountered the surprise visitor to the doorstep of the Marine Biological Laboratories.

It happened at a time when the scientists of the Station were interested in measuring underwater light intensities. For this purpose they used two light recording devices mounted on a metal frame. In January 1972 it was decided to move the apparatus. The research vessel *Cuma* was detailed to haul up the equipment from its site off the lifeboat station slipway, then to ferry it to a new station at the end of the ruined breakwater. It was a short run, and the *Cuma* was accompanied by a small rowing boat containing Joanna Jones, Michael Bates and a two-man crew. The rope slings had already been attached to the apparatus and the job of the divers was simply to attach these slings to the wire lowered from the winch aboard the *Cuma*.

The divers were in position over the submerged equipment when Mike Bates got his first sight of the dolphin — a seemingly gigantic tail disappearing into the water alongside the rowing boat. A few seconds later a grinning head appeared. The dolphin eyed the occupants of the boat for a few seconds, then submerged. On board, the two divers hastily fitted their masks. Quick checks were made, and they dived, with a great deal more splashing than the animal they were so eager to meet. Here is Mike Bates' own account of what happened next:

A few feet away I could see Dr Jones spinning round in the water, searching for the dolphin. I joined in the search but all I could see was the grey-green wall that surrounds you in mid-water in British seas. Then part of that wall solidified, assumed shape and rushed past a few inches away. Excitedly I lunged after it, only to be stopped abruptly by the rope I was holding. Only then did I remember that we had actually started out on a dive to do a job of work.

We could see the rig looming up out of the murk ahead of us. Swimming over to it, we attached the rope from the boat, which would then act as a marker for the *Cuma* to drop her winch wire on.

The dolphin reappeared with the wire. Twisting and turning, he followed it down and then, when he saw us, he repeated his express train act. While we were fixing the wire to the rope slings he stood on his head and surveyed us, first out of one eye and then the other.

When I copied the action, pushing my mask to within an inch of his eye, he became very excited and rushed around us, performing somersaults and leaps. We would rush at one another veering off at the last second so that we passed within inches of each other. It was a pity we did not really have time to get to know him better but there was a job to do and we could not very well spend the time with a dolphin, however playful he was.

We watched the rig rise slowly to the surface. As Dr Jones mounted the ladder in front of me, I watched the dolphin follow her fins until they left the water. He seemed most disappointed that we were leaving. I did not see him at all on the journey to the new site. When we reached it, Dr Jones and I went into the water again, to mark the position for the rig. Immediately he was there. He seemed as pleased to see us as we were to see him.

All the time we were placing the rig in its new position, the dolphin kept us company; weaving between Dr Jones, the rig and myself. This gave us a chance to study him quite closely. The silvery scars along his six to eight foot length made him seem quite elderly, despite his rather youthful behaviour. In spite of his size and behaviour, neither Dr Jones or myself felt at any time that he was anything but friendly and it was with a feeling of regret that we finally left the water.

That was the first of several meetings Michael Bates and Joanna Jones had with the dolphin. It would appear, often without warning, when they were working underwater, and became progressively more friendly. The two divers were struck above all by the combination of inquisitiveness and mischief in the dolphin's character. For instance, Dr Jones was one day collecting specimens, which were placed in a bucket and hauled to the surface. The dolphin watched her movements attentively and followed the first bucket when it was pulled up. When the second bucket made its upwards journey, the dolphin wagged its head excitedly and nudged the bucket with its beak, scattering the contents into the water. All subsequent loads were promptly tipped out in the same way, leaving the man on the surface fruitlessly pulling on an unloaded rope. Dr Jones was in some dilemma about whether to be amused at the playful antics of the dolphin, or irritated that her experiment had to be abandoned until tight-fitting lids could be found.

The newcomer to Manx waters was given the name Donald — Donald the Dolphin — and he rapidly established himself amongst the diving community who began to look forward to his sudden arrivals which could turn any routine dive into a memorable event.

He was identified as a male bottlenose dolphin, or *Tursiops truncatus* — the common name being derived apparently from the shape of the head, which resembles the neck and shoulder of an early wine or brandy bottle. The bottlenose is one of the largest of the dolphin family (Delphinidae), and males reach a maximum length of about twelve feet. In America bottlenose dolphins are sometimes referred to as common porpoises. This has led to some confusion because in Britain common porpoises are members of another family which taxonomists call the Phocoenidae. The common porpoise *Phocoena phocoena* is found all round the British coast, the males reaching a maximum length of only six feet. It lacks the narrow beak of *Tursiops truncatus* and has an evenly rounded snout. The teeth of the common porpoise are also comparatively small, being only about one tenth of an inch in diameter at the gum.

One person to take a particular interest in Donald was a very remarkable Manxwoman, then living in England, called Maura Mitchell. She was one of the people Henry Crellin had stayed with on his visit to England just before his encounter with the dolphin, and on the night after the incident he wrote to Maura giving her a full account of it. He went into some detail because he knew that Maura was an enthusiastic diver and that she was at the time about to move permanently to the Isle of Man.

He may also have known that she had a very special gift for handling animals, but he could hardly have foreseen that he was introducing Maura to one of the most important, and extraordinary, relationships of her life.

Just as the gift of the musical child has to be nurtured if it is to flower in later life, so the intuitive rapport which Maura had with animals was developed during her childhood. Maura had led what most people would regard as an idyllic childhood. She was born in Leicestershire, her geologist father having left his home in the Isle of Man to take a job in England. The house where she spent most of her childhood was situated next to her grandparents' farm at Evington, and she had only to cross the paddock to reach the farmhouse. She wandered in and out of the houses of her parents and grandparents, both of which she regarded as home. Old Mr Mellor, who wrote with copperplate handwriting and lived in the next bungalow, called her a "hedgerow child", a solitary child who knew where to find cowslips and wild orchids. where the best frogspawn could be found, where the birds had their nests and where the wild watercress grew. One of Maura's earliest memories was of lying on her back for a long, long time in a hayloft watching a barn owl feeding its young. She had an innate understanding of nature. To her the way in which the animals and plants of the countryside fitted together like a jigsaw was as obvious as the finished puzzle.

Her maternal grandfather always kept at least four shire horses and to young Maura their feet were as large as dustbin lids covered in hair. By the time she was ten years old Grandfather Kirby allowed her to run the carthorse shuttle service between the hayfields and the storage barns. Many other horses and ponies were always on the farm needing breaking, just riding or schooling. That was the beginning of a love of horses which she has never lost. Throughout her childhood she assimilated animal lore.

Staying with her father's parents on the Isle of Man for lengthy holidays also had a great influence on Maura. Grandpa Shimmin, a Douglas Headmaster and fluent native Manx speaker, imparted an abiding love for Manx heritage. She loved spending long summer days exploring the steep glens with their tumbling waterfalls, deep pools and darting brown trout. The rivers ended on rocky beaches with secret caves. To Maura the sea was alive. The waves breathed in and out noisily on the shingle as she searched for shells and coloured pebbles. The rock pools left by the tide were a particular delight — self-contained worlds of delicate weeds, inhabited by tiny fish, shrimps and anemonies.

Her life was not devoted exclusively to animals however, and two weeks after her sixteenth birthday she bought her first motorcycle — with her father's approval, as he had had his first riding lessons at the age of fourteen on the Isle of Man.

She later married Peter, a fellow motorcycle enthusiast who had his own engineering business. As their two young boys grew out of babyhood they took up boating and diving. Maura took to diving like the proverbial duck to water and enjoyed the spirit and companionship of the diving club. Most of all she enjoyed her diving trips to the Isle of Man where they could also watch the famous TT races. Rather than spending their lives in a city they decided to resettle in the village of Ballasalla in the south of the island.

It was only a short while after Maura had settled into her new home that she had her first meeting with Donald, a meeting that was to prove the beginning of a long and extraordinary relationship with the wild dolphin. Unlike Henry, Maura first saw Donald from the shore one evening when she was sitting on the jetty off Fort Island. The dolphin appeared suddenly, as was his way, and began playing like a huge aquatic kitten. He raced between the moored boats, turning like a slalom water skier to avoid them at the last possible moment, and sending spray and waves crashing against their rocking hulls. He hurled himself into the air with explosions of energy which Maura found exhilarating but which filled her with awe — she could well appreciate Henry Crellin's fright when a creature of such size and power had appeared totally unexpectedly out of the underwater fog. Yet although Maura could sense the enormous power required to launch Donald into the air, she was also impressed by the grace with which the dolphin could leap and the precise control he exhibited when he swam at full speed towards a boat, and then veered away with inches to spare.

So it was not without some apprehension that Maura first went into the water with so powerful a creature, when Donald appeared one day outside the Fort at Derbyhaven. Maura eventually suggested to her male companions that they should abandon their planned aqualung dive and have a snorkel swim with Donald instead. The dolphin was not in a boisterous mood, and as the trio swam slowly out from the jetty Donald made his way towards them. First he inspected one male diver, then the other, before making his way towards Maura. The dolphin was swimming gently round and then stopped. He looked at Maura head on. Maura slowly stretched out her gloved hand. As she did so the dolphin backed imperceptibly away so that she could not reach him. Then he swam slowly round her legs and she again extended her hand and stroked the dolphin very gently under the chin. This time the dolphin did not swim away but seemed to like it. Maura talked gently to Donald as she would to a horse, and the dolphin responded. The next time he swam by she held out her leg so that the rubber tip of her fin stroked the dolphin's abdomen. This he thoroughly enjoyed, and for the next thirty minutes he completely ignored the other two divers and stayed swimming gently with Maura the entire time. When all three snorkellers eventually swam back to the jetty Maura's new-found friend swam alongside until she actually left the water.

The two men, who expressed themselves as much affronted at the attention Donald had devoted to their female companion, told the story at the club room. They decided that Donald must be a male dolphin with a definite preference for female divers in wetsuits. But in a more serious vein, they noticed the extraordinary rapport that Maura immediately established with the wild dolphin.

After the first encounter Donald and Maura met frequently. Club dives took place every weekend and if ever Donald was in the vicinity he would join the divers, inspecting them all but devoting most of his attention to Maura, who spoke to him and stroked him.

Indeed, to divers and non-divers alike Donald was making his presence on the Isle of Man a source of amusement and pleasure. And those who remember him from that time were not all human. One was a Jack Russell terrier by the name of Spratt. Spratt belonged to Bill Dawson, who owned a yacht with his father. The yacht was kept moored in Port St Mary, and often when Bill rowed out to it Spratt, dressed in a red lifejacket complete with handle on top, would accompany him. Then, when Bill arrived at his yacht he would tie up to the stern and often leave the dog happily sitting in the dinghy. Donald, on his by then regular visits to Port St Mary, took to swimming around the dinghy as Bill rowed. And this in itself would set Spratt barking. One evening, when very few people were about, Maura watched Donald take what had been an established game into his own hands. She saw Donald accompany Bill as he rowed out, then, when the owner was below in the cabin of his yacht, Donald apparently decided to have a closer look at the strange four-legged creature in the red lifejacket with the handle on top. The dolphin rose in the water alongside the rowing dinghy, and with his head well clear of the water he peered in. This set Spratt barking, and he stood with his paws on the gunwale yapping at the dolphin. Donald opened his mouth to reveal his handsome set of sharp triangular teeth, and moved forward, imitating the dog's yapping movement with his own jaws. This sent the dog into a frenzy — much to Donald's immense delight.

Having elicited such a good initial response, the dolphin submerged and reappeared to look over the other side of the boat, much to the astonishment of the Jack Russell terrier who again rushed forward to defend his territory in a pose of fearlessness which Donald soon discovered was false. For when Donald made another advance with his jaws opening and closing the dog almost fell over backwards in order to escape. The two animals spent a long time playing their game of dare. Then Donald thought up a variation on the theme. He slipped quietly underwater, turned upside down and started swimming with his belly pressed against the keel. The dog burst into a new spasm of barking as soon as Donald appeared alongside to assess the effect of his latest tormenting trick. Having satisfied himself that he had extracted the maximum response from the poor dog, Donald performed a couple of spectacular leaps that sent showers of spray raining down on yacht and dinghy, then set off to find another source of amusement.

Whenever Bill Dawson set foot in his dinghy after that he was always on the lookout for Donald. If the dolphin was in the area he would come to the dinghy for a game with the dog. It was always a benevolent game — Bill Dawson was very fond of his little Jack Russell and would never have allowed him to stay in the dinghy if he had thought that any harm would come to him from the playful dolphin. Indeed, long after Donald had left the Isle of Man, Maura had a chat with Bill about the relationship between the dog and the dolphin, and Bill said that he felt sure Spratt missed Donald. The dog would often stand with his feet on the transome looking into the water as if searching for his erstwhile playmate.

In his behaviour towards the dog, Donald displayed again the irrepressibly mischievous side of his character that was to become so familiar to all who knew him. He also revealed that joyous exhibitionism that had already impressed Maura, for he seemed to be aware that people were watching him and would put on an extra special display if they were.

3: Attempted Murder

With his entertaining acrobatic displays, his endearing habit of accompanying boats when they made their way in and out of the harbours, and his friendly association with divers in the water, it would not have been unreasonable to assume that Donald's presence was a source of pleasure to everyone on the Isle of Man. Sadly, however, at least one person resented the dolphin. Not only did that person dislike the dolphin, he took steps to get rid of it permanently. On 13 September 1972 the story was told laconically in the *Daily Mirror*, under banner headlines:

> *GUNMAN'S VICTIM — DON, THE PET DOLPHIN*
> Angry animal lovers are hunting gunmen who pumped bullets into Donald, the friendly dolphin.
> For some months Donald frolicked off the Isle of Man coast and became a holiday attraction.
> But the twelve-foot dolphin was wounded by two bullets in his head and three shotgun wounds in his body.
> Mr Harold Blundell, Chairman of the Manx SPCA, said yesterday: "This has outraged us all and we want to find out who is responsible."
> He added: "There have been rumours of threats by fishermen because they thought the dolphin was causing poor catches."

The news of the assassination fell like a bombshell on Maura, her diving friends and the other folk who had come to love the dolphin.

For some the shock quickly turned to anger of a

most violent kind. They became so incensed that several of them swore severe retributions to the culprit.

Many stories about Donald's demise circulated. One was that he had been killed and eaten by French fishermen — who were intensely disliked by the Manx fisherman, partly for reasons of rivalry, and partly because of their habit of shooting seagulls and hanging the corpses from the halyards to deter other gulls.

The Manx Society for the Prevention of Cruelty to Animals offered a reward for information leading to the detection of the criminals. But although a number of suspicions were voiced none could be corroborated with evidence. The most plausible story was that Donald had played around some fishermen who were illegally netting salmon. The fishermen disliked Donald for three reasons: first because he ate their salmon, second because he could damage their nets, and third because he attracted unwanted attention to their activities. If such was the case, and as yet there is no public evidence to support the story, the fishermen were wrong on the first two counts. There is no data to support the conclusion that Donald would take salmon in preference to the other fish that are bountiful round the Isle of Man. It is also well known that dolphins are extremely clever at avoiding being caught in nets as those who have deliberately tried to net dolphins have discovered. No one could refute the third point however — for everywhere that Donald went he certainly attracted attention to himself.

One day, after the disappearance of Donald, a dolphin of about the same size was spotted near the coast, though it kept well clear of human contact. Was Donald alive after all? There were other sightings, and in time it became clear, to the relief of his Manx friends, that he was alive and swimming. Although anger at the shooting subsided, the hunt for the would-be murderers continued, and Donald kept his distance from humankind.

It so happened around this time that the European

Spear Fishing Championships were held in the Isle of Man. As is usual at such functions, a Medical Officer was appointed and the man who took on the task was Dr Raymond Goyne. Donald became interested in the activities of the spear fishermen, although he remained very wary of them. However Dr Goyne, who spent a lot of time snorkelling, gradually gained Donald's confidence and got close enough to take a photograph of him. The photograph showed a deep wound over Donald's right eye that was consistent with that which might have been expected from a shotgun fired at close quarters. Although Donald was unfortunate to have been the victim of a gunman, the dolphin was incredibly lucky that the shot had not damaged his blowhole. Without proper control of the very sensitive mechanism for keeping water out of his lungs, the dolphin could easily have drowned. Gradually, Donald became his old friendly self again, seeking the company of the Manx fishermen, getting frequently in their way and even giving them an occasional helping hand at their work. One fisherman who received the dolphin's attentions was Norman Quillan, coxswain of the lifeboat. Norman Quillan had a small lobster boat, and Donald quickly learned that there were games to be played when lobster pots were to be hauled in. He would follow the boat out from the harbour, and the dolphin always knew what was going to happen next: before Norman could grab hold of the buoy on the end of a string of pots, the dolphin would take the rope between his teeth and deliberately tow the buoy away. But Norman remembers one day on which Donald helped instead of hindering: he actually tossed the buoy that Norman wanted right into the boat!

It might be argued that the dolphin's behaviour in this case was accidental — he did not really understand what he was doing. However, most of the divers who have got to know Donald well do not take this view. Many of them can quote incidents to indicate that the dolphin is able rapidly to assess what divers are doing in the water, and then to prove his understanding by his actions. One such person is Dave Wood who was in the boat with Henry Crellin when he had his first encounter with Donald when laying the mooring lines in Port St Mary harbour.

Donald often joined Dave on dives around the Calf of Man. Usually there would be no sign of the dolphin until about half-way through the dive, when Donald would appear out of the underwater mists. On one occasion Dave's diving partner, Colin Bowen, was collecting crayfish. Donald watched carefully, disappeared and came back. Colin watched the dolphin as he swam off a short distance, and then started to swim in a tight circle. Intrigued by this unusual behaviour, Colin swam over to see what Donald was doing. When he arrived he saw that he was circling directly over a crayfish, which the fisherman promptly added to the collection in his sack, having thanked the dolphin warmly for his help.

A story perhaps even more convincing is told about a snorkel diver who was out one day catching plaice for his supper. The main mode of defence of plaice is camouflage. They lie flat on the seabed, often half covered in sand, and their backs change colour to merge with their surroundings. An experienced diver is able to see through this disguise by looking for a break in the contours of the seabed. Once he has spotted a victim he swims quietly down to the fish and then quickly impales it with a knife, or prodder of the type used by park attendants for picking up paper litter. The catch is then transferred to a sack. On this occasion Donald followed the diver, and with his usual curiosity watched him impale a fish. The dolphin then swam ahead a little, and suddenly took a nose dive at the seabed. When the diver swam over to investigate at close quarters he found that Donald had pinned a plaice to the ground but was making no attempt to eat it.

Despite these signs of returning friendliness, however, it took some time for Donald to allow himself to be approached as closely, and touched, as he had before the shooting. Indeed, it might be said that the relationship between man and dolphin was not really set right again until the drama that is recounted in the next chapter. But what is remarkable is not Donald's wariness of human contact — it is his readiness to entrust himself to it once more.

What other animal, including domestic animals with centuries of contact with man in their breeding, would have so totally unaggressive a response to so cruel an experience? What indeed is the normal response of man himself to such an attack?

One of the essential elements in the observed behaviour of dolphins recorded down the ages is in fact a complete absence of aggression towards man.

Dr David Taylor, a veterinary surgeon who has specialised in the care of dolphins, is among the many contemporary scientists who have confirmed this ancient observation. He has remarked for instance that many large animals become difficult to handle when they know they are to be injected, but that dolphins show no such resentment, regardless of how painful the procedures they are subjected to. And my own experiences in research in veterinary medicine bear this out.

In his book entitled *The Dolphin Cousin to Man*, Robert Stenuit reviewed the classical and modern literature on dolphins, and made the following unequivocal statement:

A dolphin could kill a man with a blow of its snout. It could dismember him with a blow of its jaws, because it possesses a double row of strong conical teeth, eighty in all, which sink in with precision. But never, absolutely never, has a dolphin or a porpoise attacked a man, even in legitimate defence, with a harpoon in its side, or when, with electrodes in its skull, it has been massacred in the name of science. On the contrary . . . .

Many people are killed or maimed by animals, including

pets such as horses and dogs, every year. And indeed man himself, if suddenly punched on the nose for instance, reacts immediately, by running away, or more likely by retaliating in a physically violent manner. Such an immediate response is instinctive, and involves the lower centres of the brain — those that govern the behaviour of the lower animal orders to which for example belong the sharks. A deliberate and carefully considered response will involve the higher centres of the brain which are most developed in the higher primates, including man, and the Cetaceans. Thus, in man's immediate response to aggression it is the lower centres which tend to take precedence over the higher.

Yet it would appear from a dolphin's behaviour after a sudden and unprovoked attack by man, that it is the *higher* centres of the brain that take precedence over the lower. Does this suggest that the dolphins may have made an evolutionary step not only beyond any other animal, but actually beyond man himself?

4: Stranded

The tide was slowly ebbing from Derbyhaven. As it did so, the vessels, which had been bobbing on the water with the regular rhythm of the gentle waves, became still as the keel of one after another settled on the seabed. When the tide had receded the boats were left resting on the exposed sandy flats, waiting for the next incoming tide to lift them off again.

It happens twice a day as regularly as the sun rises and it was a scene as familiar to John Moore as it is to all those who live on the coast in a tidal area. It was part of the rhythm of the sea that he enjoyed and never tired of watching. On a day in March 1973 however, the tidal rhythm held an extra special significance for both John Moore and a relative newcomer to the Isle of Man — Donald the dolphin.

John Moore was supervising new building development overlooking Derbyhaven. It was time for the mid-afternoon tea break, when his companion Willie Kneale commented that there was a seal in the haven. Willie had just seen it moving by one of the yachts. John peered in the direction indicated by Willie and could see a dark grey mass beside the white hull of the *Nemesis*. Then he saw something move. It looked more like the tail of a huge fish than any part of a seal.

"Are you sure that's a seal?" John said to Willie, puzzled by the unusual shape he had seen rise and then drop again.

"It is certainly not a seal" he commented when he had observed more closely the heavy dark mass struggling on the sand, and a tail again waving briefly in the air.

The two men left their mugs of tea. John tucked his trousers into the top of his socks and they paddled across the muddy sands towards the *Nemesis*. As they got closer they realised that the object they had seen was not a seal but a dolphin. As the dolphin struggled he sank more into the mud. He raised his tail fluke uselessly into the air and splashed it down. They inspected the huge animal and from the scar on its body they realised with mounting excitement that it could be none other than Donald. Now the poor animal, recently so nearly killed by a shotgun, lay helplessly stranded. They tried to move him manually. But as they slithered on the mud they knew that they stood no more chance of pushing Donald back into the sea than of toppling Nelson's Column in Trafalgar Square. Donald was very heavy.

The two men realised that the first thing they should do was to keep Donald alive. Already there were signs of cracking on his delicate skin. Willie Kneale ran back to the building site, collected a bucket and then ran to the receding sea to fill it with water.

John Moore was working out a rescue operation as he hurried back to the building site. The group of workmen abandoned their tea break and a couple went to help Willie Kneale with the dousing of the stranded dolphin. John Moore then headed for the mechanical excavator on the site and discussed the problem with the driver — Nigel Warren. Nigel agreed to attempt a rescue, provided the wheels of his Massey-Ferguson digger did not sink too deep into the newly-exposed mud.

The water-carrying team, who had been walking backwards and forwards to the ever more distant sea, were pleased to hear the noisy staccato chug of a powerful diesel engine as the Massey-Ferguson, with Nigel Warren at the wheel, came bumping across the sands towards them. The rescue group congregated beside the expiring Donald and decided upon a plan of campaign. Nigel climbed back into the cab of his machine and manoeuvred

Photo: Horace Dobbs

This picture taken in October 1974 shows the severe wound inflicted on the top of Donald's head when he was accidentally hit by the metal skeg beneath the propellor of a powerful outboard motor travelling at speed.

Photo: Horace Dob

Donald has as many scars as a veteran soldier. In this picture, taken in September 1976, the wound inflicted above his right eye by the gunman on the Isle of Man has healed completely. The wound on the top of his head caused by the outboard skeg has also healed and is becoming progressively pigmented from the outer boundary. If either of the injuries had damaged the delicate blow hole on the top of his head Donald would probably have died from drowning.

Photo: Horace Dobbs

Donald has an insatiable curiosity. Here he approaches Maura in Port St Mary to find out what game will be played next.

Photo: Horace D

As soon as Maura arrived in Martin's Haven, off the Welsh coast, Donald came alongside the inflatable and eyed her carefully.

the excavator so that the leading edge of the scoop bucket eased gently under the dolphin. But in this position the men could not get close enough to manhandle the animal into the scoop without damaging both the boat and Donald. So they decided the boat would have to be moved. In a few minutes a line was attached, the powerful engine spurted a volley of black clouds into the air as it took the strain, then the boat slid smoothly over the sand leaving the dolphin fully exposed, with plenty of room all around him.

Again the scoop moved in. The steel tallons along its leading edge bit into the sand, then stopped. The gang of men heaved on the fluke of the dolphin to pull him into the steel bucket. Others pushed the dolphin's head. Slowly they managed to manoeuvre Donald into a suitable position, the powerful engine throbbed again, and the steel shovel moved forward, tilted and lifted its unusual cargo with the apparent ease of a man raising a glass of ale.

Like children alongside a float in a carnival procession the team of rescuers delightedly followed the excavator as it headed towards the sea.

When the water reached a depth of two feet the bucket was slowly lowered. The life-giving sea flushed over the passive body of Donald.

But the problems were not over for the rescue team. Nigel Warren could not risk taking his digger any further into the water. So some of the men took off their shoes and socks and waded into the water. The bucket tipped and they eased Donald free. The dolphin was only half submerged and remained pressed to the seabed by the unsupported weight of his body out of the water. Each time a gentle wave came in the men pushed Donald forward.

At last, with the added push from Donald's own swimming efforts, the dolphin was free of the bottom. After that it was only a matter of seconds before he was in water deep enough for him to swim freely. But he did not swim away immediately. Instead he swam round in circles offshore. Then as if in a final gesture of thanks and farewell he turned in a tight circle, jumped high into the air and swam away out to sea.

The following day he was spotted beside his favourite boat in Port St Mary, apparently none the worse for his excursion ashore.

If Justice exists, like the statue on the top of the Old Bailey in London, then on that day in March 1973 she must have been watchng over Donald. The scales had been heavily weighted on one side by the the man who brought Donald near to death by shooting him. Now was the time to redress the balance. On the other side of the scales she put the resourceful Mr John Moore.

It is interesting to speculate on just what effects the incident would have had on Donald. For his entire life Donald's considerable body had been supported by the sea. In the sea he was weightless. So as the water became shallower and shallower the stress on his body would have been increased as the surface became increasingly exposed. The weight settling on his belly would have made it difficult for him to expand his lungs to breathe. Fortunately his respiratory system had evolved to be very economical in its use of air. Other factors however would have added to his discomfort. In the sea he was continuously bathed in cooling fluid and his metabolic rate was adjusted to keep his core temperature at the normal mammalian level of about 98.4°F. But he had no sweat glands and could not pant to keep his temperature down when his skin began to dry. Although he could control the amount of heat dissipated through the blood vessels going to the surface of his body, the thick insulating layer of blubber so essential for his survival in water could outside the water have become partially instrumental in his death. Finally, his very thin skin, uniquely adapted to help him slide through the water with the minimum of resistance, started to shrink and crack upon exposure to the air.

If John Moore and his colleagues had not spotted Donald and rescued him, would the dolphin have survived until the next incoming tide set him free again? Nobody can be positive about the answer to that question. I suspect he would have succumed like Opo, who was probably the most famous wild dolphin of the twentieth century voluntarily to befriend man. After one year's close association with people off the beach of Oponini in New Zealand, the young female bottlenose dolphin called Opo, beloved of thousands, was found stranded and dead in March, 1956.

Just why so many whales and dolphins become stranded and die is a question that has puzzled scientists and non-scientists alike for many years. One reason that has been advanced is that stranding is a voluntary method for animals to bring their lives to an end, akin to the legendary graveyards to which elephants are reputed to make their way to die. But I have been told by hunters in Africa that such places exist only in the minds of those who dream up adventure stories or write scenarios for Tarzan movies. And although many of the dolphins that are found stranded are old, relatively young specimens have also been reported. So I am inclined to discount the "graveyard theory". In Donald's case, he certainly showed a will to live after the shooting incident. And after all, if he wished to die he had only to sink below the waves and inhale.

Another, even more fanciful, reason advanced to explain dolphin strandings suggests that built into the genetic make-up of all of the whale family is an urge to get back to the land. It stems, so the proponents of the argument say, from the days way back in the dolphins' evolutionary past when their predecessors made the transition from being purely land animals to amphibians.

Such speculation takes science beyond the extent of our present knowledge. We know, for instance, that the genes within all living cells contain the master plans that govern the structure of all forms of animal life. Thus the fact that a black cat will have a white ear is written into the chemical composition of its genes, which are an intricate arrangement of amino acids, as surely as the genes will also dictate that the cat will have four legs. Basic behavioural patterns such as migrating instincts are probably also laid down in the genetic code, but in a less precisely defined way, for behaviour is also very much influenced by a host of external factors, such as the environment and the availability of food. It is possible therefore that strandings are the result of two or more influences — a deep instinctive force coupled with some unique external circumstances.

My own theory, however, is that in this case Donald's own insatiable curiosity got the better of him. He probably discovered something new, to which he devoted his attention, causing him to forget, at a very crucial moment, that the tide was receding from a flat area with a very gradual slope. The sea was calm, so there were no wave surges that he could ride pig-a-back into the sea until he got into water deep enough to swim free. His fins and his tail fluke touched bottom and he could not move forward. A small depression was scoured out alongside the vessel as the tide receded and he was trapped.

The noble efforts of John Moore and his colleagues did not go unacknowledged. They were later given awards by the Manx Society for the Prevention of Cruelty to Animals.

That incident, though perhaps the most dramatic, was only one indication of how thoroughly, within a year of his arrival off the coast, Donald had enmeshed himself in the affections of the Manx people. Already, his peculiar emotional impact on human beings, which was later to seem the most important aspect of his relationship with man, was changing individual lives. One of the first people, apart from Maura, to whom Donald was already a friend, to be deeply influenced by the wild dolphin was a fisherman by the name of Michael Kneale. Those who understand Manx fishermen will know that they are an extremely conservative and superstitious community. Many of them cannot swim. So it is all the more remarkable that one of their number should actually have learned to dive in order to get closer to the dolphin who came alongside his fishing boat when it was making its way to and from the fishing grounds.

Once he learned to dive, Michael Kneale also caught the bug that grips many of those who swim underwater and have a keen interest in the new world of Nature they see beneath the waves — that bug is underwater photography. On his birthday Michael Kneale received an underwater camera, and he delighted in the challenge of trying to get underwater pictures of Donald.

Intense though Donald's human relationships tended to be, however, they were not all friendly. At the same time that the MSPCA were considering the presentation of an award to John Moore for his rescue, another incident occurred that enraged the dolphin-lovers on the Isle of Man. It concerned a wealthy new resident to the island, owner of a thirty-foot twin-engined cabin cruiser which he kept moored off Port St Mary. And it followed as the direct result of one of the mischievous tricks that Donald played when the opportunity presented itself.

Maura Mitchell had witnessed the same trick one day when she was waiting for her husband, Pete, as he rowed back from their own cabin cruiser which was moored in Derbyhaven. As she stood on the jetty she saw the small plastic Sportykyak dinghy bump violently as Donald gave it a hefty shove from underneath. Pete, who was at first unaware of the presence of the dolphin under his boat, wondered what on earth was happening and the look of astonishment on his face caused Maura to burst out laughing. When Pete realised what was going on he kept pointing down and shouting "He's underneath. He's underneath.'' The bobbing of the dinghy stopped him from rowing properly, much to the amusement of his wife, who was still shaking in a fit of uncontrollable laughter.

Maura has an instincitve understanding of animals and the dinghies she travelled in were never subjected to the same harassment when Donald was in a playful mood. For she acknowledged the presence of the dolphin by trailing her hand, or a fin, over the side. Donald liked this attention and would follow closely under the boat swimming upside down.

But the new resident, it seemed, lacked Maura's intuitive sensitivity to Donald's playful intentions. So when Donald tried out his latest trick on him too, as he rowed out to his cabin cruiser, he was not at all amused. When he returned he wrote to the Board of Agriculture and Fisheries complaining about the dolphin. The exact wording of his letter has not been made public but it was rumoured at the time that he had reported that the dolphin was a menace and should be destroyed. An uproar shook the normally placid inhabitants of the quiet fishing village of Port St Mary when news of the contents of his letter leaked out. It was not unnatural for the local populace to resent rich newcomers who used their island home as a tax haven. And when one of these ''comeovers'', as they are called, suggested that the dolphin they had taken to their hearts should be got rid of they vented their feelings without inhibition. Many of them openly expressed the view that it was the wealthy newcomer, not the dolphin, who should be despatched.

A local newspaper investigated the accusations and reported the story. *The Examiner* quoted Mr Bill Martin, Chairman of the Port's Commissioners, as saying: "It has come to my notice that a certain gentleman has made an application to have the dolphin destroyed." He said the Harbour Board had confirmed that an application for Donald's destruction had been lodged with them.

A spokesman for the Harbour Board said "We sought the advice of the Attorney-General's Department and we were told that the dolphin is a protected fish, which is accorded something of the royal privilege extended to the sturgeon."

Although the Attorney-General's Department showed a certain lack of knowledge of the dolphin — which is certainly not a fish — the Harbour Board's stand was made quite clear in the statement reported in *The Examiner* as follows: "Therefore, if anyone does anything to harm this particular dolphin, they will find themselves in very embarrassing circumstances. There would be no hesitation to take action . . This dolphin is playful and quite harmless and it now gives a great deal of pleasure and delight to people on the Island, particularly to the children and holidaymakers. He is also very friendly with divers, and most owners of small boats don't mind it at all . . . . There is no question of doing anything to get rid of him. He is very welcome in Manx waters."

The storm of indignation subsided when the residents of Port St Mary were thus assured of the safety of their dolphin. However, they did not forget. Although the 'comeover' died a short time after the incident, feelings against him still ran high when residents were questioned by Maura Mitchell on the subject over two years later.

5: My First Encounter

Some people plot the course of their lives and direct their efforts and energies single-mindedly towards long-term goals. They become irritated and frustrated if events deflect them from their chosen path. But though I would not deny that some degree of forward planning is essential if life is to run smoothly, I have discovered that in my life the most exciting things have happened when I have let the wind of chance blow me where it will. Unexpected deviations from my general goal, rather than steps towards it, have most often led to the most interesting and satisfying adventures.

It was just such a turn of circumstances, indeed it was literally a wind of change, that brought me first into contact with Donald the dolphin and Maura Mitchell.

Underwater photography is the most popular activity taken up by underwater swimmers once they have mastered the techniques of aqualung diving. Perhaps the reason for this is that skin diving is a non-spectator sport: once the diver takes to the water nobody can see clearly what he is doing, so it is left to the underwater photographer to portray what is to be seen under the sea, to the non-divers. It was the films of Hans and Lotte Hass taken in various remote and exotic parts of the world that triggered my interest in diving in 1957. Having been awarded an Honours Degree in Chemistry at London University, mainly as a part-time student, I got a job with the Atomic Energy Authority at Harwell. For the first time in years I found myself with a few hours to spare, so I joined the Oxford Branch of the

British Sub-Aqua Club. From the moment I first put on a facemask and dived in the sea, I realised that I had made a big discovery, and that my new-found interest would enable me to combine my love of the sea with my other passion — photography.

Within a few weeks of joining the diving club I appeared at the poolside with my cameras encased in waterproof and not-so-waterproof housings. There was very little literature available on underwater photography, and I had to work out for myself solutions to the innumerable problems that were stopping me from getting good pictures. I was fortunate in having a scientific background to enable me to resolve some of these puzzles, and in 1962 the first edition of my book *Camera Underwater* was published, which has since become the standard text on the subject in Great Britain.

At the same time I gathered around me a group of divers who were keen to engage in serious underwater projects in their spare time, and with them I formed the Oxford Underwater Research Group. One day the secretary of the group, the wife of a law don, showed me a picture taken on a family diving holiday in the Aegean Sea. It was not an underwater photograph but an ancient painting illustrating an underwater scene. It was a frieze of dolphins that had decorated the bathroom of a queen in the Minoan palace at Knossos. Those stylised Common Dolphins (*Delphinus delphis*) seemed to me to capture the marvellous feeling of joy and freedom that I experienced when I was released from gravity and drifted down into clear blue water; they emanated a spirit that bridged the waters of time that separated me from the artist who painted them in 1600BC. So I incorporated one of the dolphins in the logogram of the Oxford Underwater Research Group, and painted the same dolphin symbol on my aqualungs. Thus it was that in a manner of speaking I took a happy dolphin with me on nearly all my dives after 1962. I had always had a keen interest in whales — the big cousins of the dolphins — but it was with my identification with the beautiful dolphins in that classical picture that my love affair with dolphins really began.

The members of the Oxford Underwater Research Group made the first full length underwater television documentary in which all of the sequences were filmed in English waters. The film, called *Neptune's Needle*, was highly acclaimed and won a gold medal at the International Underwater Film Festival in Brighton in 1966. A year later I changed my job and moved to North Ferriby in Yorkshire, where I named my new house "Dolphin".

Although my passion for underwater exploration and photography remained unquenched, my new post as Head of the Radioisotope Unit in a large pharmaceutical company was both demanding and interesting. I was awarded the degree of Doctor of Philosophy as an external student of London University, for some of my work using radioactive tracers to study chemical reaction mechanisms and started work on the mode of action of a series of drugs. One of them was over one thousand times more potent than morphine and was used initially for immobilising and conserving large wild animals in Africa. I was able to apply the techniques and skills I had acquired to the fields of human and veterinary medicine. It was known that the drugs I was working with had their effect in the central nervous system. Just how these drugs, present in minute concentrations, brought about their profound effects, and how they were subsequently detoxified and eliminated from the body were subjects of study which I found engrossing and stimulating. I worked closely with veterinary surgeons and doctors and was elected a Fellow of the Royal Society of Medicine.

I presented papers on my research at conferences in different parts of the world. And it was in Geneva at such a conference that I met Dr Luciano Manara. We discovered that we were both interested in underwater swimming. When Luciano announced that he was also keen on underwater photography, we established a common interest that has caused our lives to intertwine ever since.

One outcome of this friendship was that Luciano agreed to join my family on a diving holiday at Dale Fort in Pembrokeshire in August 1974. All arrangements were made. Then a day before he was due to arrive I had a telephone call to say that the holiday was cancelled as diving would be impossible because of the unprecedented force of the winds.

What could I do? One possibility was to find a new venue where we would be less affected by bad weather. Even moderate onshore winds can make diving difficult close to the coast. When the wind is blowing away from the land however, the sea remains calm close inshore and diving is possible. I considered that I stood the greatest chance of finding a suitable venue for our holiday if I chose an island, for it is axiomatic that if there is an onshore wind on one side of the island there is an offshore wind on the other side of the island. Knowing from personal experience that excellent diving was to be had round the Isle of Man, I telephoned my diving contact there — none other than Maura Mitchell.

She reported that the conditions were far from good. Then, as we exchanged our diving news, she happened quite by chance to mention that she had made friends with a wild dolphin. What were the chances of meeting the dolphin even if conditions were not too good? I asked immediately. Maura was diffident. However, in an instant I made up my mind. If there was the remotest chance Luciano and I could dive with her friendly wild dolphin, then there was only one place I would consider taking my Italian friend — and that place was the Isle of Man. Somewhat overwhelmed at my enthusiasm, Maura agreed to see if she could make arrangements for us. With what I was to find out later was her usual organisational efficiency, she rang back having booked us all, Luciano, my family and myself, into a hotel in Douglas. What was equally important was she had also made tentative arrangements for us to dive.

Luciano flew from Milan to London, and caught a plane to Yeadon near Leeds, by a hair's breadth. As soon as he arrived we squeezed the poor fellow into our four-seater car, which already had four people in it, and headed in the wind and driving rain for Liverpool and the Douglas ferry.

As we were one of the last cars to go on board, we were parked high on a flying ramp on the stern of the *Mona's Queen*. It was a vantage point almost as good as the ship's bridge. From inside the car we could look down on the deck, the dock and the River Mersey. In the shelter of the quay, conditions for the eighty-five-mile crossing appeared reasonable. It was not until we were well clear of land that the full impact of the Force Eight gale hit us. The sea was a blue-grey mass topped with a meringue of whipped spray that was occasionally flung right over our car. The car was not secured to the deck and it rocked and shuddered in the buffeting wind. Fortunately the vessel was fitted with stabilisers which kept it on a reasonable even keel. I must admit that there were moments when I questioned the advisability of staying in the car, especially when a number of the cars on the ramp leading to our elevated platform started to slither. Luciano said he had never encountered such conditions before as he struggled to open the door against the pressure of the fierce wind, and what his apprehensions were about diving in such seas I do not even know.

But we arrived safely on the Isle of Man, and all misgivings were forgotten. It was not long before I saw Maura and Donald together for the first time, and that first encounter with the dolphin and his lady friend is firmly inscribed on my memory, for it was pure magic.

It was a clear bright blue morning. The sky was dotted

with white, cotton-wool clouds pushed across the sky by a stiff breeze from the south west. Outside the harbour at Port St Mary the sea was summer blue and the waves were occasionally crested by white horses.

I parked my car on top of the harbour wall and surveyed the scene. It was one of peace and beauty. I felt inclined to regard it as typically English until I remembered that the Isle of Man enjoys an independence that is hotly upheld by its inhabitants. It has its own Parliament, and its own coinage and stamps. Placed beween England, Ireland, Wales and Scotland the harbour scene was a subtle blend of ingredients from all of its neighbours, which mixed together gave it a special character all of its own.

Small runs of ripples occasionally skated across the surface of the sea, driven by eddies of wind that sneaked past the protective harbour wall. The sea inside the harbour was quiet and had a blue-green tinge. The boats rose and fell gently as the waves at the entrance to the harbour dissipated the last of their unreplenished energy.

This place, I had been told by Maura, was where I was most likely to find the wild dolphin. Inside the car with me were Luciano, my wife Wendy and my daughter Melanie. Ashley, my son, had travelled with Maura in her car, which was parked alongside.

On the jetty a group of divers clad in black wetsuits were busily manoeuvring a red speedboat towards the slipway. The speedboat trailer was parked amidst a group of dinghies whose halyards reached into the wind and constantly rattled against the alloy masts. We climbed out of our cars and I immediately introduced myself and Maura to the divers. They had come over to the island from Blackpool for a few days diving and were anxious to get off for their dive before the rising wind made conditions impossible, so I dispensed with friendly chat and posed the question foremost in my mind.

"Have you seen the dolphin?"

"What dolphin?" came the reply.

That answered my question. But I explained that a wild dolphin had been observed in the harbour on many mornings during the past few months and I was very anxious to find it and if possible dive with it.

"Sorry, we haven't seen it," said the short stockily built man whom I had detained.

He hurried away to join the rest of his party on the slipway, as they pushed the trailer into the water and floated their boat free. A couple of the divers stood waist high in the water holding on to their boat whilst the rest of the party hauled the trailer at running pace to its parking place amidst the dinghies. Within a few minutes they were all back in the sea and climbing aboard.

We watched from our vantage point on the top of the harbour wall and I looked at my own diving bags and aqualung cylinder stowed in the back of Maura's small estate car. Even if we could not find Donald, what were the chances of getting a dive I asked myself? Slim, I concluded and looked enviously at the divers pulling at the starter on their heavy outboard engine. It fired into life and the boat turned and slid easily forward.

Fifty yards ahead of it a silver arch formed briefly on the water and disappeared in a shower of spray.

"There's Donald" cried Maura.

A few seconds later he surfaced again close by the speedboat, which had changed its course as the result of the sighting and was heading towards the spot where Donald had just surfaced. The speedboat changed course again and there was obvious excitement on board. As the pattern repeated itself those aboard quickly realised that attempting to chase the dolphin was a fruitless way of making contact with him, so they wisely tied up to one of the boats moored about a hundred and fifty yards offshore and the divers tumbled into the water.

The sighting of the dolphin had an immediate effect

on all of us standing on the harbour wall. We rushed to Maura's car and hauled out the bags containing our wetsuits.

"If they go out to sea Donald could well follow their boat out," said Maura.

Now Luciano is the most meticulous diver I know. He admits he is one of those people who needs to adjust mentally to the prospect of a dive. On many of the occasions I had dived with him in the past it had taken him over an hour carefully to check all of his equipment as he assembled it, and finally to dress in his wetsuit for a dive. It was a ritual which we all viewed with a great deal of amusement and one that he himself had christened his "countdown".

But the prospect of being cheated of our objective by the possible disappearance of Donald when the speedboat left the harbour changed the habit of a lifetime. In the urgency and excitement of the moment Luciano abandoned his normal style completely and was pulling on his tightfitting wetsuit as if his life depended upon it.

At the same time I was getting into my own wetsuit, which was nylon lined and therefore relatively easy to put on, I was instructing my thirteen-year-old son Ashley on the art of getting into his newly acquired wetsuit. His was not nylon lined and required liberal lubrication with talcum powder before it would slide over his skin. Clouds of perfumed talc billowed into the air around him as he fervently dispensed the contents of the tin into the trunk and arms. When his head finally popped through the neck seal in a small cloud of dust his hair was snow-white and his excited face looked as if he was half made-up as a clown.

Maura got into her wetsuit with a speed that would have been gratifying to any quick-change artist, and helped Ashley.

Luciano took his underwater camera and exposure meter

out of the plastic box in which it was carefully stored and joined Ashley and Maura who were already heading down the slipway carrying their fins, masks and snorkel tubes. I had decided to use an aqualung in order that I could stay underwater if I needed to. By the time I had it on my back and had got my cameras ready, assisted by Wendy, the other three were already in the water and heading out across the surface towards the area of activity around the moored boats. Excited shouts were coming from the scene as the divers caught glimpses of Donald. Fins flashed and splashed on the surface as the divers made frantic attempts to swim down to him. Donald added to the confusion by darting from one place to another in what appeared to be a completely random manner. There was just no telling where he would surface next.

At last I was ready and plodded down the slipway towards the sea. I walked into the water. When it reached my waist I fell forward into a snorkelling position and finned towards the scene of activity. I watched the gravel and sand pass beneath me as I progressed into deeper water. I looked up to make sure that I was still heading in the right direction. I could see that Ashley and Luciano, who were well ahead of me, had nearly reached the boat. Ashley raised his head. He shouted something I could not hear and stopped swimming. He trod water. Then he pointed down.

A few seconds later a shape like a grey submarine passed beneath me. In the fleeting seconds in which it took to pass it looked huge. I saw the pale, white-grey snout followed by a domed, dark grey forehead which in time widened into a massive shoulder section which was also dark grey but scratched with numerous light grey scars. Behind that came a vertical dorsal fin that passed just eighteen inches beneath me. Beyond the dorsal fin the body tapered and then fanned out again into a fishtail-shaped fluke. As the tail moved up towards the surface in a powerful vertical stroke, the head dipped slightly.

When the tail swept downwards again the head of the dolphin rose, giving the entire body a smooth undulating motion as it passed swiftly beneath. In two such movements Donald had passed into the blue-green underwater haze that represented the limit of my underwater vision, and was gone.

True to form he had come to investigate the latest happening — my arrival — in his self-appointed territory.

His introduction to me had been so swift that I had had no time to set my camera. The next time I saw him was when he surfaced briefly amidst the excited divers near the red speedboat.

The aqualung on my back impeded me and I was annoyed at my slow progress, but eventually I reached the other divers. When I had regained my breath I put the mouthpiece into my mouth, inhaled and allowed myself to sink slowly and peacefully underwater. I watched as Donald approached one of the divers who was snorkelling on the surface. With a wild flailing of his fins the diver tried to submerge quickly and made a violent grab for the dolphin's dorsal fin. But with a single powerful upward thrust of his tail fluke Donald accelerated away leaving the diver with nothing but water between his grabbing hands. Even to my untutored eye it was apparent that Donald took exception to such human behaviour.

One thing that struck me immediately as I watched the diver swimming back to the surface for air was how superbly smoothly the dolphin moved through the water when compared with the man. After that I got only fleeting glimpses of Donald as he raced from one person to the next. There was just no telling where he would appear. Then the divers decided that they had seen enough of Donald and they climbed aboard their boat and headed for the harbour entrance, leaving Maura, Luciano, Ashley and myself grouped together in the water.

That was the last I expected to see of Donald. However I had not reckoned on his special relationship with Maura. She called out to him under the water and started to talk to him gently. He was still very excited and would stay with her briefly and then rush away again. Gradually she calmed him down with a sympathetic understanding that I could sense. Maura snorkled down beneath the surface and nodded her head gently. Donald opened his mouth, giving his face an appearance extraordinarily similar to a human grin, and nodded his head in return before darting away.

I realised as I watched the two of them together that I was witnessing a relationship far more complex than that that can often develop between a girl and a horse or a man and his dog. There was something rare, and curiously exciting, about it that I could not analyse.

He came to inspect me a couple of times and stayed still long enough for me to take a few photographs. When he did so I noticed the upturned line of his jaw that gives the bottlenose dolphins their famous "smile".

The human mouth has soft lips and the shape of the mouth is one of the ways we have of outwardly expressing our inner emotions. Thus if the corners of our mouths turn down it is usually an indication that we are dejected. Conversely, if the corners of our mouth are raised and we expose our teeth it is a signal to those we meet that we are happy and pleased.

The dolphin does not have lips and cannot express emotion in this way. Some people have said that the smile on the face of a dolphin is simply a chance configuration, and that dolphins are no more happy or less happy than any other animal. But in the fleeting moments I had with Donald on this first encounter I could not decide on the validity of this theory. I thought this might well be my one and only opportunity of photographing a wild dolphin in the sea. So I concentrated on getting pictures.

After a further five minutes in the sea in which there was no sign of Donald I surfaced. None of the others, who were still snorkelling on the surface, had seen him either. Donald had gone.

That day was Luciano's birthday and in the evening we all sat in The Crow's Nest Restaurant overlooking Douglas Harbour to celebrate. Luciano was as excited as the rest of us. In his very first dive in British waters he had had an experience that does not befall many divers in a lifetime.

Our talk throughout the evening was almost exclusively of dolphins.

After the meal Maura suggested that we should meet some of the other divers on the Isle of Man who had dived with Donald. So we moved to a pub on the waterfront. The saloon bar of the "Britisher" was dimly lit with yellow light, and the air was thick with tobacco smoke, adding a further imperceptible tinge to the ceiling which had mellowed to a dark cream from a hundred other such nights.

We eased our way past the holidaymakers to a group of locals in the corner. The noise in the bar absorbed any further conversation like an additional footprint is absorbed by a Persian carpet. So we raised our voices like everyone else and listened to other tales of Donald. There was no doubt about it, every person who had dived with him had found the experience more memorable than almost any other in their very varied diving careers. These were not just divers' tales told to entertain and impress their friends in a bar. When they were all added together it was apparent to me that there was much more to diving with a wild dolphin than to encountering any of the many other creatures in the sea.

We made plans to dive with Donald again the next day.

But we had not taken into account the vagaries of the British climate. The next morning the weather made headlines, and newspapers showed pictures of the South Coast of England being pounded by gales, with columns of spray and spume rising high above cars on seaside roads. The bad weather had not confined itself to the South Coast, it had blown up the Irish Sea.

We drove south out of Douglas up the coastal road that rose high along the top of the cliffs. Huge waves lashed themselves in a thundering fury against the rocks, and whisked the water into white foam. Out from the rocks the wind whipped the surface of the sullen sea into a white mottled meringue. There was something very impressive about the elements air and water locked in battle, and we huddled in our anoraks to watch the wild spectacle.

"What," we asked ourselves, "does Donald do when the weather is like this?"

Does he run for shelter in a harbour, or does he join the giants on the battlefield of the open sea?

We pondered the answers as we plucked wet wild blackberries to which the gale blown spume had imparted a slightly salty tang. Such was the force of the storm that all prospects of diving had to be abandoned.

We never did see Donald again during our brief holiday on the Isle of Man. I felt a little embarrassed that Luciano had travelled all the way from Milan to dive with me, and all we had managed had been a single encounter with Donald. He was after all not accustomed to the resignation that must be adopted towards the weather by British divers, if they are to remain sane and enjoy their sport.

But to my delight, Luciano said that the one snorkel dive with Donald was the highlight of all his diving experiences, and that it had made the trip to Britain entirely worthwhile. He added that if ever I was to return to the Isle of Man to dive with Donald again, I was to let him know and he would join me if he could. Luciano was prepared to travel from Milan, involving not inconsiderable expense in both time and money, just to see the dolphin again! From long experience I knew that Luciano and I were both sensitive to similar "vibrations" — that was why we enjoyed diving together — so I knew that the secret feeling I had about Donald was not peculiar to me alone. The dolphin could have the same effect on other people. I resolved, come what may, to go back to the Isle of Man and get to know Donald much better.

6: Return To the Isle of Man

After that first brief encounter with Donald I resolved to go back to the Isle of Man as soon as I could, to see if I could get some photographs of Donald and Maura together. Just two days of my annual holiday entitlement remained, and I decided to use them. However there were two major obstacles to my success. The first was the weather, and the other was the technical difficulty of photographing in the relatively low visibility underwater.

The weather is always unpredictable, so the best I could do was to listen to the forecasts, get Maura's report on local conditions and then set off if the weather looked as if it might stay settled.

The underwater visibility — known as "the viz" in divers' jargon — is all-important, for it governs just what the diver is able to see. If the "viz" underwater approaches a hundred feet, it is exceptionally good, yet the same visibility on land would be equivalent to a dense fog — when the visibility is down to thirty yards driving, for instance, becomes very hazardous. Thus even in the best conditions the underwater photographer is working under circumstances that above water would be seen as very unfavourable indeed. In Port St Mary I could expect the underwater visibility to be in the region of fifteen feet, with a maximum of about twenty-five feet. Experience had taught me that to get clear pictures underwater it is essential for the cameraman to be separated from his subject by a distance not greater than one third of the visibility. In effect, then, I would have to stay so close to Maura and Donald that the standard camera lens would limit me to "head and shoulders" shots only. Full-length pictures would be so indistinct as to be virtually worthless.

The answer to the problem was to use a wide angle lens, which would enable me to get very close to the subject and, at the same time, encompass a large field of view. Nikon had recently introduced a very wide angle lens, with a focal length of 15mm, for use with the Nikonos cameras I used underwater, but its price, which was approaching that of a new small car, was completely beyond my means. And I knew of no one who had one that I could borrow.

However, one of my friends, who was working for a large photographic company, had been experimenting in his spare time with a cheaper supplementary lens that could be attached to Nikonos cameras. When I telephoned him he told me that he was indeed ready to produce it on a commercial basis, and had coined the name "Vizmaster" for it. So I ordered one of his first production models and a few days later it arrived, well protected in its box by a mass of polystyrene foam plastic chips.

It was an impressive-looking attachment with a plastic domed front about three inches in diameter, protected by a red woollen hat knitted for the purpose by his wife. It clipped on to the standard Nikonos 35 mm lens underwater, thus enabling standard shots, as well as fish-eye shots, to be taken without the need to surface to change lenses. It also came with a special viewfinder slotted into the camera accessory shoe. The viewfinder was essential, for it indicated what the supplementary lens was taking, its field of view being greater than that normally visible to a diver unless he turned his head from side to side.

Once the lens arrived I was ready to go, and decided to travel on 3 October, unless the weather forecast was very bad. When the day arrived the forecast was for unsettled weather. But I decided to take the risk, on the ground that further delay would only lessen my chances of success.

I also decided that it was more important for my son Ashley to have a few days in the company of a dolphin, than to have a few more facts crammed into his head at school. So a note was sent to his headmaster and Ashley, who was then aged thirteen, and I set off by car to Liverpool, and thence to the Isle of Man by ferry, where we were met by Maura.

The following morning we made our way to Port St Mary and were delighted to see that one of the unmanned dinghies was behaving in a very unnatural manner. It was moving forward to the full extent allowed by its mooring rope, then sliding backwards across the water apparently of its own accord. We knew no freak of the wind was moving it, so we concluded that it was being propelled by an unseen animal swimming upside down with his belly pressed against the keel. Donald was at home.

The wind was blowing strongly from the northwest, whipping up small waves that scurried into the slipway where we planned to launch the small C-Craft inflatable. We tried to shelter from the wind as we changed into our wetsuits, but even so I was chilled by the time I was ready to help carry the inflatable to the water's edge. Ashley stood in the water holding the inflatable off the rocks, while Maura and I dashed back and forth to the car to collect and load our diving equipment and cameras.

At last we were ready. I heaved my air cylinder on to my back to be ready to dive immediately, and pushed the boat, with Ashley at the oars, out into the choppy water. As Ashley started to row, I climbed in over the stern. For the first minute, with Ashley rowing as hard as he could, the vessel made headway, but the surface area presented by ourselves and the sides of the inflatable provided the gusting wind with plenty to push against, and as soon as Ashley tired, which he did after a few minutes, the inflatable was pushed broadside to wind which blew us rapidly towards the rocks despite his strongest efforts. Maura, who was close to him, jumped into the rowing seat, took the oars and with some short sharp pulls had the vessel pointing back into the wind. I sat impotently in the stern firmly anchored by my aqualung and cluttered with cameras.

My mother had brought me up to regard the female of the species as very much the weaker sex who had accordingly to be protected. She tried to instil in me a code of conduct which included carrying a woman's luggage if it was anything more than a handbag, giving up my seat to her on trains and buses, walking on the kerbside when escorting her along the road, and many similar courtesies. So good was her training that this gallant behaviour became a reflex with me.

However, when I took up diving such a code was no longer practical, because I always seemed to have more luggage than anyone else, owing to the amount of camera equipment I invariably took with me. Gradually I came to accept that females who go diving must expect to do their share of the physical work involved.

Nevertheless on this occasion I did have a pang of conscience as Maura urged the inflatable forward against the wind. It was one of those situations, like swimming against the stream, where if she had relaxed we would quickly have lost the ground we had gained and all our efforts would have been in vain. The fact that she was able to row the heavily laden boat out into the bay, until we could tie up to one of the fishing boats, made me realise just how strong she was despite her slight and very feminine frame.

Thereafter, when it came to diving, I treated Maura as if she were a man, telling her jokingly that she was a "hard woman" and that I expected her to have a physical endurance at least as great as my own. She took this in good spirit, and was almost always able to cope with my demands as a diving companion, even when they took me near to the limits of my own physical endurance.

As soon as we were tied up I rolled backwards into the sea and felt the cold water seeping into my wetsuit. Ashley handed me my camera and I slung it round my neck. I let go my handhold on the side of the dinghy, and allowed myself to sink into the cold green sea, calling to Donald as I descended. I looked around waiting for the grey submarine shape to appear out of the gloom. There was no sign of him. I called again and again but he either did not hear, or chose to ignore my cries.

After five minutes I surfaced and reported to Maura that her friend was not being co-operative. I clung to the side of the dinghy, which was bobbing up and down vigorously in the choppy swell, and between us we decided that Maura would snorkel around on the surface and call him. She slid over the side and swam with powerful strokes of her fins across the surface of the sea, rising and falling with the waves like a flexible blue log. In a few moments Donald appeared and she enticed him back to the inflatable. I could hear her talking to him. Why he had accepted her invitation but not mine I did not know, but as soon as I saw him I was filled with pleasure.

When Donald and I had made our introductions Maura joined me at the dinghy and she agreed to put on her aqualung for the underwater pictures. She put her arms over the side of the inflatable and lifted herself inboard as easily as a seal hauling itself out of the sea. I hovered just off the boat, bobbing up and down while Ashley helped Maura on with her gear. A few minutes later she was back in the sea with Donald, who was swimming excitedly in and out of the gloom. We both sank together and I watched the plumes of bubbles rising from her aqualung. Everything was set. Donald followed her down. I reached down for the camera with its new wide-angle lens, that I had slung round my neck. But it was not there. I felt again. It was definitely no longer around my neck. For a moment my stomach felt as if it had been gripped and squeezed by a pair of strong hands.

I looked up and down, as my vision was limited by my facemask, and felt all around me with my hands. I could neither see it, nor touch it. I signalled to Maura and we surfaced together.

"Have you seen my camera?"

"No. I thought you put it round your neck."

"I did."

"Well it's not there now. Does it float or sink?"

"The new lens floats and the camera sinks."

I could not remember whether the combination of the

two sank or floated. I had been bobbing up and down in the water, hanging on to the side of the dinghy, when I had put the strap round my neck. I had been so intent on getting other events organised I had not noticed whether the camera, with its buoyant dome lens attached to it, floated or sank. And I had no idea when it had come adrift.

"My guess is that it just floats," I decided.

"In that case we had better look for it straight away," replied Maura.

We looked across the water and searched intently for any sign of the plastic dome gleaming in the light. But the choppy water made it unlikely that we would see anything floating, unless it was very close by.

"With this strong wind blowing it could have drifted a long way." I groaned.

"Let's unhitch the inflatable and drift with the wind," suggested Maura.

"Good thinking, Mrs M," I replied.

We unhitched our weightbelts and aqualungs in the water and Ashley stowed them in the boat before we climbed back inboard. I untied the mooring rope from the old car tyre on the side of the fishing boat. With the three of us sitting on the inflated walls of the 'Buc' scanning the water surface we bumped gently up and down in the choppy water as the wind jostled us across the harbour.

After about five minutes, which seemed very much longer, we had drifted close to the line of fishing boats moored to the harbour wall. We looked along their waterlines and in between them, but there was no sign of my camera. The camera was black and the new lens mount was dark grey. Apart from the clear plastic dome it would be difficult to see in the water.

"Are you sure it floats?" asked Maura.

"No, I'm not absolutely sure," I replied.

"Well what shall we do then?" she questioned.

"Let's row back to the fishing boat and look on the bottom. I'll row," I replied.

As I pulled at the oars with short, hard jabs I added: "You two keep on looking."

The 'Buc' jumped over the waves and we eventually tied up to the fishing boat again without sighting the camera.

My training told me that finding lost objects on the sea bed is difficult and I should have commenced with a systematic search pattern, but I was impatient and decided to start with a random search. I took no heed of the fact that I felt a little exhausted after my row. Ashley lifted my aqualung cylinder on to my back. As soon as I had buckled the quick release fastening I put the mouthpiece into my mouth and rolled into the water. I was so pre-occupied with my loss that I did not feel the cold as I headed down into the green water.

I arrived at an outcrop of broad-leaved seaweed known as Laminaria that I recognised, and I scanned it carefully from above. It hardly stirred. That was a good sign, for it indicated that there was little current. I realised that if the camera had dropped into the kelp I would be very lucky to find it, for it would slip down beneath the brown blades that obscured the seabed like a blanket. I swam round the kelp patch and headed in the direction I thought I had taken when I first entered the water, but the seabed was devoid of any other specific features that were fixed in my memory. I glided over the muddy sand with odd outcrops of small boulders, some of which provided the necessary foothold for the holdfasts of Laminaria and other seaweeds. Donald zoomed in out of the bluegreen haze and looked at me.

"Hallo Donald," I spoke into my mouthpiece, "You've just cost me a lot of money."

He nodded at me. I continued to look at the seabed, not taking much notice of him. He swam in close to me and nodded again.

"No, I can't take your picture," I said, "I've lost my camera."

I put my hand out and stroked him gently along the top of his head, being careful not to touch his blowhole, which I knew to be a very sensitive area. He responded by shaking his head and swimming slowly forward. Without thinking I followed. He swam ahead. Then he nosed down to the seabed excitedly and, with his body vertical in the water, he flexed himself a couple of times. I looked down. There lying on the sand, just below his snout, was my camera.

I swam quickly down and picked it up.

"You clever fellow," I chortled into my mouthpiece as a feeling of intense relief flooded through my body.

I discovered that one end of the neck strap, which should have been attached to the camera via a split ring, had come free. The ring was partially open because it had been put on and off the camera several times. Nonetheless, to remove it required a deliberate rotational movement of the ring. I concluded that, although the chances of this happening were very small, it must have happened when I was bobbing in the water alongside the dinghy. What was even more remarkable, however, was the fact that I had found the camera again with its new, unused, fish-eye lens still in position.

I hurried up to the surface and waved it at Maura.

"You've found the camera, Horace," she cried, expressing with her voice as much relief and happiness as I felt inside.

"Yes, with Donald's help. He's here in the water just below me. Come on. In you come."

I decided to hold on to the camera after that, and held the viewfinder up to my eye. When I looked through it I found that my view of the underwater world was marvellously expanded. There was distortion round the edge of field where the image was curved, but the view through the viewfinder was definitely brighter and much wider than I could see through the tunnel vision of my facemask. The underwater world was much more attractive when viewed in this way, and I was fascinated because I could see both the surface of the sea and the kelp on the bottom. I watched Maura's bubbles chasing overhead to the bright silver-blue surface, and contrasted that image with the dull brown sand on the bottom. In between these two extremes the colour of the water itself ranged from dark green near the seabed, to a pale zircon blue overhead.

I realised that my new fish-eye lens was giving me a dolphin's-eye-view of the underwater world and I gazed at it in fascination. The extra view seemed to add a completely new dimension to my world, compared with the disc of vision seen through the flat glass plate of a facemask. It made me realise how much better Donald's eyesight was adapted to his environment than I had previously considered.

As I peered into the wide-screen circular picture in the viewfinder, I saw Donald's grey shape appear in the edge of the frame and rapidly become larger. Maura was visible in the distance and I swam towards her until she nearly filled the frame. My view of her seemed exceptionally clear. Donald was there too. Excitedly I clicked the shutter. Donald disappeared and I looked away from the camera. Immediately my vision contracted down to the relatively small disc normally seen by the diver, and I was surprised to see that I was only about nine inches away from Maura.

I was overjoyed. If the pictures were anywhere near the clarity of the image I had seen through the viewfinder, they would be excellent. The poor visibility underwater — which until that time I had always regarded as a barrier to good full-length photographs of people — had been cut through. I had succeeded at something I had been trying to achieve for fifteen years. I had broken the "underwater visibility barrier" with my new dolphin-eye lens.

With Donald in the water, and Maura posing for pictures with him, I was extremely happy. And those moments of joy were heightened by the small tragedy of a few minutes before, just as pleasure is always enhanced when it has been hard won.

Donald was intensely interested in the shiny, perspex dome of my new lens. He came and put his snout in contact with it and then hovered a few inches away, looking at it intently. Such lenses give a very exaggerated perspective and when I held the camera up to my eye I could see Donald's head clearly and could see the length of his body, which appeared to become tapered and thin, as if it was a long way away. I could also see Maura swimming near his tail. She too looked small. The vision I had through the viewfinder was of a huge whale in clear water, with a diver in the far distance.

Having inspected my camera Donald next moved his attention to my leg. I could feel a gentle pressure against my thigh. I looked down and could see Donald with his jaws open wide and my leg between his teeth. I realised that with his immensely powerful jaws he could probably sever my leg. In a moment of complete irrationality I said to myself, "If it's going to come off at least I will have the first picture of a dolphin biting a diver's leg." I pointed the camera towards my own midriff and clicked the shutter. Donald started for a moment and then continued to feel the texture of my wetsuit with his teeth and jaws.

In a moment his curiosity was satisfied and he swam away skittishly to inspect Maura and Ashley.

As time passed I became cold. Donald made fewer and fewer appearances, so after nearly an hour in the water in all, we abandoned the dive and climbed back into the inflatable. The wind helped to push us back to the slipway and I shivered as I pulled off my sopping wetsuit, hanging it over an upturned boat to drain. Grey clouds scudded across a grey sky as we headed for Port Erin to get our cylinders recharged with air.

As we drove along we discussed Donald. I had noticed that he had a new injury on the top of his head, where an approximately circular chunk of flesh about four inches in diameter had been completely cut out. The wound was deep and at its centre was a patch of red-raw vascular tissue. This was encircled with a ring of grey-white blubber. It did not appear to be infected.

Maura explained that Donald had been playing with a power boat when it happened. He was riding the bow wave, which would drive him forward at the same speed as the boat with relatively little effort. The dolphin probably then got into a position where he no longer had the benefit of the forward moving water, and before he could accelerate away the boat had passed over him. He was struck by the metal skeg which projects down below the propellor, with such force that the mountings of the outboard engine had been distorted and taken to Maura's husband Pete for repair.

It must have been a stunning blow, and if that skeg had hit his blowhole the dolphin would almost certainly have died from drowning. Donald seemed to lead a charmed life, I reflected.

In the height of the summer Port Erin is alive with holidaymakers who swarm over the sands, and along the streets, like ants. When the season closes they disappear, leaving the town to the locals and the seagulls.

On that cool October day Maura, Ashley and I were the only people to stroll along the foreshore. We entered an empty cafe — painted pale blue and white. Water in a chromium-plated urn behind the counter boiled continuously, waiting for the few customers who strayed in from the road. Steam condensed on the windows. Although it was not cold outside I was glad to get inside to the muggy warmth and have a hot cup of tea. The proprietor was pleased to see us and we exchanged stories. We told her of our adventures with Donald. She, on her part, remarked on the quiet at the end of the season, when Port Erin was preparing to decline into its hibernation until the tourists returned the following year. Maura, however, pointed out that it was only an apparent hibernation. Behind the surface quiet many activities went on. The divers on the island dived throughout the winter months — although less frequently than in the summer, with the influx of "comeovers".

It was mid-afternoon before we returned to Port St Mary and I was pleased to see Donald still surfacing regularly in the same area where we had seen him during our late morning dive. He still appeared to be enjoying himself and I wondered if he was ever unhappy. Maura and Ashley were pleased, as always, to see Donald but they were less enthusiastic about going in the water with him. But my ambition to get to know

Photo: David Aspinall

Above: The author introduces Donald to a rubber quoit. His lack of any immediate response to 'toys' convinced us that Donald had never been in captivity.

Below: The camera moves in to film Maura and Donald in a quiet mood.

Photo: David Aspinall

Photo: Horace Dob

Maura greets Donald as he arrives for one of our first picture-taking sessions in the harbour of Port St Mary on the Isle of Man.

Photo: Horace Dobbs

Donald swims down quietly to take a look at a picture of himself drawn by a schoolboy. When the picture was removed and the mirror behind it was exposed, Donald's attitude changed completely and he became very agitated. He knocked the mirror from Maura's grasp and would not let either of us go near it.

Above: Donald is a natural film star. He always enjoys the company of divers when they are actually performing tasks under the water. He quickly becomes bored and swims away if all they do is swim around him.

Below: 'Cue Donald and action!' Barry Cockcroft (centre) watches Donald whilst Mostafa Hammuri films a sequence for the Yorkshire Television film 'Ride A Wild Dolphin'.

Photo: David Aspin

Donald better and get more pictures of him was so single-minded that I conveniently forgot that my son was only thirteen years old, and Maura was a woman.

"Come on let's get kitted up," I said, in a voice that I hoped sounded like a request, but which concealed an order.

A fishing boat was making ready to leave the harbour and Donald was happily diving around it.

"That boat is going out and Donald will follow it," said Maura in an attempt to persuade me that getting kitted up would be a waste of time.

I pulled my soggy, cold wetsuit out of its plastic bag and hung it on the boat lashed to the roofrack of the car. Noticing me weaken at the prospect of stripping off my clothes and pulling on the cold, clammy suit, she tried quickly to push open the door of reason.

"Remember the divers' motto — a warm diver is a happy diver."

Then Ashley joined in.

"The fishing boat is leaving the harbour and Donald is going out with it," he pointed out.

For a moment I wavered. Then that streak of character — which I call resolution, and other people have been heard to refer to in my company as "stubbornness", and out of earshot as "bloodymindedness" — took control and slammed the door of reason in their faces.

"In that case we shall just about be ready by the time he gets back."

Realising that I really did intend to dive again, Maura and Ashley pulled out the bag containing their wetsuits from the car and left me in no doubt about the discomfort I was asking them to suffer on my behalf.

Half an hour later we were again loading the inflatable with our cylinders and the camera equipment. The wind was beginning to drop, as it does so often in the evening following a blustery day, and jagged streaks of sunlight were splitting the clouds overhead into multi-hued islands of yellow and white.

The boat was soon loaded and, as it nosed out of the slipway and into the harbour, a grey dorsal fin humped the sea ahead of us and disappeared. Our escort had arrived. An instant later we could see him underneath us. I refrained from saying "I told you so," but I had no doubt that Ashley read my thoughts. I also read his "Big head", or more probably "Big 'ed", unspoken retort. But no malice has ever come between us and by the time we were all in the water, with Donald sporting with us, we were a happy trio of humans and all thoughts of cold and discomfort faded from our minds.

Maura was trying to swim down, but as soon as she stopped swimming she drifted slowly to the surface. I swam up with her and our heads broke the surface together.

"I want to get a shot of you sitting on the bottom," I said.

"Horace, I'm too light. I haven't enough weight to do that. I forgot it was low tide now and I would need more lead than I had this morning."

"Have we any spare weights in the dinghy?"

"No. They're in the car."

"Can't you pick up a rock?"

"I'll try."

I watched Maura swim down to the seabed to search for a suitable rock. She soon found one with a frond of kelp attached to it and placed the rock, which was about the size of four house bricks, on her lap. I hovered about ten feet away to wait for the silt she had stirred up to settle.

Before it did, out of the gloom, came a grey torpedo shape. It hovered momentarily, watching Maura sitting on the bottom. Then Donald moved in, pushed the kelp frond with his beak and nudged the rock off her lap. Maura floated gently up from her sitting position and manoeuvred herself so that she could pick up the rock again. Clutching it to her stomach she exhaled strongly to reduce her buoyancy and allowed the weight of the rock to hold her again in a sitting position. Before she had settled Donald again moved in, pushing away the fronds of kelp with his beak. I then saw

Maura move the rock from her lap and wave her legs in a finning motion to Donald, who watched from a few feet away. I could just hear her talking to him, then she picked up another rock without weed growing on it, put it on her lap, and for the third time settled on the bottom. Donald again looked at her from a few feet away, then he nodded his head and swam away to see Ashley.

I hovered nearby and waited for the silt to settle. The next time Donald swam excitedly by I took my picture. I tried to take a second picture but when I attempted to wind on the lever would not move. I had come to the end of the roll of film. I signalled to Maura to rise and we talked together as we bobbed on the surface.

"That was strange behaviour of Donald's," I said.

"Why?"

"Pushing the stone off your lap."

"That was not strange," she replied.

"It was to me."

"It wasn't to me," she said, in a matter of fact tone. "He thought I was trapped on the bottom by the stone and came to release me."

"Only twice," I said. "Not three times."

"Didn't you see me explain to him?"

"I could see you waving your legs and I thought I could hear you talking."

"I was. I was telling him that I was in no trouble and waved my legs to prove it," Maura replied, as if this was an absolutely obvious thing to do to a wild animal that could not understand English.

"Do you think he really understood?" I asked.

"Of course he did. When I had explained the situation to him he left the rock alone. Didn't he?"

I had to admit that Donald did appear to understand what she was trying to impart. I related it in my mind to a situation when I had encountered some Italian friends who spoke no English. I spoke not a word of Italian, but we were able to communicate broad ideas, if not fine details, by a combination of gesture and sound. Yet Maura and Donald's relationship seemed to me to enable them to go a step beyond, and to one side of that. Donald had no hands, but he had expressive eyes and could nod his head. He could also make noises, some of which were in the human hearing range, though many of which were of a much higher frequency. So it is possible that he uttered dolphinese noises. But on top of all that there was something else — some kind of telepathic communication, though I hesitate to call it that, or at least a special empathy, or understanding. Their relationship one to another became more and more puzzling and fascinating.

"I've run out of film," I said.

"Shall we wind it up?" she replied.

"No," I cried emphatically. "It's perfect now. I will row back to shore and reload. You can stay here if you like and play with Donald, put your aqualung aboard."

Ashley climbed into the dinghy and we rowed back to the slipway. The wind had dropped completely and the sun, low in the sky, cast a yellow path of light over the now still water.

When I looked back across the sea I could see the dark silhouetted shape of Maura's head, and occasional ripples and dark arches as Donald lazily humped the surface nearby. In that peaceful harbour the two of them were happy to be left alone without the need to pose for pictures.

I changed the film as quickly as I could, but I had to be careful that the salt water dripping from my suit did not get inside the camera. At last the job was done, but as I rowed back across the water I realised that the sun had set and the sea had lost its yellow glow. I tied up quickly and slipped over the side. Under water it was cold and gloomy and the light intensity was too low for photography. Nonetheless I was happy. Indeed we were all happy. I remembered the old adage "Red sky at night, shepherds' delight". Although the sky was not red it had been yellow, and the portents were that the next day would be fine.

7: Maura and Donald

Most of the observations to date on dolphins in the wild have been made from the surface of the water, from ships. Occasionally the behaviour of a school of dolphins desporting themselves around a ship at sea has been recorded on film — few who have seen Cousteau's classic movie *Silent World* will fail to recall the exhilarating sight of a whole school of dolphins leaping one after another out of the water, and interweaving in the air as if in a joyous and complex dance.

But to me equally memorable were the underwater shots in the same film, taken from the observation chamber in the bow of *Calypso*. Yet although it is now twenty years since I saw *Silent World*, and skin diving has become commonplace all over the world, I know of no film showing divers sporting with free dolphins in the sea. As Robert Sternuit pointed out, wild dolphins have continued to refuse to associate with man underwater. It seems that whenever divers have encountered dolphins swimming free in the sea, and attempted to film them their plans have been cut short, because the dolphins have simply swum away. Indeed, in his book entitled *Dolphins*, Cousteau admits defeat in his own attempts to study dolphins in the wild in this way.

In order to complete a film at all, Cousteau had to adopt a compromise solution. He captured some dolphins and restrained them, in the sea, with three inflated sausage-shaped buoys linked together in the form of a triangle with a net suspended beneath them. He concedes that this capture and imprisonment caused the dolphins obvious alarm and distress. He never kept them for more than two or three days, and most of them were set free again on the same day, to reduce their trauma to a minimum. But how many dolphins died as a result of these experiments we shall never know. When I once asked Cousteau how he could justify killing dolphins in order to make a film, he replied that he would never attempt such an experiment again.

Cousteau was thwarted even when he tried to get underwater film in the sea of a 'tame' bottlenose dolphin named Dolly, who had associated with the Ashbury family in Florida since May 1971. Dolly apparently made her way one day through the numerous canals that have been cut through the coral of the islands, to the pontoon off the Ashbury property, several miles from the open ocean. When Jean Ashbury offered the dolphin a fish, she eagerly accepted it, and from that moment Dolly became a regular visitor to the Ashbury dock. Dolly swam with the Ashburys' children, and would tow them through the water if they caught hold of her dorsal fin. She was so friendly that she was seen as "one of the family".

The Ashburys' enquiries revealed that Dolly had originally been captured by the United States Navy and assigned to a dolphin training base at Key West. The "study centre" had then been transferred from Florida to California, so it was decided to release Dolly from military service, and she had been set free once again in the sea.

However, when Cousteau and his team visited the Ashbury family and took the dolphin out to sea in the hope of filming her, Dolly invariably returned immediately to the murky waters of the canal — where of course underwater filming was impossible. Cousteau never did achieve his ambition of filming the dolphin swimming freely with divers in the sea.

I thus realised how extraordinarily lucky I had been to encounter Donald and Maura. Right from the start, however, I established one principle from which I resolved I would never deviate in any circumstances: *Donald's freedom was sacrosanct*. No matter how desperate I was to get pictures or underwater film, if Donald did not like what we were doing, or just felt like doing something else, he could always simply swim away. I made this private resolve independently, but I soon discovered that it was also Maura's own: to her the idea of her dolphin being constrained in any way was utterly abhorrent.

Indeed, as I talked to her about Donald, I realised that the concept of the dolphin's freedom was integral to the uniqueness of their relationship one with another. She never attempted to impose her will on Donald, as for instance trainers of captured dolphins must do when they teach them to do tricks in dolphinariums. On the contrary, she said, when they were together in the sea Donald was always master of the situation. She drew my attention to his behaviour in the presence of divers as an indication of his complex and independent personality: he would remain interested in a group of divers only if they were carrying out some task of their own, not if they simply attempted to play with him. If they persisted in trying to grab hold of him he would swim away. Maura interpreted this behaviour as meaning that Donald was not prepared to accept any domination by human beings. At the same time, however, he did not like to be ignored completely: he liked to have his presence acknowledged, and once this was done would take such a keen interest in what was going on that he sometimes intervened and disrupted the work altogether. If he wanted to continue the game when the divers had finished their tasks he would attempt to stop them leaving the water by pulling on their fins as they tried to climb aboard their diving boat.

Maura treated Donald as if he were a very special and sensitive personal friend. And inevitably, I too thought in terms of human characteristics when I tried to define him to myself: to me he seemed like a person of very great physical strength, happy, fiercely independent, even self-willed, but above all totally free. In the sea, Donald was so superior to both of us, physically as well as in the sensitivity of his response to environment, that Maura and I acquired considerable humility in his presence. Maura always showed great understanding and tenderness for him. I think I too was sensitive to his moods, but I was less prepared to be submissive to his will.

Maura was always concerned for Donald's safety, and her diving buddies would often send in reports when they spotted Donald. Maura's special diving partner was Mike Dunning. One evening Mike was driving home from work via Port St Mary in order to check up on Donald, when he saw the dolphin in a seeming frenzy, whirling around one of the buoys. Alarmed that he might have been caught up in the buoy line, Mike telephoned Maura who immediately grabbed her wetsuit, flung it in the car, and with tea forgotten raced down to Port St Mary with her husband Pete. Mike was already kitted up, and Maura and Mike snorkelled out into the harbour with Pete observing from the shore. As the two snorkellers neared the moorings, Donald, who had been lying quietly on the surface, finned over to greet them. Maura was very relieved to find that her dolphin friend was quite unharmed.

Here, in Maura's own words, is what happened next.

"There followed a most rumbustious game, a right mad session. Mike became very anxious when he realised how possessive Donald was towards me and he feared for my safety when Donald got sexy. After a hide-and-seek session around the triple hull of a trimaran, Mike insisted I got out of the water for my own good, which I did."

On that occasion the dolphin overtly exhibited the sign of sexual arousal, i.e. erection of the penis, which is common to mammals prior to copulation. Such a display is easily recognised. Other bodily expressions of emotion are frequently more subtle and skill to interpret them is something we acquire with familiarity, often without realising it. Humans often unwittingly use their lips and mouth to express their innermost feelings. A shut mouth with the lips turned down at the corners indicates depression. Whereas lips turned up at the corners coupled with a display of teeth is a gesture, called a smile, which we all associate with a feeling of pleasure. However, although such gestures appear to be spontaneous, they may have been adopted as a result of a cultural learning process. So it can be misleading to interpret animal behaviour in terms of analogy with human behaviour. In monkeys, for instance, the showing of the teeth in an expression which we would call a smile is in fact a sign of aggression, as it is in dogs.

As Donald did not have mobile lips the line of his mouth was not an indication of his feeling at any one time. He could, however, open his mouth. If he did this several times in quick succession it was usually a sign of pleasure associated with curiosity.

It was also possible to interpret Donald's mood from the posture of his body in the water. Hanging vertically in the water with his head down seemed to indicate that he was relaxed and was interested in what was going on just below his beak.

There is one organ in all of the higher animals which can express emotion with very subtle, almost indefinable changes, to which we are all intuitively sensitive. That organ is the eye. Human eyes can display a feeling of utter despair and dejection when they become dull, or conversely a spirit of joy and vitality, when they are bright and sparkling. Poets, lyricists, film makers and photographers have all recognised the power of the eyes to convey emotion. "Your eyes are the eyes of a woman in love" is how one popular song identifies a state of mind that we all understand.

And Maura confirmed that she was particularly sensitive to Donald's inner state as it was communicated by the expression in his eyes. If he came up to her slowly and closed his eyes it was a signal that he wanted to be loved, and Maura would cuddle him and stroke him gently. On such occasions he would remain submissive and docile to her caresses. If on the other hand his eyes were bright and full of mischief, she knew that he wanted a game, and they would romp accordingly.

I had first met Maura in August 1973, shortly after she

moved to the island and settled in the village of Ballasalla with her husband Peter and two sons. She came to greet me when I landed at Ronaldsway Airport for a diving trip and two hours later I was diving from the Mitchells' cabin cruiser into clear water amidst some of the most beautiful underwater scenery with the richest marine life I had encountered during fifteen years of diving off various parts of the British Coast. I immediately understood why Maura was so enthusiastic about her new home.

I guessed at the time that she was in her early thirties, though when I later found out that she had a twenty-year-old son I realised that I was wrong. However, it was apparent from our first meeting that she was a woman of youthful appearance and even more youthful spirit. And after diving with her I realised that physically she matched her appearance.

She was very fit, she could carry her aqualung and heavy diving gear as well as a man, and heave herself into an inflatable after a dive as easily as a seal flipping up on to the rocks. However, she was of small stature but with a well proportioned figure. She wore her blonde hair straight and shoulder length to frame a pixie face, her eyes were blue and she had that undefinable quality known universally as sex appeal.

In Britain diving is still primarily a man's game. Women who make it to the top grades in the British Sub Aqua Club, as Maura had done, are rare, and those who do so usually have very exceptional qualities indeed. Maura had reached instructor grade without losing any of her femininity.

So there we were — an exceptional dolphin and an exceptional woman. And the exceptional chance that the two of them should meet in that magical underwater world that was Donald's natural environment which man was only beginning to penetrate. And I had had the exceptional good luck to encounter them both. I felt exhilarated, full of a sense that something important was happening. I was yet not clear what it was.

8: A Magic Moment

The next day dawned full of promise. Clear blue sky. No wind. Our diving suits, which had been washed thoroughly the night before, hung lifeless and bone-dry under the verandah. I am suspicious of days that begin so well. They have a nasty habit of not living up to the promises they so coquettishly offer. However, any doubts I might have had about the weather were quickly suppressed when I joined Ashley and Maura for breakfast. The sun was shining and we were all looking forward to the prospect of our next meeting with Donald.

Before our rendezvous however we had to repair a hole in the rubber floor of the inflatable. By the time this was done and the domestic chores had been attended to, the time was approaching midday. During the morning brilliant white puffs of cotton wool cloud had begun to pepper the sky, and as we loaded the inflated C-Craft on to the roofrack of Maura's Mini-Countryman the wind, which had crept into the morning as a zephyr, was already rattling the television aerials.

It was 12.45 when we drove on to the familiar jetty at Port St Mary. The wind was blowing so strongly from the north-west that even across the small fetch of the harbour it was able to raise white horses. It was close to high water and waves were swishing and gurgling up the stone slipway where we had proposed to launch the inflatable. One hundred yards offshore the red, white and blue lifeboat, one of Donald's favourite haunts, bobbed up and down, snatching at its forward mooring rope like a spirited horse on a tight leading rein.

We parked the car so that we could scan the sea. The car

shuddered occasionally when the wind caught the dinghy lashed to the roof rack. With the sun shining on to us inside the car we were as cosy as embryos in a womb. But the vibrations of the vehicle and the white crests on the waves were evidence enough that my old enemy, the wind, was out there snorting, and prodding his cold sword into any nook or cranny he could find.

We could not be sure that Donald would be in Port St Mary, and as we looked out across the harbour we realised that it would be difficult to spot him amidst the waves as he briefly surfaced and exposed his blowhole to take a breath. We carefully scanned the water around the blue boat where we had enjoyed his company the day before. Even the heavy fishing boat was snatching at its mooring lines, but with a stronger, longer pull than the relatively light lifeboat which rode higher out of the water. There was no sign of the dolphin.

On the far side of the harbour a child's inflatable boat about five feet long was bobbing up and down on the sea like a buoy. It was attached to a single white mooring line that disappeared beneath the water. Two lightweight plastic oars were permanently attached to the boat via circular rubber rowlocks which were built into the tubular sides. Thus the oars projected over the side of the boat as if held by an invisible oarsman. We hardly noticed the dinghy until a particularly vicious gust of wind picked it off the sea and held it suspended in the air, where it spun as if played on a shimmering white line by an unseen angler beneath the water. The bottom of the toy boat was coloured red and the top cream. It flashed alternately red and cream as it spun before crashing back into the sea upside down. A few seconds later the wind again whipped it into the air. Like an out-of-control kite it danced in the air before flopping down again — the right way up.

Ensconced in the car we watched, fascinated by the boat's aerial acrobatics. But we were not only the only beings to be entertained. When the dinghy landed for a third time and briefly floated on the surface a dark silver shape rose out of the water alongside. Cascading diamonds of dripping water from its body, it arched gracefully over the dinghy and splashed into the water again on the far side.

We all saw what happened, but it was Maura who got the words out first.

"There's Donald," she said, her blue eyes sparkling like sun on the sea.

She spun her head to face me.

"I told you he would be here," she said in a voice of triumphant self-vindication.

We all got out of the car. Maura's hair flew back like a horse's mane at full gallop as she stood on the edge of the jetty clinging to the rail, waiting for the next sighting. We did not have to wait long. Seconds later Donald again performed a spectacular leap. It was as if the wind had injected him with energy. His obvious enjoyment of the wind and the waves radiated from his flashing silver body. Maura shouted and waved. Donald responded immediately. He put on a spectacular display of leaps and aquabatics as if to prove that anything the wind could do with an inanimate rubber dinghy he could do one thousand times better.

Had you asked me at that moment if I thought that Donald was even aware of our presence, let alone putting on a display for Maura's benefit, I would probably have dismissed the idea as pure poppycock. Now however, with the benefit of hindsight and a much deeper understanding of the relationship between Maura and her dolphin, I would interpret his actions differently. I would say that Donald not only saw Maura, but that he recognised her and that the pleasure he derived from the wind, sea and prancing dinghy was enhanced by her presence, so that the display he now put on was not simply an expression of his own exuberance, but a sign that he was pleased to see her.

The rising of the wind had completely frustrated my objective for the day, which was to photograph Donald underwater. But my usual intense irritation and frustration at such circumstances was absent. And the reason for my

unlikely good humour was one which I have since had reason
to ponder on, and had confirmed by many others who have
had experience of dolphins: the fact that dolphins somehow
seem to exude a special kind of joy which they are able to
transmit to man. I have yet to find a man who was not happy
upon the sight of a dolphin. Many a ship's log has recorded
that the vessel was being escorted by a school of dolphins,
and to a seaman reading such a log this information
immediately conjures up a vision of a happy ship — a ship
going well. Even the most hardened of seamen will come on
deck and enjoy the sight of dolphins gambolling in the sea
alongside. And there is something in this quality of dolphins
that goes beyond the pleasure that most people feel when they
are able to watch other animals at play, domestic or wild.

Near where we had parked, a small fishing boat had been
filling up with empty scallop shells. A lorry from the nearby
processing plant poured its load down a chute on to the deck
and returned for another cargo. When the fishing boat was
fully loaded it pulled away from the jetty, turned bow first
into the buffeting wind, and headed for the harbour
entrance. Just before it passed out of sight we could see
Donald leaping out of the water in front of it. It was time for
him to carry out his escort service, a self-imposed duty he
seldom failed to perform when a vessel left his territory.

We also departed. We bought some cakes and headed for
the other side of the bay, where we found a spot completely
sheltered from the wind to picnic. As we munched our food
we looked longingly at the still clear water that idly washed
back and forth over the sand and slippery green seaweed. If
only it could be as flat as this in Port St Mary we could all
join Donald again. Overhead, white clouds slid across the sky
like leaves floating down a fast moving stream, and across the
bay we could see white horses rearing out of the deep blue
sea. But were they subsiding? I fancied they were.

Maura's husband, Peter, had decided to build himself a
new boat, after he had found a flagstaff thrown up on the
rocks near to where we were sitting. His description of

this event, and how various other components for this major project had come his way equally fortuitously, had fascinated Ashley, and fired in him an immediate interest in beachcombing. This is an occupation which I openly admit I too have enjoyed since my earliest memories, so after lunch we scrambled over the rocks, turning over the flotsam with our feet and hands to see what other treasurers providence might have deposited on the shore for our benefit.

From there we moved to the lee side of the harbour of Port St Mary. Like all working fishing harbours, it was a captivating place. The air was tinted with the smell of tar from freshly treated lobster pots, which were stacked in piles of higgledy-piggledy confusion. We picked our way amongst the coils of rope and fishing nets draped across the ground, and looked in and at the boats tied up to the jetty. The shapes, textures, sounds and smells harmonised into a living picture in which we ourselves were briefly moving figures. Maura pointed out a boat with the same hull structure — a Newhaven Sea Angler — as the one Peter was building. We discussed the construction, the line, the seaworthiness, the engine and the problems and pleasures of building your own boat. We also inspected some giant blocks of concrete that had been cast on the site. Maura explained that the harbour was being modified and extended. Little did we know at that time what repercussions these harbour constructions were to have on our lives, and in particular on that of our friend the dolphin.

As the shadows started to lengthen and the others thought of heading back for Ballasalla, my mind was gradually evolving another plan. The wind was definitely dropping. Would it weaken, as it so often does on a blustery day, to give a calm evening? If this happened there was still a chance that we could dive. I put my thoughts to Maura and Ashley. They are both of a generous nature, and agreed to have one last look at the sea from the jetty where we had previously launched the inflatable for our meetings with Donald.

When we arrived it was about five o'clock. The tide had

fallen, revealing a small stretch of yellow sand. Earlier the unyielding stone walls alongside the slipway had thrown the furious waves back upon themselves, in a turmoil of angry motion. Now the waves had diminished. They dissipated their violence without damage into the absorbent sand, and spent the last of their energy slithering harmlessly up and down the newly-exposed beach. It certainly would be possible to launch the inflatable.

But there was no sign of Donald.

We looked out at the fishing boat and the lifeboat, his adopted homes in Port St Mary. We could not see the characteristic rise of his shiny black hump.

"I wonder where he is?" said Maura. "There's no sign of him."

"I'm sure he'll turn up if we call him in the water," I said, more in hope than expectation. "Come on, let's get changed."

The sun, which earlier had penetrated our clothes and warmed us, had lost its heat and hung like a glowing tangerine in the western sky. The base of the slipway was in deep shadow. Gusts of cold wind funnelled into the slipway and pulled at the inflatable as we lifted it off the roof rack and dropped it with a bump on to the stone-cold cobbles.

I pulled my wetsuit from its plastic bag and was relieved to find that it was still warm from its cosy place in the back of the car. I caught the characteristic smell of neoprene as I pulled the yielding rubber over my goose-pimpled skin.

Maura is an efficient diver and a diving instructor. Once the decision to dive had been made she disappeared behind the car and re-appeared a few minutes later fully clothed in her blue wetsuit. Her pixie features were exaggerated by the hood which tightly hugged her face.

The three of us carried the Buc down to the water's edge with the jerky steps of people walking painfully across stony ground. Ashley held the inflatable out to sea whilst we returned for the aqualungs and other diving gear. I returned once again to the car and opened the battered blue suitcase that contained my carefully packed cameras. Having checked that they were all in order, I closed the lid and wondered what the others would have to say about all the discomfort I had pressed them to endure, if Donald did not turn up, for there was still no sign of him. I dumped my suitcase into the inflatable, while Maura was patiently holding the oars and fending off from the jagged rocks. I grabbed the transom and pushed the Buc into the waves before climbing into the stern. Five minutes later we were tied up to one of the old car tyres hanging down over the side of the fishing boat.

We should have seen Donald by now, for he invariably came to inspect any new movement of boats or people. We peered into the cold water for a sight of a friendly face looking back at us. But we saw only the dark green uninviting depths.

"I will go in and call him," I said to Maura as I heaved the metal cylinder of my aqualung on to my back and buckled the yellow harness. I picked my lead weightbelt from the water swirling over the duckboards in the bottom of the boat. The lead bit into my back as I pulled it tight around my waist. I hung a camera around my neck and drew on my facemask before finally putting the mouthpiece of my regulator between my lips. I tested that it was functioning properly. When I breathed in the air hissed into my lungs like a spitting snake. All systems were "go". I sat on one of the soft rubber walls of the inflatable and rolled back-first into the water.

The sea closed over me like a dark, cold, green blanket. I was surrounded by a cloud of tiny bubbles injected into the water by my entry and sucked down by my passage. I found my bearings after the two seconds of confusion that always follow a backward entry into the sea and watched the curtain of bubbles I had dragged down with me chasing one another erratically back to the surface. The dark brown seabed was only about fifteen feet beneath me. I checked that my camera was still in position, held the top of my mask against my forehead and exhaled gently through my nose. This cleared the few tablespoons of water that leaked into my mask. I allowed myself to sink slowly.

"Donald, Donald," I called into my mouthpiece. As I sank I revolved slowly, anxiously awaiting his appearance in response to my call.

The sea was absolutely still. It must have been slack low water.

Nearby some long dark brown fronds of seaweed lay draped over a hump in the seabed like discarded flowers on a rubbish tip. I knew their presence was indicative of a rock outcrop. So I swam over to the mound and rummaged amongst the seaweed until I found two stones about the size of Christmas puddings.

I clapped the rocks together and I could hear the sharp crack of the sound penetrating the water like a gunshot. Clouds of silt dispersed when the two stones met. I stood still and peered into the encircling green wall. There was no sight of my quarry. In annoyance I crashed the two stones together as hard as I could. One of them shattered and the pieces zig-zagged to the bottom.

"Oh come on Donald, please," I pleaded into the water. The words vanished like my bubbles.

I surfaced beside the inflatable.

"He's not here," I told Maura. "At least he won't come to me. Will you come in and call him?"

"The things I do for you, Horace," she said with a cheeky grin on her face. A few seconds later she launched herself into the cold green soup.

I could see her mouthing the word "Donald" as she descended beside me. I could just detect the disorted word mixed with the regular squeak of the air passing through her demand valve.

We swam over to the mound. I picked up two more stones and banged them together. Maura found an old tin can and bashed it with the handle of her diving knife. As she sat on the hump of seaweed singing her siren song and beating time on her tin drum, I thought I could have been watching a sequence from an unlikely movie. The next event almost convinced me that I was watching a Walt Disney cartoon. For when I next saw Maura she was still sitting on the rock calling. But this time, behind her back, vertical in the water, with his nose three inches from the back of her head was a motionless dolphin.

Donald had arrived.

I moved towards her. She looked up and raised both hands palm upwards. At the same time she tilted her head to one side and shrugged her shoulders. It was a gesture which is universally understood. It means "It is hopeless." In the underwater world of the diver no verbal communication is possible unless special equipment, which we were not wearing, is used. Maura pointed to the surface indicating that we should return to the boat. Donald remained quite still.

I now think he knew exactly what he was doing. He was quite deliberately teasing Maura.

I let on to his game by pointing at him vigorously. Maura turned. I knew without hearing that she was talking to him. She stretched up her arm and gently stroked him under the chin. He opened his huge mouth in a gesture that in human terms looked like a loud guffaw. With a flick of his fluke he arched away and returned a few strokes later for another caress and soft words from his human friend. When he saw me raise the bright dome of my fish-eye lens attached to my underwater camera he came to inspect it, putting his snout right up against the lens, thereby making picture taking impossible. Then he stood off a few feet and opened his mouth — again as if he was laughing — before sweeping round in a circle and heading for Maura. Donald was so agile and could move so swiftly underwater that we never knew where he would appear next. He would disappear outside the realms of our limited visibility with a few sweeps of his powerful fluke and reappear from a completely different direction. It was as if he knew he was far superior to us in the underwater environment. He was playing with us, not we with him.

It was then that I noticed that his pale pink penis was extended and that he was attempting to stroke it against Maura as he swam past her. Maura had told me before that Donald was sometimes "fruity", and now I could see by his actions exactly what she meant. Others who have had a similar experience in Donald's company have been more prosaic and referred to him as "A dirty old man!"

I have since thought about Donald's behaviour and have come to the conclusion that on that specific occasion at least it may have been completely misinterpreted. There are a number of reasons why this misunderstanding has come about.

One of the reasons is that when we look at animal behaviour we almost invariably attempt to find a human context in which to put it. Animal expressions and actions are translated into human expressions and actions, sometimes just in our minds, sometimes in our speech, but most frequently in cartoons. It amuses us to make such analogies. How often have you heard a person say jokingly "That dog looks just like his master." The archmaster of anthropomorphism was of course Walt Disney. It was he who saw in the timid yet woman-frightening mouse, the human-like characteristics that would turn a creature normally regarded as vermin into the lovable Mickey. There can be few houses in the western world that have not at some time or other been invaded by the rodent Mickey Mouse — and enjoyed his company. And adults and children alike have been entertained the world over by Walt Disney's film *Jungle Book*, in which we are introduced to four vultures who speak with Beatle-like Liverpool accents and a bear called Baloo with the unmistakable voice of Phil Harris. Even if Mickey Mouse may be considered in low taste in some households, I can think of no home where the animal tales of Beatrix Potter, or the antics of Toad of Toad Hall are forbidden reading in the playroom. So since our earliest childhood we have all been accustomed, and thereby conditioned, to interpret animal behaviour in human terms.

At the same time, our culture finds itself at present increasingly obsessed with sex. It is used subtly and crudely to entertain us. It is used by the media and the advertising men to manipulate us and to persuade us to buy anything from car tyres to bubble baths. Psychiatrists and Puritans offer us their — often conflicting — injunctions about sexual attitudes and sexual behaviour. We talk about it and worry about it as perhaps few societies have done before us, because from the age when we first watch television or take an interest in reading, we are bombarded with it. Sex — or the exploitation of sex — surrounds those living in cities like the incessant noise of traffic.

The morality of this situation is not relevant to the point I am about to make. It is that by anthropomorphising animal behaviour, and allowing ourselves to become obsessed with the idea of sex, we have completely misunderstood the behaviour of a highly intelligent animal — the dolphin. I suggest on the other hand that when Donald approached Maura with his penis extended he was not making a sexual approach to her, but was using his penis as a tactile organ to gain a greater knowledge of her. I am proposing that in addition to its function as a tract for urine and spermatozoa, the penis of the dolphin has a third and completely distinct role: that of a limb for tactile exploration. The dolphin can use its penis for exploring, feeling and interpreting surfaces and shapes in a totally non-sexual context. In doing so he adds to the mental picture he has of the object. The dolphin, as we have already observed, is an intensely curious animal, who gathers all the information he can about the world around him. So when he is in familiar surroundings and no harm threatens, he will use his most sensitive sense to gain a deeper understanding of his environment. Likewise, the blind man will feel with his hands the face of a friend to get to know him or her better.

How has this situation come about?

Let us consider the environment in which dolphins live. It is hostile and cold. The scars frequently seen on whales and dolphins, which are much in evidence on Donald, bear witness to the fact that the entire surface of their bodies is subject to lacerations and violent abrasion. Thus external organs must be completely protected. But a tough protective layer will inevitably reduce the sensitivity of the underlying tissue to external tactile stimuli: imagine a nurse wearing a thick pair of gloves attempting to measure a patient's pulse rate. Thus, although the dolphin's flippers have a bone structure that is distantly related to that of the human arm, and they can feel with the tips of these fins, there can be little doubt that human hands and fingers are very many times more sensitive to touch.

Humans, in common with other land mammals, have also another part of their body which is particularly sensitive to delicate touch sensations. That part is the lips. When human babies investigate an object, they first find out about it by touching with their hands. And if it is not too hostile they then subject it to further investigation in their mouths. This is not only to find out what it tastes like, but to determine characteristics such as smoothness and hardness. In later life, because they are so sensitive to touch, the adolescent human will use his lips to explore and discover his prospective mate.

Dolphins do not have lips. Their mouths are undoubtedly sensitive, but they lack the very supple, thin-skinned flesh that can detect very small differences in texture.

Male dolphins, do however, have a soft, flexible, thin-skinned member, rich in tactile nerves. During normal activities such as swimming and hunting it is kept safely retracted and protected. It can, however, be exposed when the dolphin wants to investigate and explore objects, including humans, in the fullest detail. That member is the penis.

The hypothesis is supported by the structure of the penis of dolphins. In land mammals the penis becomes erect when gorged with blood. This process is controlled by hormones which are usually released by some external stimulation, such as the smell of a female of the species on heat. Thus erection and contraction of the penis is a relatively slow process compared with most other movements which involve muscular action.

A study of the histological structure of the penis of the dolphin, however, reveals that the central section is riddled with strands of tough and elastic connective tissue, with a consequent reduction in the spongy tissue present in land mammals. Thus there is little change in size upon erection, and the erect member is relatively small compared with the size of the entire body of the dolphin. When the need arises a slit in the abdominal wall opens and the penis is flicked out by muscle action. The penis can also be rapidly retracted with the retractor penis muscle. Such muscular control, if voluntary, would obviously be beneficial to the dolphin when it uses its penis to touch and feel.

In their monograph on dolphins Cousteau and Diolé state that a newly born male dolphin is able to have an erection only a few hours after birth. Attempts at copulation take place during the first few weeks after birth and have the mother as sexual object. They state that the mother encourages copulation by turning on her side, and that this is the baby dolphin's first lesson in sexuality. I maintain that this is a false interpretation of the observed behaviour. I propose that the mother is teaching her offspring to feel and explore with his penis in a non-sexual context. It would be quite normal, on my hypothesis, for a baby to investigate his mother's breasts with his penis. As the female dolphin's breasts and genital orifice are in close proximity it is likely that both will be explored by the young offspring. This will be part of the learning process, as basic as a human baby being encouraged to put suitable objects in its mouth. Not until the dolphin approaches sexual maturity years later does its penis take on a further function — that of procreation. Throughout its life the dolphin maintains the use of the penis to feel objects, and in the same way that humans derive pleasure from touching things it probably enjoys an equivalent sensation, perhaps to a higher degree.

It is now generally accepted that men and dolphins had common ancestors about twenty-five million years ago, and that these ancestors were derived from animals that came from the sea. From that parting of the ways man and dolphin took very different paths. The dolphins returned to the sea and readopted the marine environment, but remained mammalian and continued to breathe air. During the course of evolution it is possible that the penis of the dolphin became increasingly sensitive as a retractable tactile sensor. During the same course of time our forbears evolved as upright land animals, whose hands and lips developed as their most sensitive organs of touch. Thus it is possible that millions of years ago our ancestors also used their penises as simple, non-sexual, touch sensors in addition to their function for procreation. But with the passage of time and the evolution of more suitable sensors this function has been completely lost.

Change or loss of function of particular organs through evolution is of course a process well recognised by biologists. Many parts of our bodies are now vestigial, and appear to have no role in our present stage of development, and if Darwin is correct, they will eventually disappear altogether. Perhaps the best known of these is the appendix which is thought to have played an important role when we were exclusively herbivores. Now it is sometimes regarded more as a potential hazard than as a benefit to the human race.

I must admit that all these thoughts were not going through my mind when I was watching Maura and Donald engrossed in their tactile, verbal and visual dialogue in the green sea off the Isle of Man. At that time I was totally absorbed in getting underwater pictures.

At one stage Maura rose to the underside of the fishing boat. As she did so I saw the propellor and the rudder silhouetted against the sun, which shone through the water like a broad spotlight. Where the beam entered the sea an amber disc of light danced to the time of the wavelets that rippled the surface. Donald swam round me and inspected the rudder in a mood of great apparent concentration. I drifted gently backwards watching the scene through the viewfinder, and rejoicing at the brilliant beauty of the contrast of the dark shadows with the sparkling light. I pressed the shutter.

Donald swam away and I drifted slowly down waiting for him to return. He did so a few minutes later and I swam back towards the keel of the fishing boat to get some more pictures. When I arrived the scene had changed completely. The sea now appeared to be illuminated from inside by a pale diffuse green light. The sun had set. Dusk was falling. The magic moment of sunset had gone.

It was time to go.

9: Masterpiece of Evolution

The animals that now inhabit the earth are the products of millions of years of evolution. They can be divided into groups which form the branches of an evolutionary tree. Each main branch, which we call an order, divides into sub-orders and families, often with wide variations.

In the course of the growth of the evolutionary tree some branches died and the species became extinct. Now only one species of man inhabits the earth — *Homo sapiens*. His branch stands out of the evolutionary tree as a single spike, not like a much-divided twig as do many other orders. It has been argued that the reason why there is now only one species of man on the earth is that our ancestors exterminated similar but non-aggressive branches from our evolutionary stem. That this inbuilt aggressive characteristic, which has dominated our evolution, is still present is supported by the manner in which, even within our own species, we continue to destroy these individual tribes and ethnic groups, such as the Australian Aboriginals, who show signs of being more pacific than the rest. Thus a single, highly intelligent, but basically aggressive mammal — *Homo sapiens* — now dominates the land masses of the world.

Approximately two thirds of our planet, however, is covered with water, and the dominant order of animals in the sea is undoubtedly the Cetaceans — the whales. The whales range from the 100-feet-long blue whale, to the five-feet-long harbour porpoise. And it has been argued that this order is so enormously diverse because, unlike men, it has built deep into its genetic make-up a trait of non-aggression, which allowed variations brought about by the processes of evolution to survive and develop along their own lines. This trait of non-aggression is certainly apparent in the lack of reaction of whales to the hideous injustices inflicted upon them by man. With aggression so central to our own make-up, it is sometimes difficult for humans to comprehend a species in which external threats and inflicted pain do not raise an aggressive response.

The Cetaceans are evolved from mammals that roamed the land 25 million years ago. Like all mammals, they breathe air — it was for this reason that Donald surfaced regularly and made his characteristic sound, which was like a diver blowing powerfully to clear his snorkel tube. They divide into two broad groups — the Mysticetes and the Odontocetes.

The Mysticetes, which, literally translated from the Greek, means 'whiskered whales', have within their membership the largest animals ever to have lived on the earth — far larger than the now extinct land mammoths of pre-historic times. At the top of the scale in terms of size is the blue whale. There is a lifesize model of a blue whale in the British Museum of Natural History in London which is as long as one and a half cricket pitches. Models may be all that future generations will see, for these magnificent creatures have been hunted near to extinction.

These largest animals in the world feed on some of the smallest animals in the world — tiny planktonic larvae in the sea. The whiskered whales sweep gently through the sea filtering off enormous quantities of krill through cartilaginous sieves composed of baleen, or 'whalebone'. These filtration slats are not in reality composed of bone, but are modified mucous membrane.

In the heyday of the whaling era, the baleen or whalebone found its way into many products. Perhaps best known are the whalebone corsets into which Victorian ladies squeezed their reluctant midriffs. But these animals were not hunted for their whalebone, that was a bonus. The major prize was the oil — which was used both as a food and for lighting — as much as 26 tons of it from one animal. Nowadays everything that is taken from the carcasses of these animals can be obtained from alternative sources, so it is no longer only need, but man's avarice, that drives the fishermen who hunt these and other large whales to the edge of extinction. It is sad to think that two of the richest nations in the world, the Japanese and the Russians, still kill these wonders of evolution.

The same fate has befallen many of the other category of whales, the Odontocetes, which means 'toothed whales'. When one looks at Donald's impressive array of triangular teeth, it is obvious that he belongs in this classification, whose members range from the sixty-feet-long sperm whale to the relatively small common porpoise.

When mammals took to a life in the sea, their weight was supported by the water and they became virtually weightless. The skeletons of their forbears, which had evolved both as support structures and for movement, were now required to adapt to the needs of a swimming mammal. Over the millenea the skull changed completely from the usual mammalian pattern. The nasal bones were reduced to two small nodules, and a new passage was evolved that opened to the exterior blowhole on the top of the head. There was a complete loss of the hind limbs, to facilitate streamlining. The fore limbs retained the same elements as land mammals but in greatly modified form. All trace of horny finger tips was lost. Freedom of movement was restricted to the shoulder joint, and the modified fore limbs (flippers) took on the function of controlling direction and acting as brakes. They were not used for propulsion. That function was left exclusively to the tail, which was assisted by an increase in the number of vertebrae in the lumbar region. This gave greater sensitivity and flexibility of movement to the tail. The propulsive power of the tail was also increased by the development of longer vertical processes (neural spines) for the attachment of the tendons of the powerful tail muscles.

The more I saw of Donald the more impressed I was with the dolphin's superb adaptation to life in the sea. All external protuberances which might impede the efficient passage of the dolphin through the water have been biologically modified to maintain perfect streamlining. The external ears have been reduced to two small pinholes. The eyes do not protrude. The male reproductive organ, the penis, is normally retained in an abdominal channel and is completely hidden from view behind a slit in the skin which is kept closed. In females the mammary glands are likewise located within the body, and the nipples retracted behind two so-called nipple slits on either side of the female genital opening. (The sex of a dolphin is thus not immediately apparent, as it is with most other mammals.)

The "bends" have caused the deaths of many human divers. Nitrogen in the blood dissolves when he dives deep, and may reappear again in the form of bubbles of gas in the bloodstream when he surfaces. If the bubbles block blood vessels, the supply of essential oxygen to nervous tissues may be stopped, giving rise to paralysis which can be fatal. The Cetaceans however have evolved a complex system of oil droplets in the bloodstream with a high capacity to dissolve nitrogen rapidly under pressure. The nitrogen dissolves into the oil droplets during a deep dive and is harmlessly released again when the animal comes back to the surface.

The dolphins have also evolved a respiratory system that enables them to inhale and exhale extremely quickly. They can move five to ten litres of air in and out of their lungs during the 0.3 seconds of the active part of their breathing cycle.

However, most remarkable of all of the evolutionary processes of adaptation to a marine environment, is undoubtedly the dolphin's development of a completely new communication system. Although men have spent millions of dollars on research into this system, there are still enormous gaps in our knowledge.

The need to adapt arises of course from the differences between air and water as conductors of light and sound. Whereas water is a less efficient conductor of light than air is, it is a better conductor of sound. Accordingly it is no surprise that the dolphin's primary communication system, both for collection and transmission of information, is based on sound; and his perception extends to frequencies much higher than can be detected by the human auditory senses. The external ears which serve in humans for collecting and reflecting aerial vibrations are absent. All that remains of the ear holes of the dolphin's land ancestors are two pinholes, which are extremely difficult to locate and are about two inches below and behind the eyes.

Without an air passage and an eardrum to vibrate, how does a dolphin hear? That is a question which is still being debated. Commercial divers will be aware that bones conduct sound for they will almost certainly have used "bone mikes" which are tucked inside the rubber hoods of their diving suits. A "bone mike" consists of a small loudspeaker enclosed in a tiny watertight capsule. When the signal is received by the loudspeaker (usually instructions about the task in hand), it is transposed into vibrations. These are transmitted through the case of the "bone mike" and the skin of the diver to part of the bony structure of his skull, and thence to the ear-bone complex of the inner ear. These vibrations are in turn converted into signals which are passed along nerves to the brain.

It has been proposed by one eminent delphinologist that dolphins use their jaw bones to intercept water-borne sound signals, and then transmit them to the internal ear-bone complex. Dr Kenneth Norris evolved this theory after finding a perfect porpoise skull buried in the sand, with all of the fine bones intact.

Land mammals produce sounds by the passage of air through the larynx during inhalation and exhalation. But although a dolphin can exhale underwater, and we have seen Donald do this on numerous occasions through his blowhole, this is not the manner in which he produces sound. The precise mechanism by which the dolphin makes sound signals is simply not yet understood. There are air cavities within the heads of the Cetaceans, and it is thought that sounds may be produced by the passage of air from one cavity to another, past tissues which vibrate rather like the reeds in musical wind instruments. The air in the upper nasal passages can be internally cycled, thus enabling the dolphin to emit sounds regardless of the duration of a dive. And one school of thought proposes that the domed foreheads, called the melons, in bottlenose dolphins act as "sound lenses" which beam the sound out in a given direction. If this is so, concentrating the sound beams in this way would considerably increase the efficiency of the dolphin's auditory system.

Man, of course, has to depend on his very restricted vision, and mechanical sound aids to communicate underwater. But nowhere is his inferiority to the dolphin more obvious than when he moves. Whenever I compared my own clumsy performance with Donald's extraordinary grace and speed, I was struck by the evidence of his superb adaptation to the sea.

It is the peculiar quality of the dolphin's skin that is thought to be a key to its amazing manoeuvrability and ability to swim at very high speeds. It has been suggested that very small quantities of the outermost layer of the epidermis, which is composed of flat cells, actually slide off the dolphin when it swims through the water. This process is assisted by secretions of a very fine oil. Thus when it swims through the water fast the dolphin is literally swimming out of the outermost layer of its skin, thereby virtually eliminating the drag produced by turbulence. This is typical of the subtlety with which dolphins have apparently evolved to adapt to an underwater environment.

The loss of the outer layers of skin is not of course unique to underwater mammals — it also occurs constantly in humans, whose epidermis is thicker than that of the dolphin, and consists of an outer layer of dead cells that rub off and are continuously replaced by new cells growing underneath.

If you press your fingers to your forehead and move them up and down you will feel the skin moving over your skull. Can you imagine what would happen to the skin on the head of a dolphin if it were equally mobile? When the dolphin swam fast through the water the drag would tend to pull the skin back towards the tail and small ridges would form. This in turn would set up turbulence which would destroy the smooth flow of water over the skin and reduce swimming efficiency. Such an effect would not be restricted simply to the head of the dolphin but to its entire surface.

What Nature has done is to effect a remarkable adaptation to eliminate this effect. The thin epidermis is keyed into the underlying layer, the dermis, by numerous fingers of tissue called papillae, which efficiently lock the dermis to the epidermis. These dermal papillae are arranged in ridges. A study of the ridges has enabled physiologists to determine just how water flows over the dolphin's body when it swims. Their research has shown that the direction of the water flow relative to the body remains the same on both the upward and the downward stroke of the tail. The upward stroke is the power stroke. This movement produces a low-pressure zone on the underside of the fluke, which draws water over the head and chest and down across the ridge behind the dorsal fin. This flow of water effectively moves the dolphin forwards and downwards against the hydro-planing action of the front flippers. The down stroke is simply a return stroke during which the extremity of the tail fluke is relaxed and water is allowed to spill across it.

When scientists first seriously investigated the extraordinary swimming abilities of dolphins they calculated that a dolphin would have to develop nearly two horse-power to push itself through the water if the flow of water across its body was turbulent. For a man to equal this performance in terms of muscle power he would have to be able to climb a mountain at a rate of well over thirty miles per hour. Yet an investigation of dolphin tail muscle showed it to be very similar to other mammalian muscle. Thus the investigators

Photo: Horace Dobbs

In the Turks and Caicos I discovered a new level of trust had been reached between a wild dolphin named JoJo and a young American, Dean Burnal.

Photo: Wendy Dobbs

Photo: Horace Do

Above: Diving in the canal at Dolphins Plus in Florida reminded me of the upper reaches of the River Thames.

Below: The author in one of the pens at Dolphins Plus.

Photo: Wendy Do

Photo: Horace Dobbs

The dolphins at the Dolphin Research Center could easily have jumped over the retaining fence.

Photo: Horace Do

Above: Dr David Nathanson gives two-year-old Bill, a Down's Syndrome child, a lesson, after which (*Below*) he swims with the dolphins in the company of his mother.

Photo: Horace Do

concluded the dolphin did not derive its extraordinary swimming performance from "super-muscle", but as the result of laminar, i.e. non-turbulent, flow of water across its body. Since that time much money has been spent on research in an effort to simulate a "dolphin skin" for submarines but so far man's technology has not matched Nature's ingenuity.

10: Boy on a Dolphin

Many of the events which have had the most profound effect upon my life have in fact been the results of a mishap that in the end has turned out a happy chance. The happening on the Isle of Man on the 6 October 1974 was one of those.

In that instance the mishap was a misunderstanding concerning the times of the sailings of the ferries to and from the Isle of Man.

I had booked a return passage to Liverpool on the 12.00 o'clock sailing from Douglas. I was very happy with the way my trip had turned out, and hopeful that I would have some fine pictures, particularly those taken on that last evening, just before sunset. Admittedly, I had not been able to shoot any 16 mm. film, but that had been a low priority anyway. The timing of the ferry was such that I would be able to pack my diving and photographic equipment in a leisurely manner. Once back on the mainland I would have a comfortable drive across the country to arrive in the early evening at my home in East Yorkshire. Everything seemed to be in order until I decided to check the time of sailing.

Quite by chance and to my surprise and consternation I discovered during my telephone conversation that, unlike British Rail and all the aircraft companies, whose timetables were based on the 24-hour clock, the Isle of Man Steam Packet Company was still operating on a 12-hour clock. I was booked on the boat that sailed at midnight, not midday. The significance of the situation dawned on me as I put down the receiver. I had another twelve hours on the Isle of Man. I stopped packing immediately and announced to Maura and Ashley that we had time to pay Donald another visit before we departed.

It was an opportunity I could not miss, and I took my 16 mm ciné camera into the water to film the dolphin we had all come to love.

Donald appeared so quickly I got the impression he had been waiting for us. I framed him up in the viewfinder and pressed the shutter release. As soon as the camera motor started to whir Donald came straight for me, and pushed his snout on to the front of the camera housing. I stopped filming and tried to push him away, but as he was much larger than me I succeeded only in pushing myself backwards.

Manipulating and filming with the 16 mm. camera underwater is a two-handed operation. I let go of one of the handles and stroked him gently on the front of his head. He looked at me for a few moments and I told him to play with the others, which he did after a short time. I pulled the camera viewfinder up to my mask. The instant I started filming again Donald shot like a bullet towards the camera and peered intently at it. I could barely hear the camera motor with my ear actually touching the camera housing. Yet Donald could obviously hear it quite distinctly from ten feet or more away. His behaviour reflected not only his very acute sense of hearing, but his fascination with mechanical sounds. However a succession of shots of Donald's nose pressed against the camera lens was not what I wanted.

When he had fully satisfied his curiosity he swam off to inspect Ashley, who was snorkelling down to take the dolphin's photograph with one of my still cameras.

Ashley's antics then set Donald into a frenzy of excitement. From below I could see showers of bubbles as the dolphin leapt clear of the water and splashed in again within inches of my son. I continued filming from underneath, but when I saw the dolphin make a headlong rush for Ashley I feared that Donald's exuberance might override his gentle nature, and I hastened to the surface to tell Ashley to get into the dinghy. As I surfaced I saw a sight that is now etched on my memory.

Ashley rose gently out of the water.

At first his expression was one of incredulity and slight apprehension. Then when he realised what was happening he relaxed. He looked in my direction. His snorkel mouthpiece dropped from his lips and he gave me a broad grin. As he did so he held both of his hands in the air whilst sitting perfectly balanced on the head of the dolphin. Donald accelerated away from me with Ashley riding, legs astride Donald's head. The dolphin gradually increased speed until he was moving at an impressive rate. He took the course of an arc that swept round the harbour and then brought Ashley back to near where he had started.

Then the dolphin sounded, leaving Ashley to sink slowly in the water again like a water skier who has released the tow rope after a run.

That beautiful and spontaneous act — Ashley said afterwards that it came as a complete surprise to him — on the part of the dolphin left me with a joy which even now I am inadequate to describe. The simultaneous power and gentleness with which the dolphin lifted Ashley so smoothly and held him as safely as if he had been on a hydraulic chair in a barber's shop, forged a bond between Donald and me as strong and tender as the trust between lovers.

The mystery and enchantment of that image of the boy upon the dolphin's back had something primeval and mythological about it that set me thinking and reading again about the ancient relationship between men and dolphins. And once more I turned to the legends of the ancient Greeks, who seemed to have had a love and reverence for dolphins that succeeding civilisations have lost. Sure enough, I found the tale about the poet Arion, who lived in the seventh century BC and was recorded two centuries later by the historian Herodotus. Herodotus confirmed the story in Corinth and saw with his own eyes in the Sanctuary at Cape Tainaron, the bronze statuette of a boy riding a dolphin.

Arion was a native of the island of Lesbos, who went to Corinth, to the Court of King Periander, to win fame and fortune. Such was his talent that he became a top entertainer and went on a tour of the Greek island and colonies. One of the places he visited was Sicily, to take part in the famous festival that has been likened to an Olympic Games of the musical arts. His performances were superb and he reaped many prizes. Everyone wanted to hear him sing. So he stayed on in Sicily after the festival, moving from estate to estate entertaining the noblemen and their guests who rewarded him with gold and gifts. Then he became homesick. So he chartered a Corinthian vessel to take him and his amassed fortune back to his homeland on Lesbos. On the journey the sailors coveted his wealth and threatened to kill him. The murderous crew would not agree to his plea for mercy but they did grant him a final wish — to dress in his best costume and sing for the last time. With his last wish granted, and the pirates for an audience, Arion tuned his lyre and began to sing.

He sang in a high pitched voice. So beautiful was his music that it attracted a dolphin who swam alongside the vessel. Suddenly, taking his would-be killers by surprise, Arion jumped overboard. The dolphin took the poet on its back and carried him to the shore at Cape Tainaron (now named Cape Matapan). Arion made his way to Corinth and told his story to Periander who was sceptical and asked for proof. When the ship arrived back in its home port the sailors said they had left Arion behind. But when Arion presented himself their guilt was proven. In gratitude Arion offered a bronze votive figure of himself astride the dolphin to the temple of Tainaron.

Another story about a boy and a dolphin was told in about 200 AD by Oppian, in his poem "Halieutica". The poem tells of the love and friendship that developed between a boy who grew up in the port of Porosolene, and a wild dolphin. According to the story the boy was the fairest in the land and the dolphin surpassed all the creatures in the sea for its good nature and grace. The young man would row his boat out into the middle of the bay and call the dolphin by name. The dolphin would gambol to his friend, leaping from the water as he made his way towards the boat. He would raise his head beside the boat and the boy would stroke it tenderly as they greeted one another. Then the boy would leap into the water and the two of them would swim side by side, touching one another gently. The boy would often climb upon the dolphin's back, and the dolphin, understanding the child's wishes, would take him wherever he wanted to go.

The story of Arion and the poem by Oppian are two romanticised accounts of boys riding dolphins. But they belong to a golden age, some two thousand years ago, and I know of no comparable tales recorded since. Indeed, had I never encountered Donald, I think I might have assumed, as others have assumed, that they belonged to the world of myth and legend, and not to the world of real experience at all. But I have seen a boy ride upon a dolphin, and my concept of what is possible, has changed accordingly.

Ashley's ride on Donald's head was a fitting conclusion to our visit to the Isle of Man. For four days we had spent every minute we could in the water with him and at the end of that time I was beginning to feel that I really knew him and he really knew me.

When we climbed aboard the midnight ferry in Douglas I told Maura that I had used all of my leave and that Ashley and I would be back to see her and Donald as soon as we could in 1975. The date was 6 October 1974. As the ferry sailed across the sea, which was as flat as the Serpentine, there was no wind and the moon rose high in the sky. I thought of Donald resting in the dark, still waters of Port St Mary.

I stood beside the ship's rail watching the black water rushing past the hull and listening to the muffled swish that it made. When the chill of the night air started to filter through my clothing I made my way below decks, stretched out along one of the seats and pulled a blanket over myself. I was too excited to fall properly asleep but was lulled into a state of semi-consciousness by the regular throb of the engine after the tiring events of the day. A I drifted contentedly into the limbo between sleep and total awareness I compared Donald's life with my own. I had a vague sense of an identity between us, a connection between his fate and mine.

Donald seemed to be thoroughly at home in Port St Mary, with occasional visits to Port Erin and even Douglas for a change of scene. His early misadventure with the man with a gun seemed to have been completely forgotten and the ride he had given Ashley was a sign that he was prepared to associate even more closely with humans — especially ones he knew. He had become a character who was almost taken for granted by the local people, and the dolphin could be relied upon to set alight with pleasure the relatively few visitors who came to Port St Mary. Nobody knew where he had come from and everyone assumed he had settled. To the Manx people in general he was "our dolphin", to Maura Mitchell he was "my friend Donald" and it looked as if her bonds with him would grow even tighter.

I too felt satisfied, and at peace. I had a very successful career in medical and veterinary research and had reached a position in the senior management of a pharmaceutical company. My hobby of underwater swimming coupled with photography and a deep interest in all aspects of sea life, particularly dolphins, provided me with the relaxation I needed to escape occasionally from the pressures that all people in such demanding professions experience. I was happily married with a son of thirteen and a daughter of sixteen. I had a nice house, could afford to run a modest car and enjoyed my job. Yes, my life was stable and my future secure. With this enjoyable senses of wellbeing, I slipped contentedly into a light sleep.

It is perhaps as well that we do not know what the future holds in store for us. For Donald's life and my life were by no means as secure and peaceful at that time as I thought. In fact they might be compared with sister volcanoes that were only passing through a quiet phase in preparation for major devastating eruptions.

11: The Volcanoes Erupt

At the time of my encounters with Donald I held a position in an international pharmaceutical company. One of my titles was Veterinary Services Manager, and part of that function involved lecturing to veterinary surgeons on a very powerful animal immobilising drug I had investigated in detail and introduced into the market along with its antidote. I was enthusiastic about the product because it was a powerful analgesic in addition to being an immobilising drug and so able to relieve stress in domestic and farm animals that were often in pain and in need of surgery. In November 1974 I spent an evening in Chelmsford with a regional association of veterinary surgeons and showed them the two films I had made on my research into the drug and its effects on both large and small animals. Most of the audience had used the drug and the evening developed into one of lively debate. It was after midnight before the last veterinary surgeon left the meeting place.

The following morning I caught a very early train from Chelmsford in order to spend a few hours in my office in Hull before returning home. In the warm comfort of a first class compartment on an Inter-city train I wrote up some notes and enjoyed the satisfaction of knowing I had done a good job. In his closing remarks the Chairman had thanked me warmly and said the drugs I had pioneered were now regarded as indispensable by veterinary surgeons. I had made a major contribution to veterinary medicine and I was proud of the achievement.

It was 28 November, so Christmas decorations were beginning to make their annual appearance, and a general spirit of bonhomie was in the air. Life was good. I sat back and pondered the stimulating events of the night before and looked forward to the festivities to come. There were no dim rumblings to indicate the imminent eruption in my life.

For Maura Christmas was a happy time. It was the time that she briefly dried out externally. Throughout most of the months of the year she spent hours every week on or under the water, fishing, sailing, water ski-ing, snorkelling or aqualung diving. But these activities were at a minimum from November to March, and she and her family became caught up in the swirl of local parties and social events. As Maura enjoyed cooking, Christmas was a time for producing large quantities of mince pies and other goodies. The winter months were also the time when the wine, which she had made the summer before, and the summer before that, was broached.

Her younger son was at home and he brought into the house a stream of friends, who enjoyed the uninhibited hospitality of the Mitchell household. Her elder son had just married and was busy setting up his new home. Maura had fashioned a lifestyle that embraced her children but was not centred on them. She was happy to see all of the members of her family making their own way in the world and leading full lives.

So the winter of 1974 promised to be a happy time. There was however one thing that worried her. She had a feeling, deep down, that all was not well with Donald. She tried to discover what it was in moments of quiet contemplation. But the questions she asked herself could not be answered in precise terms. All she could identify was a rather vague feeling of unease.

On my return trip from Chelmsford the train was late arriving at Doncaster station, and I missed the connection from the last leg of the journey to Hull. I telephoned my office to let them, know that I would be delayed, and one of my colleagues told me that the Medical Director had been asking after me. There was nothing unusual about that.

Anticipating that he might require an account of my activities, I marshalled my thoughts on the manner in which I could report on my meeting.

Eventually the small local connecting train arrived and rattled its way to Hull. I arrived in the Medical Department offices in good spirits, and was told that the Medical Director wished to see me as soon as I came in.

I pressed the appropriate digits on the intercom on my desk and announced my arrival. A minute later I was in the Medical Director's office being told that my job had been made redundant.

I was dumbfounded.

A situation where jobs are threatened and cut is like one of war, it brings out both the best and the worst in men. It raises the question of survival, and there is nothing like the threat of death to reveal the true characters of men. And it brings into play that potential for vindictiveness and corruption that can come with power — particularly the power to control one of the most vital elements of a man's life — his livelihood.

As I evaluated and re-evaluated my situation, in the context of the changes that were taking place within the company, I found myself not only distressed by my own dismissal, but sickened by the struggle I saw going on around me. I seemed to be tangled in a net, enmeshed in a system which played on avarice and envy simply to survive. The men of power were manipulating stress and tension — their own and others' — for gain. The whole social system, geared to more and more consumer production, more and more greed, suddenly disgusted me. 'Affluent' or not, it was no happy place for the majority.

The contrast between the fraught situation in which I now found myself and the freedom I had enjoyed in the sea with Donald a few weeks before, was never greater. I thought of Donald without possessions and responsibilities, leaping for joy in a blue wind-tossed sea, the waves capped with white foam. And I began to feel that somewhere within me a choice had to be made.

I had no way of knowing that Donald too was in distress. And that the source of his distress was not his own kind, but man.

I felt no resentment to those of my colleagues who had been spared the axe and who would take on the work I was doing when I left. I worked out my four weeks' notice to the full. Christmas came and went and I joined the ranks of the unemployed.

During this period I had no news about Donald from Maura, and felt some slight unease about him. Then the thought was pushed to the back of my mind by my own preoccupation in losing my job. Her Christmas card made no reference to Donald, which stirred my suspicion that all was not well with him, but my concern was overwhelmed by the Christmas festivities which proceeded with their customary energy in the Dobbs' household.

I decided not to rush headlong into any new job but to let events take their own course for a while, so I started to make contact with friends and acquaintances who could give me more work as a freelance lecturer, writer, film-maker and photographer. Eventually I telephoned Maura and told her what had happened. She immediately tried to console me, stressing how much happier she and her family had been since her husband had given up his motor-cycle engineering business and adopted a more relaxed life-style on the Isle of Man.

When I mentioned Donald I sensed that Maura was reluctant to add to my problems, but she did tell me that she was worried about Donald. She said that he was acting differently from usual, spending more time away from land and harbours. He had taken to rushing from place to place, and could not be seen regularly in Port St Mary as before.

I was by now aware that Maura was exceptionally sensitive to Donald's moods, and that she had an uncanny ability to communicate with him by a means which I could not identify precisely but which I thought of as some kind of sympathetic understanding. I asked her if she knew anything about why he should be behaving so strangely. Then she broke the news to me that underwater explosives were being used in the course of work to deepen the harbour at Port St Mary, to enable more fishing boats to come alongside the harbour wall.

The method used was to drill ten to fifteen feet into the rock bed of the harbour with a compressed air drill mounted on a pontoon. The drill, painted with red oxide and black bitumen, was called Tarroo Ushtey — which is Manx for Water Bull, a legendary creature with flashing red eyes and a shining black coat that came out of the sea to cause trouble and stress on land. Sausages of explosives were dropped into the holes, the tubes removed and the wires connected. About ten holes were drilled and prepared per session. Two banks of charges were detonated per day, the first usually at about midday. Bill Ash was the man who carried out most of the work, and early in the programme he had seen the dolphin watching the noisy drill biting into the rocks under the sea. On one occasion Donald had nearly become tangled in the connecting wires. A white dinghy fitted with an outboard engine was used in an attempt to entice the dolphin clear of the harbour before the explosives were detonated.

Work on the harbour improvement started in November 1974. Complaints received from the residents of Port St Mary indicated that the explosions were sufficiently violent to rattle the cups on their sideboards.

We both knew what a traumatic effect all this would have on Donald, who had a super-sensitivity to underwater sounds. We also realised that if he happened to be close by when a charge was detonated he would be killed. Knowing how curious he was and how he loved to investigate new objects placed in the sea, the thought that he might actually have his inquisitive face close to a charge when it exploded was a prospect that filled both of us with horror.

The days passed. The day of 18 March 1975 was not of

great significance to Peter's mother, who lived on the Isle of Man. She went for a walk in the afternoon and saw a dolphin swimming fast, occasionally leaping out of the water, offshore from the jagged coastline of Langness. She noted the incident in her diary, and gave the matter no more thought. But hers was the last sighting of Donald on the Isle of Man.

The following day Maura and Peter were having a drink in their conservatory, which was warmed by a weak March sun. Peter was drinking a coffee from a mug with a dolphin motif on the side that Maura had bought specially for him. The mug slipped from Peter's fingers and crashed to the floor, breaking the handle. Maura felt so cold she started to shiver uncontrollably.

"Peter," cried Maura, "something has happened to Donald."

"Don't be daft," said Peter. "What could happen to him?"

"I know it's silly," she said as she started to regain her usual calm composure, "but I feel inside me that something has happened to Donald."

"It's just your imagination," said Peter, "he'll be in Port St Mary to-morrow — you'll see."

"Perhaps he's been injured by the explosives," said Maura, pressing her point.

"I'm sure he hasn't," said Peter.

Not wishing to invite more ridicule than necessary, Maura said no more about the incident, but she still felt uneasy as she picked up the handle, thinking it might be possible to mend it with adhesive.

Many of those who live on the Isle of Man are very superstitious, and Maura's Manx ancestry would not let the thought that the incident with the dolphin mug was some sort of portent slip from her mind. She remembered an incident a year earlier, when she found that a plant that had been given to her by an aunt was broken. When she saw it her skin had prickled. And two days later she learnt by letter that her aunt had died. Maura was relieved that the mug was not shattered, for that, she felt, might signify that Donald was dead — with the handle gone, it probably meant that a link was broken.

The feeling that something was wrong stayed with her all through the night, although she said no more about it to her husband. The next day as soon as Peter had left for work, she put her wetsuit into her car and drove to Port St Mary. From the jetty she looked out towards her dolphin's favourite resting spot beside the lifeboat. There was no sign of his hump rising in the water and blowing. She looked carefully at all the moored boats. They all lay quietly bobbing in the water. None of them were moving out of harmony with the others.

The days passed and still there was no sign of Donald. Her anxiety grew. She knew he would not be able to resist investigating any divers laying charges. Surely, she argued with herself, none of the divers would let off the charges with the knowledge that the dolphin was nearby? On the other hand, she reminded herself, commercial divers have a hard job and they are not the sort of people to let anything get in their way when they have work to do.

She knew that shock waves travel considerable distances underwater, and that a diver may feel the impact of even a comparatively small explosive charge fired underwater over a mile away. Donald, with his super-sensitivity, would be much more severely affected if he were anywhere in the vicinity of Port St Mary when a charge was exploded.

The effect would of course be related to the distance between him and the explosion. If he were far enough away it might cause him only momentary discomfort, but if he were close by it could cause pain, and risk of internal injury. If he were very close, the explosion would kill him. She read the local newspapers every day to see if there was any news of a dolphin's body being washed ashore. No such news appeared. On the other hand, if he had been injured by an explosion he might have rushed away from Port St Mary in a frightened state and even now be lying lonely and wounded off a remote part of the island far away from the sight of man.

"If he is still safe and sound and as intelligent as I think he is, what would he do if the peace of his adopted home was shattered by explosions?" she asked herself. The answer seemed obvious. Move somewhere else. That raised the question: Where?

She telephoned her friends at the Marine Biological Laboratory at Port Erin, but they had no reports of dolphin sightings. She asked her friend and diving partner, Mike Dunning, to maintain his look-out for their mutual friend, as she was to be off the island for a while.

She was reluctant to leave, but on 19 April 1975, over four months since she had last been in the water with Donald, and still with the fear nagging her that some disaster had befallen him, she left for the Shetland Isles on an expedition which was part of David Bellamy's project "Countdown". She had been in the Shetlands a week when a package arrived addressed to her. There was no note inside, just an inflatable blue and white plastic dolphin. It was a sign from Mike to tell her that Donald had gone.

Spring matured into summer. With the coming of the warmer months came the basking sharks. These gigantic fish, often more than twenty feet in length, cruised just below the surface, sweeping the sea with their colossal mouths, scooping and sieving the plankton. Following the sharks came the Scandinavian fishing boats, with harpoon guns mounted on the bows. The sight of one of these boats in a Manx harbour always filled her with fear for Donald. The men aboard harpooned the sharks as they cruised along on the surface of the sea. The oil and vitamin-rich livers were removed, and the carcasses were then tossed back into the sea to rot.

The prospect of her beloved and gentle Donald being accidentally or deliberately killed by a harpoon filled her with horror. She thought how in all innocence he might go out to a vessel to play in the bow wave, and of the agony he would suffer when the harpoon smashed into his sensitive body. She shuddered at the thought of his searing pain as he sounded and hurled himself to the depths. There he would stay for as long as he could, but he would be forced to return to the surface for air. When he surfaced, would he spout blood from his blowhole, like countless others of his cousins, the whales, had done at the hand of man? How long would it be before he finally died? The picture was too cruel to imagine but it remained gnawing at her subconscious mind. She knew full well that if such had been Donald's fate she was unlikely ever to hear the truth.

12: Reflections on Men and Dolphins

When I was made redundant I realised that external events had taken hold of my life. I imagined my fate rather like that of a toy yacht which had been gently sailing on a set course, then is suddenly picked up out of the water by a boy. With the tip of the mast between his fingers he keeps it swinging, deciding where next to drop the vessel into the stream.

My encounters with the wild dolphin had caused me to begin to formulate questions about my life-style, and the quality of my life. However, they had remained largely unvoiced, pushed into the dark recesses of my mind by the relentless pressures of my job. Now, suddenly, those pressures had evaporated. I found myself with time to look at my life, look at my values, and decide just what it was that I wanted from living. I asked several people what they would do if they were suddenly given a completely free choice. To my surprise none of them knew. When I asked myself the same question, I realised that I too did not know the answer. I felt the answer was in some way connected with dolphins, but if the solution was there, it remained unrevealed. Meanwhile other questions raised themselves concerning the meaning of my encounter with Donald, and more generally about man's relationship with his fellow creatures.

In those uncertain days I took to cycling along the banks of the River Humber which flowed past the village of North Ferriby where I lived. I would cycle on my daughter's bicycle along the road to the construction site of the new Humber bridge at Hessle, and then make my way back home along the muddy, bumpy footpath beside the wide expanse of the tidal river.

During the ride I would think about the days in my youth

when I spent hundreds of hours on my bicycle in the early post-war years, exploring little known paths in Sussex, Surrey and Kent. I revelled in the solitude of the river bank, the lapping of the dark brown water as it eddied round the banks at high water. I loved to watch the wild geese and the seagulls rise from the reed beds. I would sit on the bank, enjoying the subtle warmth of the early spring sunshine, and let my mind wander, whilst tugs and cargo boats chugged past on the tide.

Slowly the mists around the answers to my questions started to clear. One incident which helped to drive them away was an unexpected meeting on the river bank. Very few people made the journey along the riverside between Hessle and North Ferriby, and I was surprised one day to encounter a man in his fifties, wearing a bowler hat, and sitting on an upturned crate. He was brewing an enamel kettle of what appeared to be tea on an open fire, and tinkering with a clock he had found on a nearby rubbish tip. I stopped and said "Good morning" in a cheerful polite manner and noticed that he had established a camp. His bedding was hidden under a nearby bush and various objects he had collected from the rubbish tip were placed at strategic positions around his camp site. At first he said little, and clearly did not welcome my presence as I leaned on my saddle and asked him about the river and the weather and the ships and barges sailing up-stream. He did not reply to my questions, but he asked me abruptly where I worked. When I told him I was unemployed he immediately became more responsive and told me that he also was between jobs — although my guess would have been that he had had his last job at least twenty years before.

I had seen him several times in the past, cycling at a good pace through the village, his bowler hat decorated with plastic fruit and flowers, and sometimes carrying a placard on his back with an unintelligible message painted on it. He wore one Wellington boot painted white and the other black. Everyone said he was harmless, but little children were quickly rushed indoors if he dallied nearby. he seldom spoke to the villagers except to buy food in the shops.

Our first meeting was brief. But as the weeks passed they became longer. He was not always there. One day, as I stood looking down at the charred sticks that remained of his fire, I realised that he was free to wander according to the whim of the moment. I did not envy him his hard existence, but with it he had certainly bought a kind of freedom that is a rare commodity in our society.

The words 'tramp' and 'vagrant' do not conjure up the right picture. He was always clean-shaven; he usually wore dark clothes and though they were not smart, they fitted him well and were not ragged. From a distance he looked like a slightly down-at-heel London business man. He was well built but not at all flabby. He had a good set of teeth, which were stained and wearing down, like those of an ageing horse. He appeared to be fit and strong, and after seeing him pedalling furiously along the road I concluded that he was also of good wind.

Gradually our conversations got deeper, and he informed me he was writing a book. Then he launched into a diatribe that at times was crystal clear, then would suddenly become unintelligible. If normal prose is a photograph then he put his words together like an abstract painter. A splash of metaphor here, a turn of phrase there blended together in sentences that were individually coherent yet when added together left my mind searching for a meaning. He could have been a scientist giving a brilliant specialist paper on nuclear physics to a lay audience. As he rattled on fluently, and my brain tried to reorganise the words into something I could truly comprehend, I realised how thin is the line between genius and madness. I also accepted how little we understand the nature of the distinction. Until we could bridge such gaps among ourselves, it occurred to me, how could we hope to cross the much wider gap between the brain of man and the brain of a dolphin?

Thus it was that the encounter with the stranger on the

banks of the Humber brought me back to Donald, and helped me to recognise that whatever I was going to do with my life would have to make room for my obsession with the dolphin, and in particular for my concern with how the dolphin perceives and communicates.

Dolphins are known to hear and emit sounds underwater. Many investigations have been carried out to discover what roles sounds play in the lives of dolphins, and the results have sometimes been surprising. Scientists have found that dolphins emit sounds with frequencies up to one hundred and fifty three kilocycles per second. Thus much of the sound emitted by dolphins is at a considerably greater frequency than the twenty kilocycles per second which is the highest pitched sound that can be heard by most men.

It has been discovered that dolphins use this high-frequency sound to pass information one to another, and they are thought by some scientists to have a whistling language. However, despite very sophisticated research involving the use of computers, nobody has so far succeeded in unravelling the mysteries of delphinese — which is what the whistling language of dolphins has been called.

What is clear is that enormous amounts of information can be passed in the form of high-frequency sound signals. Just how much the dolphin's large brain is able to utilise this potential is something scientists will speculate upon for years to come, but most of them are already agreed that if dolphins have a language, it is such as would make our speech by comparison appear like a recording played at a very low speed. That is, our deep verbal rumblings would probably register as dull and tediously slow to the dolphin's lively mind! Indeed our own brains are capable of taking in and comprehending information at a faster rate than through normal speech: our reading speed, for instance, can be much faster than the spoken word.

What is perhaps even more intriguing is the evidence that the dolphin uses sound to provide an 'acoustic picture' of his surroundings. It was found in one set of experiments that a blindfolded dolphin could locate a target as small as one inch in diameter with unerring accuracy across a tank thirty-five feet wide. The sounds used by the dolphin for this purpose were analysed and shown to consist of clicks about one thousandth of a second long.

The manner in which dolphins interpret the sounds bounced back by the objects around them has been likened to underwater sonar. Sonar is used by trawler fishermen to detect shoals of fish — the images the skipper sees on his sonar readout result from the changes in the signal when it intercepts the air bladders of the fish in the shoal beneath him. Thus the tell-tale signal is produced not just from the outside of the fish, it also comes from their internal structures. On the basis of this analogy it has been suggested that dolphins can use their sonic vision to see *inside* objects. If this is true, then the dolphins have evolved a sonic sense which gives a three-dimensional sound picture of the internal as well as the external features of the object they are "looking at". Although we have compared this sense with our sonar systems, it is probable that we will never fully comprehend it because our brains have not evolved to interpret such nerve impulses directly. Our mental quandary can perhaps be understood if we consider the plight of a person with normal colour vision attempting to explain to another person who has been blind since birth the qualities of colour.

As a scientist I too have speculated on the possibilities of the dolphin's proven ability to differentiate between objects of different density but the same external appearance. I recalled seeing one of the first demonstrations of a hologram at a Physical Society Exhibition at Alexandra Palace. An object was illuminated with light from a laser, which was split into a reference beam and an object beam. The reference beam was directed at a photographic film and the object beam reflected off the subject was reflected on to the same film. Where the beams met and overlapped interference was produced and recorded. When I looked at the processed film illuminated with a beam of coherent light I saw a totally three-dimensional reconstruction of the subject. To my eye and brain, conditioned to the fact that light travels only in straight lines, the experience was a little short of uncanny. The science of holography is still in its infancy, but already the principal is being applied in medicine and engineering. Its first application in the film industry was in a film starring Michael York called *Logan's Run*. And in March 1977 the Royal Academy in London put on an exhibition of holography. At night laser beams probed the skies over the city projecting words and images into the clouds. Inside the exhibition itself was an illusionary Concorde flying through space. There were no mirrors, no strings and no screen. Yet the image appeared solid and three-dimensional, and changed shape according to the angle from which it was viewed.

Logan's Run and the Royal Academy exhibition were to come later, but as in the spring of 1975 I sat on the banks of the Humber, I could clearly recall the hologram I had seen some six years before at the exhibition of the Physical Society.

Could the acoustic image seen by a dolphin come about by a process similar to that by which holograms are formed, I asked myself? If a dolphin emits a coherent beam of sound waves, and then compares the phase difference between the output beam and the reflected beam, I concluded, it is indeed possible that this would form a sonic hologram image which would reveal internal as well as external features.

I took my riverside speculations a stage further. Armed with the knowledge that dolphins have a brain equal to our own, on a weight for weight basis, and that they have traditionally a special empathy with man, I tried to imagine what it would be like to think like a dolphin and to see sonic pictures like a dolphin. To do this I set out to put my own brain inside Donald's head, as it were, and relive that first fateful encounter with the diver Henry Crellin in Port St Mary on 26 March 1972.

This is the story, as I told it to myself.

Donald was first attracted to the site by the sound of an anchor going overboard — a sound with which he was familiar and which had always interested him. It was part of the world of sound in which he lived and which always surrounded him. But when a new shape appeared on the radar of his brain his insatiable curiosity was aroused beyond repression. What was this new animal that had come into his sea? Was it the mammal he was looking for: an animal with clumsy movements that breathed air like a dolphin, but was neither a dolphin nor a fish?

His instinct for survival told him to stay out of visual range and first investigate the newcomer with sound. He beamed a short burst of sound at the unfamiliar animal and his brain immediately translated the reflected sounds into a three-dimensional picture indicating the internal structure of the new animal.

The sound picture revealed an animal with two very large air sacs, surrounded by a relatively thin-walled body. There were more air cavities in a bony structure — the head — and the mouth was very small with few teeth. The new animal did not adopt the usual horizontal attitude of a fish. Indeed, it behaved in a very unfishlike and undolphinlike manner. It appeared to have two tails which ended in fins that were used for propulsion. The two tails were very inefficient at moving the animal through the water when compared with his own single tail or even those of the fishes, which were a lower order of animal than himself altogether.

All of these things were unusual to him. But the

most unusual features of all were the parts of the body that corresponded to his own front flippers which the dolphin used for steering. The flippers of the new arrival were long and could be articulated in any direction. They ended in long paddles that the new arrival used for moving the chain, when the dolphin would have used his mouth. The clumsy newcomer was not much of a swimmer but his ability to manipulate the chain was most impressive.

Another thing that puzzled the dolphin was the major dense thin-walled air sac from which the two-tailed mammal drew an apparently everlasting supply of air. When swimming the two-tailed mammal used its air supply at a prodigious rate compared with the dolphin's respiration rate of about once every two minutes.

Having established an image of the inside structure of the two-tailed mammal, the dolphin considered the danger the new animal presented. It was apparent that it was very poorly adapted to live in the sea. An inefficient swimmer with a most interesting respiratory system, and manipulative flippers that divided into separate limbs, did not appear to pose much of a threat.

Curiosity urged him to move in close enough to obtain a visual picture of the outside of the animal. He swam slowly past and briefly saw that the intruder had a black skin, which he knew from his sound picture was cellular and about one quarter of an inch thick. It was very much thinner than his own layer of blubber, and a far cruder method of reducing the heat loss from the mammal than the dolphin's combined blubber and vascular system of temperature control.

Through the water he could hear the two-tailed mammal's heartbeat. The information fed into the memory bank of his computer-like brain. Just as he came into visual range the heartbeat of the two-tailed mammal raced and the water carried the alarm signal to the dolphin as quickly as a telegraph message. Then the panic-stricken newcomer rushed to the surface in a frantic flurry of its fins and was followed by the exhaust bubbles it had left behind.

The dolphin was both amused and saddened that he should have caused the two-tailed mammal such a fright. The frightened mammal had climbed into the flimsy transporter that had brought him to this part of the dolphin's new territory. Through the rubber floor of the inflatable came the deep slow sounds of the mammals communicating with one another. He observed that the language of the two-tailed mammals was very much slower than the dolphin's high-pitched information transmission system. Although he knew otherwise, it seemed to the dolphin at that moment he could have little to fear from the air-breathing animals.

They were physically close, but were separated from him by twenty-five million years of evolution that had dictated that he should stay on one side of the air-water interface above his head, and they should remain on the other. Now they were invading his environment, which would give him an opportunity to study them more closely. That was what he wanted, but he would not be able to do so if he frightened them.

He decided to surface gently near their transporter in order that they could visually identify him. Once they knew he was a dolphin they would surely be aware that there was no cause for alarm.

That, for the moment, was as near as I could get to imagining myself into Donald's first encounter with man. But I was pleased with my piece of fantasy. It seemed that I had made the first steps towards bridging the gap in consciousness between myself and another species, and I felt somehow that I had also taken an important step in defining my own life.

13: Moment of Decision

Having failed to introduce Luciano properly to the thrills and hardships of diving British-style in the summer of 1974, we agreed to try again in August 1975 when I was scheduled to run an underwater photography course at Dale Fort. Dale is an attractive village that lies on the further-most south-west tip of Wales, in a county that once had the romantic name of Pembrokeshire, but has now been renamed Dyfed.

The fort at Dale is situated at the extremity of a high peninsular and is an obvious defensive position for the deepwater harbour of Milford Haven. It was built in the mid nineteenth century from huge blocks of stone as a defence against a possible foreign invasion, and has none of the classic castle-like lines of many of its romantic predecessors in Wales. It was designed to house guns, not human-propelled missiles, so it was therefore given a low profile that blends in with the natural line of the headland. The original stone fortifications have now been supplemented by other buildings, and it has been used for many years as a Field Station by the Field Studies Council.

In 1975 Peter Hunnam was director of diving, and he welcomed Luciano and me when we arrived by car.

The Field Studies Council owned a redundant lifeboat which we should have used for our diving expeditions. It was moored just off the jetty at the base of the cliffs immediately below the fort. However, as one of its engines was out of commission, an old steel-hulled boat, owned and skippered by an Australian, was engaged as a substitute. The *Conshelf*, as she was called, was a working boat and looked it. She was painted black and had no frills on her whatsoever. She was

used as a general work boat and as a diving boat. It was easy
to jump overboard from her fully kitted-up with diving gear
as the deckline was close to the water.

This time the weather was kind and Luciano sampled his
first real dive from the *Conshelf* off the Island of Skomer.
There were strong contrasts between the underwater worlds
of the Bristol Channel and his native sea. First, even when it
was flat calm, the water off the Welsh Coast was far less clear
than that of the Mediterranean, the maximum visibility being
thirty feet (in the Mediterranean the underwater visibility is
often in excess of one hundred feet). It was also much colder,
and where we swam near the bottom clouds of silt were
stirred up at the slightest disturbance by our hands or fins,
and remained suspended in the water.

We swam down over a forest of kelp, which Luciano had
never seen before. Kelp plants are like miniature palm trees
with dark green leaves attached to long rubbery stalks that
cling to the rocks with root-like looking structures called
holdfasts. We examined the holdfasts, which provide a home
for a host of small organisms, and passed on our way down
into the deep. At a depth of about thirty feet the kelp
disappeared completely and we entered a completely new
zone populated by sponges, sea urchins and many other small
organisms, including the tiny Devonshire cup corals. Our
flash guns fired as we drifted down into the quiet depths. A
three-pound crawfish, which Luciano immediately identified
as a relative of the Mediterranean langouste, inspected us
with its long antennae banded with alternate light pink and
dark pink stripes. I hovered as quietly as I could to take a
picture, but found I was not quite in the right position. I
attempted to reposition myself with a gentle movement of my
hands. But despite the utmost care the turbulence caused a
flurry of silt particles to float up into the water. During the
one-thousandth of a second in which the flash fired I saw it
illuminate the particles like stars in the night sky. For the
merest fraction of a second the dark underwater world had
burst into colour, but that was time enough for it to

register on my mind, as on the film. Then the light was gone and the scene resumed its blue-grey tone.

After twenty minutes Luciano signalled that he was getting cold, by clasping his arms together across his chest as a man does on a cold day. We headed back towards the surface.

The following day there was no wind and the sea was flat calm. We again headed for Skomer. Conditions should have been perfect for diving, but we were frustrated by the not unusual idiosyncrasies of the British climate. This time it was fog. Thick grey swirling mists that would have blown away with a puff of wind, engulfed us. The temperature dropped. It seemed that Luciano's diving in British waters was again to be blighted by the weather. The waters around Skomer are very treacherous and visibility was so bad that even if we had anchored off the island we could easily have lost sight of a diver if he or she had surfaced very far from the boat. So we abandoned the dive and headed back for the mainland, planning to hug the coast as we made our way slowly towards Dale.

"We could dive in Martin's Haven," said Peter Hunnam, keen to ensure that our group of divers would not be completely disappointed. Although the fog horn was still blaring regularly, the fog had indeed lifted slightly when we nosed quietly into Martin's Haven.

I was in the stern of the vessel chatting to the other divers about techniques of underwater photography prior to our dive, when suddenly I heard a familiar loud puff alongside the boat. I rushed to the side to see a dark shape disappearing into the green water. I couldn't believe it. We had a dolphin alongside. My bag of diving equipment was with me and in a few moments I was in my wetsuit. I leapt into the water, and Luciano followed close behind. What I saw next was almost unbelievable, for out of the misty waters came the cheeky grey face of Donald. I recognised my old friend from the Isle of Man immediately. He came to inspect me briefly, nodded his head and flashed away. From his movements I knew there was no mistaking him. There could only be one Donald. But who would believe me? We were over two hundred miles from his old haunts.

There was however one way of making a positive identification — the dreadful wound on the top of his head caused by the skeg of the outboard. So the next time he reappeared I swam over the top of him so that I could clearly see the crater on the top of his head. Skin had now covered the wound, which earlier had been red raw, and the new scar tissue was a vivid white. Close inspection revealed that the edge of the crater had become pigmented a dark grey colour. Eventually the pigmentation would cover the entire cavity. Then the only external signs of his encounter with the boat would be another dent in his otherwise smooth contours — like the one on the side of his head which resulted from his encounter with a gunman.

The visibility was poor, ten feet at the maximum. So even when face to face with Donald, when I looked down the length of his body, the end of his tail disappeared into a green fog. It is virtually impossible to get first-rate pictures under such conditions, since the camera cannot photograph what the eye cannot see. To get the best pictures it is necessary to get as close to the subject as possible, and at the same time to include as much of it as possible in the field of view of the lens. Knowing that Luciano wanted a photograph of a diver and Donald in the same picture, I passed him my fish-eye lens attachment and viewfinder to fit to his underwater camera. Then, so he could get Donald and me in the same picture, with some interest in the background, I submerged to the propellor and rudder of the *Conshelf* and started to tap on the hull with the handle of my diving knife, hoping that Donald's curiosity would bring him in close. It did. As I tapped away I was aware that the end of his beak was just a few inches from my hand.

I talked to him as I tapped, and for a few minutes he hovered, watching what I was doing with his bright inquisitive eyes. I knew that Luciano was taking pictures. After a few minutes, however, Donald tumbled to the fact that I was not doing anything more interesting than tapping, so he swam away. I looked up at Luciano. I could see his eyes alight in his facemask and knew he was thrilled with what had just happened. His pleasure was enhanced by looking through the fish-eye viewfinder, which expanded his field of vision to make the scene appear much more dramatic.

Luciano expressed his delight in the only way he could. He touched the tip of his forefinger with his tip of his thumb so that the two formed an 'O'. It is the diver's sign for 'OK'. Luciano made the sign three times in quick succession, indicating that he was not just OK, but trebly OK.

Later, when we were back on board the *Conshelf* and Luciano was still excited, he commented that the chance of diving with a wild dolphin in the sea was about as high as winning first dividend on the football pools. Luciano had dived only four times in British waters, at two locations two hundred miles apart and one year apart in time, yet on both occasions he had had an encounter with perhaps the only truly wild friendly dolphin in the world.

"It is like winning first dividend on the football pools not once but twice," he announced happily, "I think I am Lucky Luciano."

Everyone on board became caught in Luciano's enthusiasm, and he told them the story of the original Lucky Luciano. From that moment everyone on the boat referred to Luciano as Lucky — and that is how he was recorded in the diving log.

For me the totally unexpected appearance of Donald beside the *Conshelf* in Martin's Haven turned out to be the apparently inconsequential but in fact deeply significant event needed to crystallise my thoughts about my own future. I had by now been out of full-time employment for eight months, and during that period had undertaken various jobs on a freelance basis. As time had passed I had enjoyed more and more my new lifestyle. It was certainly precarious financially, but the variety that came as a result more than compensated. And above all else I had at last gained a feeling that I was in control of my own life. I was no longer a digit to be manipulated by a computer in a multi-national company.

I was me, I was exulted, and I was free.

And I would no more give up my freedom again than would a wild animal, as I surmised, exchange his die-or-survive situation for the constrained but well-fed existence in a cage in a zoo.

At first I had been hesitant, but now I knew what I was going to do. I was going to run for freedom. When the decision was finally made I felt a great sense of relief. Twenty years were lifted off my shoulders. I felt as excited and as eager as a young man stepping out to conquer the world, and confident that I could do it.

When I told my wife, Wendy, of my decision not to seek full-time employment again and that this would introduce a high degree of financial uncertainty into our lives, she said she had complete faith in our ability to survive. My wife is a pragmatic person, not strongly religious or given to belief in the occult, so her next comment came as a surprise.

Fate, she said, had decreed that I should devote at least part of my life to understanding dolphins.

She went on to tell me that she felt my reunion with Donald must have been predestined. It could not have come about had I not been made redundant, so redundancy too was part of the overall fate which had manoeuvred me to the coast of Wales. She could not explain her conviction. It was just a feeling that sprang from somewhere within her. To back up her theory, however, she argued that I was really admirably equipped to take advantage of the unique position for studying the dolphin in which chance had placed me, pointing out that I combined diving ability with a great deal of special experience in handling animals both large and small, acquired during my research in veterinary medicine.

I had to admit that the chance that had brought

The shallow lagoon was a wonderful playground.

JoJo the wild dolphin allowed his mouth to be opened by Dean.

Above: The Kiss. A touching illustration of the gentle, loving relationship between Dean and JoJo.

Below: Dean had his own method of formally introducing humans to his dolphin friend, JoJo.

JoJo enjoyed underwater games with Andrew Dalton, the marine biologis from the Conch Farm.

Donald and me together on two occasions with Luciano was so extraordinarily far-fetched as to invite a mysterious explanation of some sort.

I telephoned Maura on the Isle of Man to tell her of my unexpected reunion with Donald. I had also to give her the less pleasant news that he was by no means safe in his new home.

Before my return home from Wales I had set about the task of finding out as much information as I could about Donald's presence in Pembrokeshire. Once I made my interest known and was able to throw some light on Donald's previous history, several people came forward and told me stories about the newly arrived dolphin. He had already aroused in them the same kind of affection that he had inspired on the Isle of Man, and he had been named by the local people 'Dai'. But it emerged that some friends were fearful for Donald on the grounds that his life was now being threatened by the fishermen. One local fisherman had claimed that when he was shooting his herring nets the dolphin had swum right through them tearing great holes in the mesh. The same man had also complained that when he was working on mooring buoys the dolphin would continually rise and sink between the work boat and the buoy chain, blowing bubbles as he went. To this fisherman, Donald was simply a great nuisance, and he proposed a simple solution to the problem — to shoot the dolphin. No move had yet been made by the irate fishermen against Donald, but once more it seemed, he had his enemies.

Once I had told Maura all of the news I could have predicted her next question.

"How quickly can I see Donald?"

I explained that I had only just come back from Wales and that Dale Fort was about as far away from my home as any part of Wales could be.

"But I've got to see him," she persisted.

"I knew that's what you would say," I replied,

"so I have made loose arrangements for us both to go back to Dale Fort and stay there."

"How soon?"

"That depends upon how soon you can get away."

14:   Maura in Martin's Haven

A few days later I collected Maura from the Douglas Ferry at the docks in Liverpool and we headed south-west, the car loaded with cameras, the boat and diving equipment. It was approaching midday the following day when I drove up a steep narrow high-hedged road from Dale village to the fort. I parked the car just outside the entrance to the Field Centre, and we disembarked at the head of the steep path leading down to the jetty. We looked down on to Dale Roads spread beneath us. It was a chocolate-box view. The day was crystal bright and there was not a breath of wind to disturb the oil-flat surface of the sea. The *Lord Hircomb*, the redundant lifeboat now used as a diving and general service boat by the Field Centre, sat on the water as still as a souvenir on a mantelshelf. Only the edge of the sea moved, as it slid gently back and forth over the wrack-covered rocks with the slow gentle rhythm of a waving cobra.

We looked expectantly down towards the water, hoping to see an arch of silver that would indicate the presence of Donald, but nothing stirred the almost baize-flat surface. We had been hopeful that we would spot him immediately upon our arrival, because I had been told on the telephone the night before that he had been round the lifeboat. The group from the Field Centre had been trawling a plankton net off the jetty, and had had some difficulty completing their studies because of Donald's antics. Apparently he had done everything he could, short of actually grabbing it in his teeth, to obstruct the passage of the net. Having failed to stop the study he had rounded off the evening with a spectacular display of aquabatics. Now there was not a sign of him. We stayed at our lookout for ten minutes, enjoying the tranquillity of the world but disappointed that Donald was not there to greet us.

"He's probably round at Martin's Haven," I said as we discussed his whereabouts with Peter Hunnam.

"I will bring the Zodiac round," said Peter, "I want to collect some samples from Martin's Haven anyway."

So we drove round the twisting roads to the tiny inlet and pulled into the car park at the head of the track leading to the sea.

The fact that a friendly wild dolphin was sometimes to be seen in Martin's Haven had been reported in the local paper, the *West Wales Guardian*, and the resultant extra influx of cars carrying hopeful dolphin viewers clearly did not please the local car park attendant. When I enquired about Donald the man's non-helpful reply was matched by his abrupt manner. He softened slightly, though only slightly, when Maura spoke to him, and we concluded that he really did not know whether Donald was in the vicinity or not, and would have been happier if we had kept our questions to ourselves and happier still if we had not inconvenienced him by coming.

Somewhat taken aback by our rebuff we decided to investigate for ourselves. We walked down the road and then clambered high on to the headland which commanded a view of Martin's Haven and the surrounding area. The island of Skomer, lichen-patched and sea-bird colonised, floated on a deep blue sea. A small boat carrying birdwatchers, reduced to toy size by distance, was edging its way into an anchorage. Had Donald followed the ferry out to the island? I strained my eyes to see if I could detect any signs that would indicate his presence, but could see none. Northwards, St David's hovered on the far horizon. A small fishing boat glided silently towards the open sea followed by the white tail of its wake. If Donald was out there playing with the fishing boat I knew there was no chance that I could see him. Maura said she would go down and talk to the few people on the beach at Martin's Haven whilst I climbed to the end of the headland to see if I could detect any signs of his whereabouts from a higher vantage point. As I walked alone over the heather I breathed the air deep and thanked the circumstances of life that had brought me to such a beautiful place on a self-appointed mission. From my seagull view I looked down on to the turquoise green water below. The mooring buoys lay on the surface of the sea like orange balls on a bowling green. To one of them was attached a small wooden pram dinghy, to another a small sleek cabin cruiser. I looked at each of the moored boats in turn, hoping to see a dark grey lump appear alongside, but nothing happened. I remembered Donald's habit of pushing moored boats until the mooring line was stretched taut and then letting them slide back again to resume a balanced position. But none of the boats moved.

A verse from 'The Ancient Mariner' flashed through my mind:

> Day after day, day after day,
> We stuck, nor breath nor motion;
> As idle as a painted ship
> Upon a painted ocean.

Changing my viewpoint to cover every corner of Martin's Haven, for fifteen minutes I continued my vigil. But not a single sign could I see, so eventually I scrambled down to join Maura. She had been chatting to Terry Davies, the boatman who transports visitors to Skomer Island. He said Donald was not around.

It seemed that our luck was out. Donald was neither at Dale nor at Martin's Haven. Just as we were about to depart, however, an inflatable loaded with a group of divers, their black wetsuits still shining with water, rounded the headland and ran their boat ashore. They were university students who had been out collecting specimens.

"Have you seen the dolphin?" asked Maura.

"Yes," replied one of them, "he's been swimming around us when we were collecting specimens."

"Where was that?" asked Maura.

"Just round the headland, close inshore," he said,

pointing to the very headland on which I had been standing. I had not seen them simply because they had been so close inshore. Whilst we continued our interrogation of the man who appeared to be in charge, the remainder of the group carried their equipment and specimens on to the beach in plastic buckets.

"What happened when you left?" I asked.

"He got hold of one student's fins and tried to pull him back into the water."

"What happened next?" I continued.

"He followed us in," he said.

"Where is he now?" asked Maura.

"Out there under a boat," he said, pointing to one of the moored vessels with a cathedral hull.

"Will you take us out to him?" pleaded Maura, "Please."

By this time the boat was empty and the divers were ready to hand it ashore.

"OK," said the black-clad figure, "In you get."

He backed the inflatable slowly away from the shore, taking care that the propeller did not hit any submerged rocks. Once clear he accelerated forwards, swinging round in an arc towards the moored boat.

Before we reached it there was a puff alongside. Donald had come to see us.

"Stop," cried Maura and our boatman put the engine out of gear. The lightweight inflatable came to a halt almost instantly. As soon as it did so a dolphin face appeared alongside.

"Hello Donald," said Maura and then she started to talk to him in a quiet but very relaxed and happy-to-see-you voice.

For a full thirty seconds Donald remained stationary, with his body vertical in the water and his head back in the air just about one foot away from the side of the inflatable. He looked at Maura and then looked inside the inflatable. He shook his head a few times and opened his jaws as if replying to her conversation. Then, when he had finished welcoming her, he dived and a few seconds later appeared on the other side of the boat and again raised his head above the water and looked in. It was the first time I had seen him do this, although Maura had seen him do it several times before. After a further brief conversation he dived and swam away for a quick circuit of the stationary boat moored twenty yards away from us.

We could keep our boatman away from his companions no longer, so he put the engine into gear and headed back to shore. All thoughts of lunch were forgotten and we hastened back to Dale Fort to tell Peter Hunnam to bring the Zodiac for a proper reunion in the water. One hour and a half later the Field Centre's Land Rover with the trailer behind was bouncing its way down the steep rocky approach to Martin's Haven.

As soon as the boat was launched Donald came alongside and escorted us to one of the moorings. When we stopped, he again put his head right out of the water to inspect Maura. It was a pleasantly warm sunny afternoon and Maura, who was wearing a bikini, leaned over the side and talked to Donald whenever he surfaced. Once, still only in her bikini, she slipped over the side of the inflatable and I took some pictures, but the water was very cold and she soon climbed back inboard.

Since his arrival in Wales, Donald had quickly made a name for himself, and all of the divers who had encounters with him had stories to tell of his behaviour. Some of them said that he had a definite preference for female divers and that he had made uninhibited advances of a directly sexual nature to some of them. As virtually all those who dive in British waters wear wetsuits complete with hoods, it is often difficult to tell a female diver from a male diver underwater, and this raised the question, how could Donald tell the difference between male and female divers? However, his apparently sexual advances, as I knew, were not directly exclusively to females — I had myself been investigated with his penis — so I felt that the reason why females attracted his attentions more than males was usually because female divers were gentler and more understanding towards Donald, more motherly if you like, than male divers.

Having taken some still pictures we went ashore to collect the 16mm camera in its underwater housing, for I wanted to shoot some film of Donald and Maura for television. By the time we had loaded the wooden box containing the camera into the inflatable, and Maura had put on her wetsuit, she was warm enough for another immersion. During our trip ashore other activities in the Haven commanded Donald's attention. However, as soon as we were water-bound he swam alongside, we slipped into the water and I was soon filming Donald and Maura swimming happily with one another. But their session together did not last long because after a few minutes Donald disappeared. I surfaced and we both looked around. Fifty yards away was a very sleek white cabin cruiser. A girl with blonde hair, her black wetsuit unzipped to her waist, was draped over the cabin catching the rays of sun whilst her male companion in a wetsuit long john was frantically pulling at the starter of the outboard engine. As he did so a dolphin face appeared alongside to watch the performance. Donald was obviously delighted at the new form of entertainment. When the man took the cover off the outboard and started to tinker with the engine the sound picture of tools clumping into the fibreglass hull would have been transmitted into the sea very clearly and were obviously of great interest to Donald. He dived and circled the boat, leaving us swimming in an empty sea, getting cold even though we were wearing wetsuits. We needed a counter attraction.

"Peter," I called out, "In my bag there is a tin full of stones with a handle on it. Would you please find it and give it to Maura."

Peter rummaged in my diving bag and produced the "dolphin rattle" we had used on the Isle of Man.

Maura took the handle and shook my home-made rattle under the water. In a few seconds — as inquisitive as ever — Donald appeared and inspected the source of the new noise. His stay was short-lived however. Having got his engine running the man in the cruiser was hauling up his anchor. Even from where we were we could hear the sounds of the chain rattling and true to form Donald again disappeared to investigate.

I realised that if Donald followed the boat out of the harbour I would not be able to shoot any more film. So as the boat cruised out I got Maura to shake the rattle vigorously. Whether it was the attraction of Maura or the rattle I know not but Donald did remain in the Haven. However he soon again became restive and would appear out of the sea only for a few seconds, before speeding off again. Athough I am sure he was pleased to renew his acquaintance with Maura he was exhibiting a side of his character which I was only now coming to understand: his passion for activity, and his need for constant mental stimulation. Unlike that of dogs, who seldom seem to tire of fetching a ball, Donald's attention was very difficult to command for long periods. I interpret this characteristic as being proper to a highly active brain. Having seen and heard some phenomenon, and assimilated all it had to offer, which he did in a very short period, he needed to move on to the next experience. He became rapidly bored and like a child with a lively mind, he needed new interests, he needed to be intellectually stretched.

We were getting cold and tired so I decided to wind up the operation, and handed Peter the heavy camera into the boat. I next removed my weight belt and was handing it into the boat when one of the weights slipped off and dropped to the seabed thirty-five feet below. I asked Peter to lower a weighted line overboard so that I could follow it down and retrieve my lead weight. So I put on the weight belt again, deflated my life jacket completely and swam down. At a depth of about ten feet I became negatively buoyant, and allowed myself to sink very slowly, waiting for my ears to clear — which always took a considerable time. As I neared the bottom I saw a tail fluke, and there vertical in the water with its tail uppermost was Donald, carefully inspecting the weighted line. Donald was stationary and was in a perfect pose for photography. The frustrating thing was that all of my cameras were now in the boat above. I gave him a friendly stroke under the chin and told him I had come to look for my lost weight. The seabed was flat and sandy and I spotted a scallop, its eyes peering like an even row of bright marquesites in the water. As I was over it the two shells slammed shut. I swam in ever increasing circles about the scallop, followed all of the time by Donald. Then I spotted my weight and triumphantly picked it up, still watched by the dolphin. As I swam back slowly to the surface he must have decided that that was the end of the action, so with two powerful flicks of his tail he disappeared into the blue green horizon.

The following morning I drove into Haverfordwest to put the film on a train to the BBC, and to post an article which I had sat up most of the night completing for the magazine *Photography*.

It was midday before I got back to Martin's Haven. When I arrived I could see the Zodiac out in the haven with Maura aboard. Peter Hunnam was obviously diving. As I walked down I spotted another Land Rover, and upon peering inside saw some packages of 100-foot spools of 16mm film. I must admit that I did not welcome the prospect of competition from what appeared to be a television unit. I identified the group from the Land Rover at the water's edge, and went over to find out who they were. It turned out that the new arrivals were not from television, but from the Whale Research Unit and Institute of Oceanographic Sciences of the Environment Research Council. A member of this expedition explained that the Pembrokeshire Parks Warden had told them about the unique wild dolphin who befriended divers along the coast around the islands of Skomer and Skockholm. The group had been so intrigued by the report that they had come to Wales to study and film the dolphin above and below water, as part of their general research information programme.

I explained my own interest in — or more accurately my

obsession with — "my" dolphin Donald. I realised that it would be in neither of our interests to compete with one another to film Donald that afternoon: although it might be highly amusing to Donald, if there were two camera crews in the water he would simply get so excited, and flit from one to another with such speed, that we would both find it difficult to obtain usable photographs.

The leader of their expedition, Christina Lockyer, agreed that I should go in first and that they would come out later. As we spoke I watched the Zodiac and could see Donald surfacing regularly. Then I saw Peter surface, climb aboard the Zodiac and a few minutes later he and Maura were on the beach.

"We've had a lovely time," said Maura proudly.

"Donald has taken a keen interest in my collection of specimens," said Peter, who was carrying out a survey on very pretty tiny creatures called nudibranchs.

"I've spent ages playing with him," continued Maura.

I was keen to find a better way of "calling up" Donald when we visited his territories. To date I had been extraordinarily lucky, but I knew if I could find a way of attracting his attention and identifying myself without getting into the water it could possibly save some future frustrating immersions. I reasoned with myself that the call should be interesting from Donald's viewpoint. For an animal that lived mainly in a world of sound my call sound would have to be subtle enough to compete with whole orchestras of other fascinating noises. The most effective method I had found to date was to rattle a tin full of stones.

My reasoning was to a certain extent vindicated by some later studies by Dr Robert Morris, who attempted to attract Donald with a series of single-frequency notes known to be audible to dolphins and played into the water with hydrophones when Donald was near. Donald showed no visible response to the sounds. My interpretation of the dolphin's apparent lack of interest is that sound of a single fixed frequency is like a single blotch of one colour in a sound picture as complex as a garden full of flowers — it is not sufficiently arresting to warrant his attention. The sounds from my dolphin rattle or the clockwork motor in my underwater ciné camera, which he came to inspect at very close quarters whenever I ran it in his presence underwater, on the other hand was variable in frequency and therefore far more interesting.

After a brief picnic lunch, we loaded the Zodiac. I picked up the dolphin rattle, which until then we had used underwater only, and shook it vigorously. Almost immediately Donald surfaced in the sea and looked in our direction. I continued to rattled the tin and Donald gazed at us. Then he turned round and headed towards the shore.

I know it could be argued that it was pure coincidence that Donald should surface and look in our direction when I rattled the tin. I think not, partly because we had already used the rattle underwater, with exactly similar effect; and partly because his appearance was so beautifully on cue. I believe that he heard the rattle, associated the noise with us and came towards the shore in anticipation of some more interesting happenings.

I wanted to study how Donald responded to visual images, so the last thing to be packed into the Zodiac before we moved away from the shore was a mirror mounted in a wooden frame. Donald, who had been idly cruising round the Haven when we were loading the inflatable, surfaced briefly alongside as soon as we were in deep water. I slipped over the side with my still camera and Maura followed immediately. Donald appeared and disappeared in his usual manner. When he had been away for a longer period than usual, Peter gave Maura a small brass bell which she tinkled under the water. When I was close to her I could hear it quite distinctly. So too did Donald. He came, had a very quick look at it and disappeared again. Despite further efforts on Maura's part, the bell seemed to be of only very fleeting interest to the dolphin.

To explain this lack of interest I tried once more to put myself inside the mind of a dolphin. I remembered how on previous occasions I had watched Donald's fascination with the regulator on Maura's demand valve, which being of the twin-hose variety was located on the top of the air cylinder she carried on her back. The regulator had a few moving parts, which controlled the escape of the air from the very high-pressure cylinder into the inlet breathing tube. When she exhaled, the exhaust air flowed out in a spurt via a one-way valve into the water, making the characteristic plumes of bubbles that will be familiar to those who have seen films of divers underwater. Maura's exhaust valve was also situated behind her head. I asked myself what, as a dolphin, I would have found more interesting: the tinkle of a bell, or the noise of a demand valve which was composed of a mixture of sounds including the flutter of the rubber diaphragm, the movement of levers and the reverberating sounds made by the passage of air through a tube? The answer seemed obvious, and to confirm Donald's own preference for the valve. But why? Would the regulator's sound appeal to his aesthetic sense, to the pattern-making capacities of his brain, as a human responds, say to wind instruments? Or would the sheer complexity and variations in the sound stimulate him? My intuition told me that the answer would be a mixture of both — but proving this in a scientific manner would call for controlled experiments which I was not prepared to contemplate, for I was determined that I should never attempt to reduce the relationship between Donald and myself to the level of researcher and guinea-pig. Controlled experiments were out. Nothing whatsoever was to interfere with the dolphin's total freedom, so the choice about whether or not he would co-operate in my studies was always to be his. If he did not like what I was doing at any time, or became bored, he could simply swim away. Anything I learned about him was to be only a bonus on top of the friendship he had with Maura and me.

I did not know what reaction to expect when Maura took the mirror into the water. On a number of occasions territorial fish have had mirrors placed within their boundaries. Upon seeing their own reflections the fish have adopted aggressive attitudes towards the images, which they have taken to be intruders. Filmed sequences have shown fishes attacking the illusory invader in an attempt to drive it away. I suspected that Donald would not be so easily fooled, and he wasn't. Indeed, although Maura tried to position the mirror so that he could see himself, he appeared to take no notice of the small part of his own image that I thought he could see. Instead he nibbled at the wooden frame with his teeth — which was his way of establishing its texture. Then he shook his head and swam away.

Later events showed how completely wrong it is to draw conclusions from a single observation. His behaviour on the later occasion when confronted by a mirror was violent, and so disturbing that I was really scared with Donald underwater. However, in Martin's Haven I was perfectly satisfied with Donald's undramatic reaction, and content to conclude only that he was not narcissistic and that vanity was therefore probably an exclusively human characteristic!

By the time we had finished with the mirror it was time to let the Whale Research Unit make their observations, and they came to join us in their inflatable. Donald was delighted to have some more action and immediately took an interest in the newly arrived vessel and its occupants. One of those on board was Arnold Madgwick of the Institute of Oceanographic Sciences, who was keen to obtain surface ciné film of Donald.

When the inflatable swung round in an arc Donald followed. The person at the controls opened the throttle. The inflatable responded immediately and rose on to the plane. As it did so the water parted at the keel, and formed two waves that followed the course of the boat as closely as a shadow. Donald positioned himself just ahead of the waves, so that he could be pushed forward by the water rising continuously behind him. As the inflatable swung into curve after curve, Donald rode the waves like a surfrider, revelling in the mastery of his element, and the innate sense of balance and movement through water, that enabled him so effortlessly to keep himself in the correct position to benefit from the man-created wave. The sensitivity with which he manoeuvred with his tail and flippers reminded me of a seagull delicately fingering the air with its wingtip feathers, as it soars high on the upwelling air created by an onshore breeze deflected by a cliff.

From our Zodiac we watched fascinated as the other inflatable passed by.

As the boat raced past us we could clearly see Donald just below the surface, riding the arm of one of the V-shaped waves that followed the boat. We noted that he rode the waves that followed, and did not position himself to ride the bow waves. Perhaps he remembered the incident in the Isle of Man when he was hit by the outboard skeg.

When the inflatable again pulled up alongside us, Donald swung away and performed a couple of spectacular leaps to show his appreciation. He moved at such speed and was so unpredictable that attempts to photograph and film proved very frustrating. Running the 16mm camera all of the time was out of the question — the 100 feet of film it contained would run for only two and a half minutes at twenty-four frames per second. So with Maura acting as dolphin spotter I tried to follow her pointing hand as she desperately attempted to indicate his position when he was rushing along just below the surface. Anticipating when he would surface and perhaps leap was almost impossible. So I watched Maura's hand with one eye and attempted to keep the camera pointed in the right direction, whilst peering through the viewfinder with the other eye. When I saw him surface I would slam on the shutter button in an attempt to get the most spectacular sequences I could with the limited amount of film I had available. I longed for the use of a camera with a 400-foot magazine, and for the resources to enable me to make a really good film of Donald in one of his exuberant moods. And not being in the fortune-telling business, I had no way of knowing that the stars were set right for this ambition to be realised at a later date.

From our conversation with members of the Whale Research Unit, it was apparent that Maura and I had a lot of information on Donald that would help them fill in background details on their new subject. So when they heard that we were to leave the next day, Christina Lockyer suggested we all get together during the evening.

When the arrangements had been made we headed back to shore, to the task of loading all of our gear back on the Land Rover. A few hours later we approached The Griffin, still not quite sure what to make of the sudden interest in Donald by a group of professional scientists.

The Griffin is in the middle of the village of Dale. The entrance opens on to the road. There is no footpath on the opposite side of the road, just a low wall and beyond that the sand and the sea. In the summer months the patrons flow out of the pub door and spread over the road and along the sea wall, and as we approached in the car the crowd parted and closed behind us again as if some invisible force, like surface tension, was holding it together.

Inside, a juke box in one corner pumped out the latest pop tune, competing with the hubble bubble of raised voices. In one corner I recognised the Dale Fort people. The noise level was so high that a comfortable conversation with any person at a distance greater than six inches from one's mouth even when speaking at full volume, was impossible, so our exchanges on the subject of dolphins were limited. In any case I suspected that this unit, which contained some of Britain's acknowledged authorities on Cetaceans, were likely to be rather wary of me, and perhaps slightly resentful that a mere enthusiast, with no recognised expertise on whales, should engage in their specialised field of study.

I for my part was certainly suspicious of members of this expedition, for I had heard rumours that they intended to capture Donald and fit instruments to him. Having just completed ten years of research in human and veterinary medicine I appreciated very well that research workers might indeed regard Donald as an ideal subject for a host of scientific studies. I knew also that every effort would be made to ensure that he came to no physical harm; but I was certain that if they interfered with him, they would greatly change, if not destroy altogether, the purely spontaneous relationship he, and I emphasise that it was *his* choice, had established with humans in general and with Maura in particular. Thus I needed to know precisely what was the purpose of their visit.

Shouting at the top of your voice in a packed public house is not an ideal way of conducting a diplomatic exchange in which each side is attempting to uncover the intentions and aspirations of the other party without giving away too much information itself. So I think we were all relieved when 'time gentlemen please' was eventually announced and Annette, one of the young lecturers from the Field Centre, invited us all to her room for coffee.

Her room was in part of the fortifications and it had a high vaulted brick ceiling. The men and women assembled there were all keenly interested natural historians, and throughout the two hours we spent sipping coffee and eating freshly made shortbread the conversation hardly deviated from dolphins and their related species. As the minutes unwrapped themselves, to reveal unknown upon unknown, I realised how little information the experts really have about the life of the dolphins and whales in the sea. It was obvious that a lot of research material had been gathered on captive dolphins but on wild dolphins living free in the ocean man clearly knows extraordinarily little. What I found perhaps even more surprising was how limited was the information on whales: an entire world-wide industry had been based upon whales for over a hundred years, had thrived and declined; yet that enterprise had been so totally commercially based and conducted in such a free-for-all manner that it was not until the 1920s that any real attention was paid by those directly involved to the life history and the survival of the hunted species.

Over the past fifty years, scientific studies have been published, many in the industry's journal *Norks Hvalfangst-tidende*; and Britain has had a Whale Group working on whale biology since 1925. Yet these efforts are surely small compared with the magnitude of the industry in its heyday, and the magnitude of the insult it inflicted upon the wild life of our planet.

Nonetheless, research work in the present century has made some contribution to our knowledge of the sea's largest inhabitants. Some whales were tagged with stainless steel markers as part of one of the research programmes of the National Institute of Oceanography in the nineteen thirties, and this work has continued ever since, the information gathered from these and other studies being analysed to indicate that most species of whales make annual migrations. It has been shown for instance that distinct populations of southern humpback whales feed in the summer in the plankton-rich waters of the Antarctic. They then migrate northwards up the coasts of the continents of South America, Africa and Australia as the winter sets in. In the shallow warm water they mate and give birth to their young. We do not have similar information on whales in the northern hemisphere. And details on the populations and movements of dolphins are even sparser. Even the apparently simple question "What is the world population of bottlenose dolphins and where are they to be found?" cannot be answered with any degree of accuracy.

The main source of data has been that gathered from reports of strandings, that is of animals washed ashore, or dead animals found on beaches. However, deductions made from such observations must obviously be cautious: numbers may reflect for instance a tendency of a particular species to become stranded (or a preference for a shallow water habitat) rather than population density. Species that steer well clear of the coast when migrating will appear to be less common than those which may exist in relatively small numbers, but hug the coastlines when they migrate. By law in Britain all stranded whales and dolphins should be reported to the British Museum of Natural History at South Kensington. Their records show that there were 174 strandings of bottlenose dolphins between 1913 and 1966, i.e. about three a year. The bottlenose dolphin is third in order of frequency of strandings off the British coast, following the common porpoise and the common dolphin. Most reports of the bottlenose dolphin came from the south and west coast of England, and it has only rarely been reported from the North Sea. Reports of strandings from other parts of the world indicate that bottlenose dolphins are most widespread in temperate seas.

Another major source of information is of course the sighting of the species in the wild. Here again we must ask ourselves "How accurate are the data?" How many of those who see wild dolphins in the sea are able positively to identify the species from a brief glimpse as the dolphin surfaces or leaps out of the water? Knowing of Donald's love of following boats, just how much does the frequency of bottlenose dolphins' sightings depend on a bottlenose dolphin species characteristic: the tendency to associate with vessels that move through the waters?

These were just a few of the problems we debated that night in Annette's room at Dale Fort. And when we came to considering the social behaviour of bottlenose dolphins in the wild, we concluded that the information from which valid deductions can be made was even more hopelessly sparse. The reason is simply that men have never been able to get in the water and study dolphins at close quarters, as they have on land with wild animals such as lions.

Since man first sailed the seas he has observed that dolphins sometimes congregate in groups or schools. And a few incidents have been reported which indicate that a dolphin school is a mutual aid society in the wild. One su. incident was described by two trained observers, members of the staff of the Living Sea Gulfarium at Fort William Beach in Florida. They noticed that an underwater dynamite explosion had injured a bottlenose dolphin in the bay. The animal rose to the surface in distress and then sank. Immediately two other dolphins came to his assistance. They positioned themselves on either side of their wounded companion, put their heads under his flippers, and carried him to the surface for air. In this position they were unable to breathe through their own blowholes. They therefore had to let go of their casualty from time to time to catch a breath themselves. They returned to their first-aid stations the moment they had filled their own lungs.

The incident in Florida was one of the rare instances where observations have been made on spontaneous dolphin behaviour in the wild. On the other hand, many studies have been made on the social behaviour of dolphins in captivity. But any conclusions drawn from this source must be viewed with circumspection. Confinement in a dolphinarium may impose such severe conditioning on the captive dolphins that their behaviour may bear little resemblance to the social order of a free life in the sea. How far would a study of Jews in a concentration camp help in the understanding of life in Israel?

Thus the presence of Donald off the coast of Wales was of special interest to the Whale Research Unit: it presented a very rare opportunity for close-up observations to be made on an unrestricted animal.

As the shortbread biscuits disappeared from the plates and the coffee vanished from the cups, I came to realise that there was after all no conflict between Christina Lockyer's group's interest and ideals and mine. They merely wanted to observe and record Donald's behaviour and movements. When I was assured that these studies would definitely not involve Donald's capture, or any interference with his freedom, my apprehension melted. And when they realised that Maura and I were primarily concerned for Donald's wellbeing, I think any reservations they might have had concerning our contact with the dolphin were also dispelled. Indeed, we found that our respective pools of information were mutually beneficial. The members of the Whale

Research Unit had considerable knowledge of the scientific work that had been conducted on other dolphins, in which both Maura and I were keenly interested. Maura and I on the other hand had a great deal of background information, especially dates of incidents and sightings, on Donald which was of interest particularly to the member of Dr Gamble's team, Christine Lockyer, assigned to compiling a record of Donald's past.

It was well past midnight when we all eventually left the Field Centre. The Whale Research Unit expedition party were camping nearby. Maura and I were staying in a guest house in Dale, and I crept into the silent house to collect an album of photographs of Donald that had been taken in Port St Mary in the Isle of Man, to show Christina. The headlights of the Land Rover were switched on and we squatted on our haunches in the road leafing through the book. Christina Lockyer was also interested in the rate of healing of wounds in wild dolphins, and we examined the photographs to see if we could identify any of his old scars and relate them to existing marks. She was particularly interested in the wound on Donald's head, which we could date precisely. When I had first seen the photographs taken shortly after the incident, I had been distressed because the wound detracted from the beautiful smooth line of his shape and made him look rather battered. Now however, on a road in Dale in the early hours of the morning, I looked at the pictures of the ugly wound from a new viewpoint. First, they provided uncontrovertible evidence that Donald and Dai were once and the same dolphin — a question which we were often asked. Second, by comparing Donald's present condition with that indicated in the photographs we could see how wonderfully the wound had healed spontaneously without any interference from man. We anticipated that over a period of a further year or two the entire area would be dark grey and the only external sign of the accident would be a permanent depression about six inches behind, and slightly to the right (looking forward) of, his blowhole. Third, the photographs confirmed my view that we could learn a great deal about dolphins in the wild without subjecting Donald to the rigorous controls usually deemed necessary by research scientists. We would gather our information merely by observing and photographing him.

A friendly meeting with scientists from the Institute of Oceanographic Sciences and the Whale Research Unit was a rewarding way for Maura to end her reunion with Donald. We agreed to exchange information and photographs freely. When the Land Rover eventually departed and the red rear lights disappeared round the bend into a black Welsh hillside, we departed happily to our respective beds, happy that so many people were taking a friendly and above all protective interest in our dolphin.

The next morning we collected our wetsuits, which were still sopping wet from an overnight downpour of rain, from the clothes line at the Dale Fort Field Centre. We thanked Peter Hunnam for his help and headed for Harlech Television Studios in Cardiff. One of the films I had shot underwater was processed whilst we had lunch, and during the afternoon we tele-recorded a news feature. It was Maura's first visit to a television studio.

A few days later when she was back in the Isle of Man, she was able to pick up the item when it was broadcast. For a few minutes she again relived the pleasure of being under water with Donald, sad that he had left the Isle of Man, but pleased that he appeared to have settled happily into a new home.

15: Call to Cornwall

The circumstances that have brought Maura, Donald and me together have often been linked by the most curious contacts and coincidences.

Quite by chance I sat next to a very attractive young lady with long brown-blonde hair at lunch at the British Sub-Aqua Club's Diving Officers Conference in London. We were introduced by a mutual friend and I was told her name was Hazel Carswell. She had the clear looks of natural English beauty. I was not surprised when I later discovered that for part of her young life she had been a shepherdess. As we sat and chatted at the lunch table, I learned that she was now making a living with her husband Bob, running a boat called *Aquanaut* which they chartered for diving trips out of the tiny Cornish fishing village of Mousehole. When not taking out divers they collected sea urchins, the tests (shells) of which were sold to tourists. As I had just been appointed Conservation Officer of the British Sub-Aqua Club and had made an appeal requesting divers to restrict what they took from the sea she naturally was a little apprehensive as to how I would react when I found out that she was denuding the sea bed of some of its sea urchins. So on the principle that the best mode of defence is attack, she took a slightly aggressive attitude towards me. However, I have always taken the view that rules are mostly for guidance and not necessarily for strict observation, and had no inclination to condemn her for what I knew was a very hard source of living from the sea, especially when she told me she had given up gathering gorgorian coral which was a lucrative business, when she learned of its very slow growth rate.

I recognised her immediately as one of those special women

whom I had met occasionally in the diving community, and who, once they take up the sport, stick at it come hell or high water. Those who believe in astrology will not be surprised to learn that her birthday was 10 March, the same day as Maura's. And the coincidence did not end there. Both their mothers had the same birthday, 6 March — all under the sign of Pisces — the fish. I told her that I had often dived in the Plymouth area but I had never dived the far west of Cornwall, and we discussed the possibility that perhaps one day I could arrange to dive from the *Aquanaut* if I could fit it in with a trip to the West Country.

What I did not know as we sat eating lunch together on 15 November 1975 was that a few weeks later I would receive a letter from Penzance telling me that a wild dolphin had arrived in the area. I was told that Bob and Hazel Carswell had befriended the dolphin and if I wanted to see it I should contact them.

Just how long it took for Donald to make the trip from Dale Haven to Cornwall I do not know. The first person to observe his arrival was a man called Geoff Bold, the mechanic of the Penlee Lifeboat.

He had spotted a fin between the breasting buoys which are used to guide the lifeboat back up the slipway after a launch. At first Geoff thought it was a basking shark — a "basker" — but then he realised that it was the wrong time of year because basking sharks are seen in the area only in the summer. The next possibility he considered was that the fin moving between the buoys belonged to a small whale. The following day however there was a lifeboat exercise, and when the new arrival was attracted by the sounds of rattling chains and the activities of the launching and came to gambol in its characteristic way about the lifeboat, he recognised it as a dolphin. Geoff kept a log of some of the activities and movements of his newfound friend. Thus the date of his arrival is precise. It was 10 January 1976.

Geoff was born in London and became a highly skilled tool maker. He earned good money, ran a fast car, had a wife and a son. Everything should have been fine. But Geoff was one of those people for whom the pressures of city life irritate and corrode like an abscess in the mind. He grew so embittered, and so short-tempered with his wife and the son whom he adored that the family eventually split up. Freed from home ties he was given a job in Cornwall, which he completed in record time. The man for whom he was working said, "Why don't you take some time off?"

With nothing but sad memories to attract him back to the city he explored the area of Cornwall west of Penzance, fell in love with it and decided never to go back to London.

He met a dark-eyed Cornish girl called Liz, married her and took the low-paid job of lifeboat mechanic which carried with it a tied cottage in the beautiful fishing village of Mousehole. Again, everything seemed set fair for him. But as the years drifted past Geoff discovered that as a stranger he was not readily accepted into the tightly knit community of the fishing village, and that the claustrophobic atmosphere of the village could be as stressful as the anonymity of the city. His wife wanted to travel but Geoff had had enough of travelling. His wife whom he adored became very stressed and the strain was telling on Geoff. It was then that Donald the dolphin sailed into his life.

From the way he himself described the experience to me later, it would be no exaggeration to say that Donald's arrival transformed Geoff's life in much the same way that both Maura and I felt he had transformed ours. Geoff is a man with a super-sensitivity to his environment, and to the people who create the emotional atmosphere in which he lives. It had brought him much mental pain but it had also made him aware of the undefinable emanations that appear to come from Donald and that experience, from the beginning, made Geoff happy.

When he tried to describe what he meant, Geoff gave as an example one day when he was feeling particularly depressed. He was greasing the steel runner, down which the lifeboat slides when it is launched, and was wondering why he, a skilled mechanic, should be doing such a dirty unskilled task. Then suddenly the gloom that enveloped him lifted, and he found himself continuing with his work in an unusually cheerful frame of mind. As he became aware of the change, and asked himself why he should suddenly feel in such good spirits, he looked round and noticed that Donald was watching him from the water a few feet away. Geoff made the point strongly that he was quite unaware of the dolphin's presence until after his depression lifted, and that he saw his feeling of wellbeing as springing directly from the arrival of Donald. When Donald was off the slipway of the Penlee lifeboat station Geoff Bold was a happy man.

Right from Donald's first appearance Geoff studied the movements and behaviour of the dolphin, much of which he recorded in a log book.

He had a keen interest in natural history and was in a unique position to observe Donald's behaviour. As the days passed Geoff noticed that Donald had settled by the right hand buoy which he seemed to use as a territorial marker. Geoff evolved a theory that Donald used the buoy chains as sonic reflectors which enabled him to set up a kind of sound fence in which he could trap fish when he was feeding. When the fishing boats from nearby Newlyn approached on their way to their mackerel fishing grounds, the dolphin would become very active and would frequently break the surface, though he seldom followed the boats out to sea. The fishermen for their part often deviated towards the lifeboat slip from their homeward course especially to see Donald, and toss him fish, which he appeared to accept. (Maura and I later made observations underwater, however, that suggested that he did not in fact eat them, but let them sink to the seabed). Westward Television got wind of the story, and sent a cameraman to the lifeboat station to record the scene.

In due course news of the dolphin's arrival at Penlee reached Malcolm Cullen, a warden of the Pembroke National Parks, who was missing him from Martin's Haven. Malcolm was anxious to identify the new friendly dolphin as Donald, so he contacted Geoff to check on his markings and scars, and Hazel and Bob Carswell were called upon to dive with the dolphin off the slipway, to observe him at close quarters. Their report left absolutely no doubt that Cornwall's gain was Wales' loss.

As before, Donald was making new friends, and in addition to Geoff Bold one of his favourites turned out to be Hazel Carswell. Hazel was as near to the kind of human friend he had had in Maura as Donald had met since he left the Isle of Man. Since Hazel and Bob took the boat out of Mousehole harbour nearly every day, his encounters with them were frequent and he joined them on many of their dives. And it was from Hazel and Bob that I learnt most about the dolphin's adventures in Penlee, and about what I was to come to see as his ever-deepening relationship with human beings.

One of the incidents which most moved Hazel took place off the Carswells' boat, *Aquanaut*, when a group of divers from Colchester had chartered it for a day. In the morning they were practising lifesaving drill in the water. Such aquatic activities bring out the mischievous spirit in Donald — who had been christened 'Beaky' in Cornwall — and it was not long before he was totally disrupting the exercise by putting his nose between the divers to separate them, and on occasions actually pushing the "victim" in the opposite direction to that in which the "rescuer" was trying to tow him. Donald's involvement in the practice exercise was so energetic and disruptive that the lifesaving drill had to be abandoned. However, on the same afternoon, the group were diving a wreck in Mount's Bay when one of their number, a student teacher named Keith Monery, got into difficulties and surfaced. His lifejacket was punctured and full of water, so it failed to function. Keith shouted for help and started to sink. Hazel, who was acting as safety lookout, was then horrified to see Donald swimming towards the diver — would the dolphin behave in the same manner as in the morning, and push the distressed man around making his plight even more serious? She threw herself into the water and swam towards the drowning man.

Although Hazel is a very experienced diver, she admits to being a not exceptionally strong swimmer, and as she made her way towards the victim she realised that although she could cope with the man she would be quite unable to save him if Donald interfered. When she reached Keith Monery she found that Donald was indeed with him. But instead of teasing him, the dolphin was gently supporting Keith from beneath. Hazel grasped the coughing and spluttering student from behind, calmed him and towed him back towards the *Aquanaut*. As she did so she found that he was being gently supported from below by Donald, who also managed somehow to help Hazel tow him back to the boat. And when she stood on the diving ladder helping to get the man aboard, Donald did not pull at her fins which he often did when she was leaving the water after a dive, when he wanted her to stay and play longer. Instead he stayed beside the boat with his head out of the water watching the scene. Keith Monery made an uneventful recovery.

When Hazel told me the story afterwards, she said she was absolutely convinced that Donald knew that the diver was in distress — that he had been able to differentiate between a real life drama and mock operation. Thus, she concluded that the dolphin was able in some way to 'sense' that the vibrations made by the diver were genuine distress signals and not simulated distress signals. Certainly other aquatic animals have this sense; I witnessed it in operation myself in the Persian Gulf when I was floating on the surface watching a snorkel diver about sixty feet below me spear a fish with a harpoon gun. I had seen no sign of sharks for the entire morning, yet within two seconds of the spear hitting a fish two eight-foot-long sharks arrowed in out of the blue. One "bumped" the fish, the other

swam straight at the fisherman and bumped him with
its snout. Then both sharks disappeared again as
quickly as they had appeared. There was certainly
no time for the blood from the fish to diffuse through
the water towards the sharks. It was as if the speared fish had
shrieked with pain and the prowling predators, aware
of our presence but keeping out of sight, flung themselves instinctively at the distressed creatures, which they
investigated by ramming them with their snouts. One
of the creatures they investigated in this manner was
not the fish but the spear fisherman, and since the
fisherman's reaction, which was aggressive, was not an
expected response, the sharks, being cowardly creatures,
pressed their investigations no further and disappeared
into the safety of the blue haze of the sea that was all
around us.

If relatively primitive creatures, the sharks, possess this
ability to sense distress vibrations, I would be surprised
if dolphins cannot do likewise. Indeed, I would expect
the dolphins, with their exceptional sensitivity to sound,
to be even more alert to distress signals. And if a dolphin
is able to sense a human's personality, which is what
our experience of Donald already suggested, then why
not also his moods?

Bob Carswell subsequently had an experience with Donald
which he saw as further evidence of Donald's ability to
'sense' human temperament.

When Donald encounters, or more often, is approached
by a group of unfamiliar divers he may not want their
company for very long, and after allowing them to play
with him for a few minutes he usually moves away. With
divers with whom he is very familiar, however, he likes
to play for long periods, and he resents it when they
pay no attention to him. He also has a keen interest
in any underwater activities in which the divers may
be engaged, and ideally he likes a combination of work
and play, with the divers periodically breaking away from

the job in hand to take notice of him. One day Bob was diving in about sixty feet of water collecting sea urchins, and Donald was swimming around him. As Bob was preoccupied with the need to make a living he concentrated exclusively on picking up the urchins and putting them in his sack. After about ten minutes of being thus ignored. Donald swam over him and pinned him firmly to the bottom for what must have been a few seconds, but which to Bob seemed like a long time. Although he was surprised by the dolphin's actions, Bob was not unduly upset, and did not struggle or behave in a distressed manner. He told me that he realised the dolphin was only taking him to task for neglecting him.

If however Donald had done this to a less experienced diver, or had pinned a diver with a more excitable temperament to the seabed, the outcome might well have been disastrous. At the very least he would have given a less cool diver palpitations and some very anxious moments. Bob suggested that in fact the dolphin can hear heartbeats through the water, and that he associates a high heart rate with distress. If this is the case, it is unlikely that he would have persisted in pinning a frightened diver to the seabed.

Bob Carswell stressed that at no time has he felt any fear when Donald has been in the water with him, and indeed that for no other creature in the sea has he felt the same warmth and affection. He has often for instance been in the water with basking sharks up to twenty feet long, which are plankton eaters and therefore not considered dangerous, but he has no warm feeling towards them like he has for Donald.

With news that Donald had found a new home and a new set of friends, Maura and I were naturally keen to visit him. Our opportunity came following a short broadcast I did for the early morning radio programme *Today*. Details of my interest in Donald reached Yorkshire

Television, who wanted something special to include in the first of a new series of 'Don't Ask Me' programmes. Having failed to get a large live shark into the studio they opted for what they considered to be the next best thing — a live dolphin in the studio. When they heard about the relationship that Maura and I had with a wild dolphin in the sea, they pulled out all the stops to include a feature on Donald and Maura to link with studio sequences. By the time the full television crew was mobilised, however, I was leading an underwater photographic safari in Kenya, and it seemed that my entire journey along the coast of Kenya was accompanied by a series of telephone calls, each of which seemed to take an extraordinarily long time to reach me. There was always some confusion at the switch-board when the calls arrived, and someone else with a name similar to mine would be hunted for whilst the transcontinental telephone minutes ticked by. When the mistake was eventually discovered I would hasten to the telephone to answer such impossible questions as "How long will it take you to find the dolphin?" and "Do you think you will be able to get any really good underwater footage?" To which I would reply that Donald was a totally free wild creature living in the sea, so I could guarantee nothing, but I would do my best. It was the sort of situation that gives nightmares to a programme producer with a budget to keep to and a deadline to meet.

Meanwhile it was up to my wife Wendy to carry the administrative role from my home. She contacted Maura and the Carswells, and the entire operation was teed up for my return from Kenya. As soon as the jumbo jet from Nairobi touched down at Heathrow I bade a rapid farewell to the members of my safari and was whisked away to where the Yorkshire Television helicopter was waiting to fly me to my home in Yorkshire to collect my underwater ciné camera and diving equipment.

I sat next to the pilot and as we rose in the air

I felt as if I was sitting in a magic chair high above the countryside. It was April and the weather was cool and showery. The multi-hued green landscape below contrasted vividly with the dun-coloured expanses of the game parks of central Africa through which I had been travelling a few hours before. We flew at a height of about one thousand feet and at one point passed over Woburn Abbey. From my kestrel-eye view in the sky, I could see the tracks and the animals in the Safari Park. It looked minute compared with the twelve thousand square miles of the Tsavo Game Park over which I had flown two weeks earlier, and the sight raised once more in my mind the question of the morality of confining animals, whose natural habitat is the vast plains of Africa, to the confines of English parks, or even worse, the tiny cages of a zoo. The same question was to come right into focus later when I saw the dolphin in its pool in the television studio.

When I saw the familiar tall white pillars of the new suspension bridge that was under construction I knew I was nearly home. I looked down on my village of North Ferriby, which is still dominated by its church, and savoured that 'it's nice to be back' feeling that one has after a long journey away from home — no matter how exciting the expedition has been. As we flew over my house I noticed a strange apple-green car in the drive beneath the trees I loved, which were in their new spring foliage. The grass of our landing field flattened and bits of straw were whisked into the air as we touched down. News of our arrival had spread through the village and a small crowd had gathered in the drizzling rain at the edge of the field. My seventeen-year-old daughter, Melanie, rushed up to the helicopter before the blades had stopped rotating and flung her arms round my neck as soon as I stepped out.

Wendy, had prepared a superb homecoming lunch which was eaten between excited talk about the trip

: John Maddrell — Manx Press Pictures

If cats have nine lives then Donald's history of encounters with death suggests that dolphins have even more. One of his lives was used up in Derbyhaven, and the story is told in this series of pictures taken by John Maddrell.

Above: The tide runs out leaving Donald stranded.

Right: Donald is dowsed with water to keep him alive until he can be rescued.

John Maddrell — Manx Press Pictures

Above: Donald is ignominiously scooped into the bucket of a mechanical digger and his journey back to freedom in the sea begins.

Below: First attempts at putting Donald back in the sea without putting the expensive digger at risk are unsuccessful.

John Maddrell — Manx Press Pictures

o everyone helps to manhandle Donald, who probably weighs 600 lbs, to deep water. Donald eventually swam away with one fewer of his ves in the Bank of Providence.

Cartoon: Mike

WE HAVE SEEN BEAKY THE DOLPHIN

Wherever Donald goes he becomes a local celebrity and can be relied upon to entertain the locals and visitors alike. Mike Green, a comic strip artist in St Ives, seized the opportunity of Donald's visit to produce a comic postcard that sold in thousands to the trippers in the summer of 1976.

Donald in a boisterous mood in Martin's Haven.

Photo: Arnold Madgwick, Institute of Oceanographic Sc

I had just finished and the new one I was about to make. I was introduced to the owner of the strange car in the drive. She was Yvonne Ingham from Yorkshire Television who was to drive me and my equipment to Cornwall.

Two-and-a-half hours after my homecoming I waved farewell once more to the family and we sped to Manchester Airport where Maura, who had flown over from the Isle of Man, was waiting patiently for us. Our driver was a vivacious blonde whom Maura liked immediately, and they later became firm friends.

It was nearly midnight when we eventually arrived in Penzance. I was exhausted.

The next morning dawned a sullen grey. I rose early before the rest of the crew were awake, and walked along the deserted seafront. The sea which lapped quietly against the wall outside our hotel was the colour of lead.

Arrangements had been made for Bob and Hazel Carswell to bring their *Aquanaut* across from Mousehole to the quay in Penzance, near to where the *Scillonian* was due to depart for her daily run to the Scilly Isles. Compared with the *Scillonian* the *Aquanaut* was minute. She was a typical fishing boat of the region, about thirty-five feet long and painted the traditional blue. The influence of Donald on the Carswells was already to be seen for there was a bold dolphin painted in silver on the forecabin. Then, as we began to bring our diving equipment and underwater camera onto the *Aquanaut* it started to drizzle: conditions for photography above or below water were far from ideal.

I was a little fraught, partly as the result of the long journey and a general lack of sleep, but mainly because of the uncertain outcome of the expedition. I watched the white mass of *Scillonian* start to move gently out of the harbour and could see the dark water turning in whirlpools round the stern as her powerful propellors bit into the sea. Then suddenly a small black hump broke the surface and disappeared in a second. The *Scillonian* inched forward. The hump appeared and disappeared again. Donald had arrived on cue. The television crew watched excitedly as the dolphin frolicked around the vessel which was slowly moving away from the quay. My anxiety started to evaporate, but the day was not yet won.

The one thing that now concerned me was whether Donald would maintain the daily pattern of movement which our researches had shown he had established, or whether he would choose today to go out with the *Scillonian* and join the fishing boats far out to sea. We watched him disappear as the *Scillonian* sailed quietly across Mount's Bay. It was still drizzling, but I was in high spirits, delighted to see my friendly dolphin again.

The arrangements for our rendezvous with Donald were complicated by the fact that the team from the Whale Research Unit and the Institute of Oceanographic Sciences, with whom we had made contact in Wales, were also in Penzance for a brief stay to continue their own observations of Donald. Dr Robert Morris of the Institute of Oceanographic Sciences wanted to investigate what sounds Donald would react to. Each of the teams was keen not to upset the other, and none of us wanted to interfere too much with Donald's routine, so we agreed to limit our filming session to the morning only, leaving the afternoon free for the scientists to pursue their interests We also offered them space in the *Aquanaut* for any observations they might care to make, and Christina Lockyer and Arnold Madgwick came aboard. Once these negotiations had been completed we were faced with the not inconsiderable task of tracking a wild dolphin in the English Channel and then getting both above water and underwater film of him — this task to be completed in the space of a few hours.

I had been told that Donald sometimes went out as far as St Michael's Mount. As we waited for our aqualung cylinders to arrive I looked across the bay at the famous landmark. It stood out of the sea like a picture in a fairy story book — a rugged triangular island topped with a castle. That day it was painted grey and just visible through the mist. There was the whole vast expanse of Mount's Bay in which Donald could hide himself. Our main hope was that he would go straight to the Penlee Lifeboat Station.

So when our fully-charged aqualung cylinders arrived we set off for Penlee. Maura and I got kitted up in our wetsuits while the rest of the crew huddled under their anoraks. It was a far cry from the scorching sun and heat of the tropics I had recently become accustomed to.

I could soon see the two parallel strips of grey concrete, that make up the Penlee slipway, rising out of the sea to a lifeboat station, nestled close to the rocky coastline. Offshore from the slipway were two buoys. This is where we were told Donald might be. But there was no sign of him.

Maura did not put on her aqualung but slipped quietly into the water. And miraculously, within half a minute Donald appeared. Their reunion was very gentle. Donald was quiet and the two of them swam slowly side by side. Maura put her arms round Donald and crooned to him in a quiet voice and told him how glad she was to see him again. Donald lay quietly his eyes tightly shut. "I could see his eyes, under the lids, rolling in ecstasy" said Maura afterwards. She continued "He lay alongside for a while, then we finned along gently together, with one of my arms across his neck."

I followed Maura into the sea with my cameras, and swam very quietly towards the two of them. Donald took no notice of me, which was most unusual, for he normally inspected every person entering the water. I had never seen him so relaxed before. Later, Geoff Bold, the lifeboat mechanic, explained to me his theory that Donald had adopted the buoy outside the lifeboat station as a territorial marker. He pointed out, that if any boat headed directly for his buoy, Donald would become excited and swim vigorously towards the vessel, as if to deflect it from approaching too close to his territory. I was myself to see this behaviour pattern exhibited very clearly at a later date, when Donald had moved to a new site and adopted a new territory. This place was his haven, a place of security. His peace of mind was in no way disturbed by the *Aquanaut* because it was a very familiar boat in his adopted territory, and an old human friend "dropped in" from the sky could be welcomed with confidence.

I glided quietly past and looked closely at his eyes. Maura put her arms round him and cuddled him and he shut his eyes in bliss. Those eyes really were extraordinarily expressive. The eyes of fishes are permanently open and cold, but a dolphin has eyelids which can be opened and closed like those of most other mammals. The eyelids are parts of the small area of a dolphin's body where the skin does not have a thick underlayer of blubber.

Donald stayed with us for a few minutes and then dived quickly and disappeared. We waited in the cold water for his return and called him. When he did not reappear we swam back to the *Aquanaut* where the television cameraman wearing a wetsuit was standing on the lower rungs of the diving ladder with his feet submerged. Donald was just beneath him looking at the rubber bootees dipping into his territory. Then he darted away, swung in a tight circle and returned to the steps again to see what was happening.

The cameraman was a young Jordanian named Mostafa Hammuri. What I did not know was that I was witnessing the first steps in the formation of another quite positive relationship between Donald and a fellow human being. For fate had decreed that Donald and Mostafa would meet again and this in turn would lead to Mostafa and I becoming firm friends. However, that was hidden in the mists of the future.

The entire television crew were excited at seeing the dolphin so close, and having got his above-water shots Mostafa insisted on joining us in the sea. He was not wearing a hood on his diving suit, the water must have felt very cold. He swam as if the devil were chasing him, finning rapidly and sweeping his arms vigorously through the water. He swam diagonally down, then raced up again. He was breathing at an incredible rate, the air rushing from his exhaust valve like a steam locomotive at full speed. A services diving instructor would have gone into a state of apoplexy if he had seen a novice diving in such a manner.

In contrast, Donald was delighted with the newcomer's company and the two of them were soon embarked on a whirlwind of underwater activity. Which of the two was the more excited I could not say.

Mostafa was a law unto himself, and we were told later that he had a reputation halfway round the world for total disregard of his own safety. On one occasion, it seemed, hand-holding his heavy camera, he had stood on the pillion of a motor cycle going at full speed in order to get a film sequence. For such people the normal safety laws simply do not seem to apply — it is on risks that they thrive, even if their adventures are sometimes brought to an untimely end. In a society where we are increasingly cosseted from birth to the grave, and where what I would see as the right of the individual to expose himself knowingly to personal physical danger is being constantly eroded, people like Mostafa are few and far between, and it is not surprising that they are often regarded with a little envy by the less venturesome amongst us.

Mostafa's stay in the water was brief, and he handed his aqualung back into the boat a few minutes later. His encounter with Donald was in complete contrast to that of Maura who was now wearing an aqualung. She swam over to the buoy for me to get a sequence of Donald by the chain which was covered in interesting marine growth. Donald appeared for a few seconds, then disappeared again. We waited patiently for his return but the cold was beginning to get through the neoprene rubber of my wetsuit and I started to shiver. When Donald did not reappear I signalled to Maura to surface.

I looked across at the boat where I could see the cameraman was still on the ladder with his feet in the water. It was obvious from what he was saying that Donald was just beneath him.

I yelled over to the director. "Would you please get Mostafa right out of the water."

The director asked the cameraman to climb aboard and I again sank beneath the sea into the grey depths. Then Donald reappeared and circled us. My camera whirred satisfactorily. When Donald again swam away and did not return I gave Maura the sign to surface and we made our way back to *Aquanaut*. I was cold but Maura still felt warm enough and energetic enough to go for a final snorkel. So whilst I clambered aboard she swam over to the lifeboat station to talk to Geoff Bold.

When it was time to leave I called Maura back to the boat. As she snorkelled across from the slipway she was unaware that Donald followed her all of the way, with his snout about two feet behind her gently oscillating fins.

Having got both the underwater and above-water film footage of Donald that they required, the television film crew departed from Penzance. But Maura and I wanted to learn more about Donald's experiences in Cornwall, so, armed with a couple of bottles of wine, we made our way to the Carswells' house in Mousehole.

Their home, locked on to the steep ground above the harbour, was one of a row of tiny houses built of local stone and weathered into harmony one with another, and with the surrounding land and seascape. The room into which we squeezed ourselves was full of trophies the two of them had collected from the deep in the hundreds of dives they had made together from *Aquanaut*. However, much as we enjoyed the tales of their adventures on wrecks, it was their stories of Donald that interested us most. By now we could anticipate their account of their surprise at their first encounter with Donald. But how, I wondered, would two people who spent their working lives, day in and day out, winter and summer, in Donald's own environment, view him, and their continued experience with him? How would their attitudes towards him compare with Maura's and mine? I have had a keen interest in whales and dolphins for many years and had read widely on the subject before I ever encountered Donald. So my views on his behaviour may to some extent have been influenced by what I had read. I was anxious to discover whether Bob and Hazel Carswell, who perhaps did not have a special interest in dolphins before they first met Donald, interpreted his behaviour in the same way as Maura and I had done.

As the hours passed it was apparent that their views and attitudes were very similar to those of Maura and myself. Indeed it was almost as if Hazel had taken Maura's role and Bob had taken mine. They both now regarded Donald as "their dolphin" and both had developed a deep love and enormous respect for him. Bob commented on the great understanding that Donald had for what was going on around him and Hazel was sensitive to the gentleness and affection that sprang from him. When we heard this, and about the relationship the dolphin had established with Geoff Bold the lifeboat mechanic, we were delighted that he had found the company of such sympathetic people. We felt that if he was otherwise undisturbed Donald was likely to stay in the area for some time, an idea which pleased Bob and Hazel enormously. As it turned out we were wrong and Donald's peace was to be shattered once more, but that was to come later.

The underwater film I had taken of Donald for the television programme was to be linked with sequences of a captive dolphin in a tank in the studio, and a few days later Maura and I were in the Yorkshire Television studios in Leeds with my old friend David Bellamy who was the 'human' star of the show. The 'animal' star in this instance was to be Pixie, a young female bottlenose dolphin who was confined to a small tank. She had been tranquillised and brought from a local zoo. The poor creature was daubed with violet antiseptic along her body, and on the leading edge of her dorsal fin where the skin had been damaged. Before Maura and David got into the tank with Pixie I studied her carefully and quietly from the side. Although she had the right shape for a bottlenose dolphin, I had to ask myself if she was really of the same species as the creature we had seen and enjoyed in the open sea. Where was the zest for life we knew so well? Where was the emotional warmth that we could feel when we were near Donald? I could just sense it, but it was to Donald's fire like the dull smouldering of a pile of damp burning leaves. Where was the bright mischievous eye of Donald? Pixie shut her dull eyes and opened them again listlessly. I touched her skin, expecting to feel the silky texture of oiled velvet. It was slippery and unpleasant — more like the skin of a fish than a dolphin. She swam in a never ending circle. Wheel upon wheel of utter dejection.

"My God," I thought to myself, "what have we done to you?"

The morality of keeping dolphins in dolphinariums for public display is a subject worthy of consideration. If, as I believe, dolphins are creatures with a brain and sensitivities different from but of an order as high as man's, if not higher, then what moral right have we to imprison them in tiny pools? Consider such subjections from the dolphin's point of view. He is an animal that lives in a world of sound. The sea is full of natural sounds, probably as diverse to the dolphin as are the shapes and colours of the wild flowers in a hedgerow to us. Some of these sounds we can hear underwater when we are diving — ranging from the rasping sound of a crawfish, or spiny lobster, to the roar of the waves advancing and receding over a pebble beach. In some areas the sea has a constant background of crackles and pops the source of which we cannot identify. Any new sounds interest Donald immediately. Those made by man he finds particularly fascinating: the rattle of chains, stones in a tin, the throb of an engine, and probably many more which we cannot hear or give no thought to, but which he listens to attentively. For example, if the dolphin, like the shark, can hear the sound of a wounded fish — what sound does a shoal of fish make to his highly evolved auditory system?

But what sounds does the dolphin imprisoned in a dolphinarium hear?

The dolphin is also aware of textures and shapes — of that we are certain. We also know that he has a very highly evolved brain. We do not know that he gets the kind of aesthetic joy from his environment that we expect from a walk along a cliff path, say, to feel and smell the breeze and see Nature's complex pattern of life. But if he does, what happens to his higher senses when he is confined to a concrete box totally deprived of sensory experiences? We know that man, in situations of extreme sensory deprivation, risks madness.

It is thought that migrating fish such as the salmon find their way back to the rivers in which they spawn by the taste of the water. This too must indicate a sensitivity of a very high order to detect minute traces of dissolved substances. Do dolphins have a similar sensitivity to the taste of their environment? Man is prepared to expend considerable money and effort in producing tastes to please his palate. Does the dolphin enjoy the different tastes of the sea? If so, what does dolphin taste in a dolphinarium the water of which, if it is not filtered and changed at a considerable rate, will contain above all an unnaturally high percentage of the dolphin's own excrement?

Anyone who has seen dolphins in the sea cannot fail to observe how thoroughly they appear to enjoy the freedom of the seas about them. Their bodies are superbly adapted to moving through water and they spend much of their time travelling. That same instinct to travel is certainly present in many men, and we all suffer immensely if we find our movement severely restricted. Do dolphins have an inbuilt urge to move on and see new places and experience and enjoy new tastes and sounds? If so, what happens to those urges when the animal is confined to a minute world bordered by concrete walls?

An observation made by many dolphin trainers is that dolphins tend not only to learn tricks by mimicking the behaviour of other dolphins, or of their trainers, but that the dolphins invent tricks themselves. In other words the dolphins themselves create their acts — not their trainers. If this is so, who is training who? Are the dolphins manipulating their captors? Imagine a highly intelligent man conscripted into the lowest ranks of the services, where all scope for thinking things out for himself is removed. Such a person may well deploy considerable effort, both mental and physical, to devise ways of avoiding duties. He will often put more effort into avoiding a duty than fulfilling an order, merely for the intellectual satisfaction of "beating the system". Would a captive dolphin, finding itself faced with the irreversible prospect of confinement to a dolphinarium, adopt a corresponding attitude? And if so, how would it act? Would it for instance explore the limit of possible experience within the confines of its new environment — which we would interpret as learning new tricks? Dolphins will certainly not perform the same tricks endlessly. Dolphin trainers have found that it is necessary to change routines and to "rest" dolphins after a series of shows. And this need for rest is not seen as related to physical exhaustion. Sometimes dolphins simply refuse to perform. So who is the master — man or dolphin?

Dolphins, like humans, have different personalities and some will adapt to a captive life more readily than others. However, it is not widely known that in fact many dolphins do not survive long in captivity. Maura has heard that the average life expectancy of a captured dolphin is only about six months. Gastroenteritis is common — which may be due to the fact that the animals have to eat dead fish which are not fresh — before humans eat fish they cook them and kill any harmful bacteria. But in many cases there is no sign of disease and the dolphins do not die for want of proper food.

If however dolphins have only some of the mental and emotional needs and sensitivities I have outlined above, I put forward the hypothesis that confinement to a small tank compresses their minds to such an extent that they may die of intellectual and emotional starvation.

16: Ride a Wild Dolphin

Barry Cockcroft is a busy and successful man who always has a full schedule ahead of him. He is a freelance film director, under contract to Yorkshire Television when he was asked in 1976 whether he would like to make a film about a man who had been made redundant and had become friendly with a wild dolphin, he agreed to look into the possibility and I told him my story over lunch at Rowley Manor. My son Ashley joined us, and Barry Cockcroft introduced me to his production assistant Julie O'Hare. I found Barry a charming and sympathetic person, and by the end of the meal we had decided to go ahead with the project and agreed a contract. I made it clear from the start that at no time should we consider restraining Donald in any way — he was to be left free to swim away at any time. Cockcroft agreed. He knew that making the film would be a gamble. So did I.

I felt reasonably sure that we could get under-water footage, but I could not be sure that it would be exceptionally spectacular. Barry Cockcroft's chosen cameraman, on the other hand, was none other than the amazing Mostafa Hammuri, whom I had already seen in action in Penzance. Balanced against the fact that we might not get spectacular underwater footage was a track record — and I place considerable value on a track record. For Barry Cockcroft — director — and Mostafa Hammuri — cameraman — were a very successful team with a string of television awards to their credit. I had also heard that Barry Cockcroft was incredibly lucky when making documentary films.

Thus overall I felt our chances of success were reasonable.

With the possibility that Donald could disappear at any time, once the decision had been made arrangements for a full television camera crew, plus Maura and me, to visit Penzance were put in hand immediately.

Telephone calls between us were not frequent, so one day when I rang Julie O'Hare after I had sent her a list of possible film sequences, she answered the 'phone with the abrupt question:

"Have you rung up to tell me what I already know?"

"What's that?" I answered rhetorically.

"The dolphin has moved," she replied.

"Oh, no," I groaned.

"The last report was that he is in St Ives — I am just going to check up on that."

"What does Barry think of the situation?"

"He thinks we should go ahead."

"So do I."

The die was cast.

That was the last I heard from the Television Centre in Leeds before I set off to collect Maura from Manchester Airport in the middle of what turned out to be the longest hottest summer Britain had known for 200 years. It was 30 June 1976 and the countryside in the Midlands and South West already had an arid appearance. The drive to Penzance was more like a drive through the South of France than through England. The sun shone down from a sky of unbroken blue. I wore shorts and the backs of my legs were sticky with sweat where they touched the plastic car seats. We stopped for tea after we had passed Exeter, and the freshly picked strawberries were still warm from the sun when we smothered them in delicious Devon cream. Although it was six o'clock in the evening the sun still felt fierce on our bare skin when we stepped out of the log cabin café to resume our journey to Penzance.

The following morning we were awake early to make the journey over the big toe of England from Penzance to St Ives, which was where Barry Cockcroft was staying and where we hoped to meet up with Donald again.

Bob and Hazel Carswell had brought the *Aquanaut* round Lands End from Mousehole, and were as pleased to see us again as we were to renew our acquaintance with them. I did not realise just how many people go to make up a full television crew, and when we were assembled all together I was reminded of the old nursery rhyme:

> When I was going to St Ives,
> I met a man with seven wives,
> Each wife had seven sacks,
> Each sack had seven cats,
> Each cat had seven kits,
> Kits, cats, sacks and wives,
> How many were there
> Going to St Ives?

Unlike the catch solution to the nursery rhyme (there was only one man actually going to St Ives) there seemed to be a multitude of us. It was obviously a very expensive operation, and Yorkshire Television had clearly gambled a not inconsiderable sum of money on the prospect of finding and filming an animal that was free to roam anywhere in the English Channel.

Barry Cockcroft is the antithesis of the archetypal autocratic film director. When we met him in St Ives he was cheerful, dressed in casual holiday clothes, and outwardly as cool as the proverbial cucumber.

"Any signs of Donald?" I asked as we walked together towards the stone jetty which is known locally as The Pier.

"Oh, yes," replied Barry reassuringly. "He's around alright."

He was right. Donald was there just outside the harbour entrance, surrounded by a crowd of small hire boats with outboard engines that we immediately nicknamed 'buzz boats'.

Bob Carswell told Barry the tide was falling and he would have to get his crew on board the *Aquanaut*, otherwise it would be grounded until the evening. It was then that I realised the benefit of having a large well co-ordinated team, for in a very short time we were all on board and nosing out of the harbour with an inflatable boat towed by a rope at the stern. Donald obviously still followed his previous habit of acting as escort to boats moving in and out of his territory. He appeared as soon as we were clear of the harbour wall and we could see his dark silhouette moving from side to side under the inflatable. Our dolphin stayed with us until we were well clear of the harbour and then he left us to sport with the buzz boats that swarmed around him like wasps round a jam pot. The open sea just outside the harbour of St Ives was calm and as busy with small craft as the Serpentine on a Sunday afternoon. With so many distractions I had a feeling that filming with Donald was going to be difficult. And I was right.

Maura and I were soon kitted up and Donald joined us immediately we jumped overboard. However he was in an excited mood and swam quickly between us. His reunion with Maura was quite unlike their previous encounter off the Penlee lifeboat slipway, when the dolphin had been completely docile and relaxed. He allowed himself to be stroked a few times and then darted away to play with the buzz boats which kept coming uncomfortably close to us. Knowing that the drivers of the boats were holidaymakers, who were probably quite unaware of the hazard their whizzing propellers were to divers, I was anxious for our safety as well as that of Mostafa, who was having difficulty with his diving equipment and the cumbersome underwater camera he was attempting to film with.

Whilst we were in the water the wind started to rise and the sea became choppy, making it even more difficult to film. As the sea became rougher those on board the *Aquanaut* began to feel the effects of the rolling motion of the boat. The buzz boats were recalled by a man who came out in a speedboat fitted with a very powerful outboard. Donald disappeared. So after consultation with Barry we decided to abandon filming. The harbour of St Ives had dried out completely and we were rowed ashore by a local fisherman, whilst Maura snorkelled in through the waves, leaving Bob and Hazel Carswell alone on their boat, which would have to remain at anchor and ride out the waves in the open sea until the incoming tide allowed them to sail back into the harbour.

Remembering our experiences on the Isle of Man, when Donald was usually in his most co-operative mood in the evening, and counting on the habit the sea had of calming down late in the day, we postponed our next attempt to film until five o'clock.

As the afternoon progressed the wind started to abate and the sea crept slowly back into the St Ives harbour. The running lines of green, algae-covered ropes and chains that stretched across the sand were again awash with salt water. The boats, heeled over at the harbour entrance, started to rise. The sea that slid into the harbour was crystal clear and the sand was the bright yellow colour of a railway poster. Gradually the wind died, leaving the ocean as flat as ice.

We rejoined Bob and Hazel aboard the *Aquanaut* and Bob told me that on a number of occasions he had attracted Donald's attention by blowing on his foghorn, with the end of the trumpet submerged. He tried it and within a few minutes Donald appeared. He was in a very happy and playful mood. He seemed to particularly enjoy playing with our "dolphin rattle" and nibbling at it.

It was sheer joy to be in the water with him and I soon shot the 100 feet of film in my camera. Then, after I surfaced to hand in my 16 mm camera and start taking stills, Donald disappeared. We called him again and again in vain, we tried the dolphin rattle and the foghorn, but he did not return. So we decided to finish filming and headed back for the harbour and berthed alongside the pier. Events had not gone perfectly on our first day, but we had made a start, Barry was happy with our progress and we were optimistic as we dined together that evening in his cottage in the back streets of St Ives.

We agreed on an early start the following day to gain maximum benefit from the tides. It was a grey day and right from the start I felt uneasy. Maura, who is normally very cheerful and easy going, was on edge.

I had a premonition that something was going to go wrong.

By the time we got to sea the buzz boats were again out in force and we decided to attempt to entice the dolphin beyond the buoy which was supposed to indicate the limit of the hire boats' excursions into the open sea. The *Aquanaut* was crowded and we had an additional cargo of two young ladies lured aboard by a couple of the camera crew — no doubt with promises of stardom. Bob tried attracting Donald by rattling a chain overboard just as we were about to dive. His ruse worked, but as soon as he had inspected the chain the dolphin swam off again, before we had a chance to get into the water and carry out an observation I had planned.

As a result of an article I had had published in the *Sunday Times*, a class of school children of about seven years of age had sent me letters. Many of them had drawn pictures of Donald, and one of them had shown my son Ashley sitting astride the dolphin's head. I was curious to see how Donald would react to this picture of himself, especially in view of the past historic associations between dolphins and children. I always felt that as the minds of children were less conditioned than those of adults, they are better able to transcend the gulf between dolphin and man. And if dolphins have the intellect I suppose them to have, it was possible that Donald might appreciate the primitive caricature of himself.

I had placed the drawing in a transparent polythene bag and attached it to the wooden frame of a mirror in such a way that the reflections from the mirror were completely hidden. When she launched herself into the water Maura was carefully carrying the picture mounted on the frame. However to assess Donald's reaction I needed his presence. So I tried to attract him first by blowing through the foghorn, then by using our dolphin rattle, but he did not respond to our calls.

I reasoned with myself that as Donald was intelligent he already knew we were there, but that just swimming around would be boring to him so he would not return unless we could offer him a new experience. Then I remembered that Donald always took a keen interest in divers actually performing a task underwater. I sank down to the seabed, which was flat and featureless apart from a large congregation of spider crabs wandering across the sand in an apparently aimless manner, took the diving knife from its scabbard strapped to my leg, and attempted to see what I could dig up from under the sand. I had not got very far with this project when I was aware that I was being watched. I carried on digging and within a short time a dolphin snout was six inches from my hole. Donald had arrived and his eyes sparkled with curiosity.

I stopped digging and Maura diverted his attention to the picture stuck to the mirror. He eyed it intently and I could hear Maura talking to him and telling him about the picture. He seemed to understand what she was saying and to take an amused interest in his likeness.

What, then, I wondered, would be his reaction to his real likeness? So when Donald had finished looking at the child's drawing of himself I took the mirror from Maura and removed it from the polythene bag. Maura called Donald back and this time held the mirror up so that he could see his own reflection.

Up until that moment I had dismissed from my mind the premonition that all would not go well. But the instant Donald saw his own reflection his mood changed completely. He became extremely agitated and knocked the mirror out of Maura's hand. As he did so the edge of the mirror struck Maura a glancing blow that dislodged her facemask and bruised her face. The mirror fell to the seabed and landed reflective side downwards.

Maura was hurt and intensely upset by Donald's frightening and sudden change.

By the time Maura had returned safely to the boat Donald had disappeared. I went below again to collect the mirror, and as I returned to the surface with the mirror tucked under my arm I realised that Mostafa, who had been around part of the time when I was filming Maura and Donald, was no longer in the water, but I suppressed any further feelings of unease in my concern about what had just happened between Maura and Donald.

It was Barry who called me quietly over and told me that Mostafa had had to go ashore. I agreed that we should suspend all diving activities and take the *Aquanaut* back into the harbour whilst there was still sufficient water for us to get alongside the pier. At the time I thought it strange that Mostafa should take it into his head to want to get ashore. I had heard him refer to an acid stomach, and simply assumed that he was suffering a little from the motions of the boat and probable ingestion of seawater.

I found out later that Mostafa had run out of air and had surfaced rapidly, holding his breath at the same time. When he surfaced his facemask was half-filled with blood, much to everyone's alarm, including Mostafa's. Fearful that he had done himself some serious injury Barry had called Julie on shore with the intercom, and she had immediately arranged for Mostafa to see a doctor as soon as he landed.

The news of this event was broken to me over a drink in the 'Schooner' when we were having lunch, only minutes before Mostafa himself made a dramatic entrance, bright and breezy as ever. But his brave countenance was a front. The doctor had told him that he was not to dive again for a week. It looked as if the famous Cockcroft luck had run out.

Mostafa objected furiously to the doctor's advice, and made clear that he intended to ignore it. Barry consulted me, as the most experienced diver in the group, and I told him that one of the first laws of aqualung diving is that one should never hold one's breath and rush to the surface, because the air trapped in the lungs expands and may rupture the alveoli. If the bubbles then get into the blood system the results can be very nasty, and sometimes end in death. However, it seemed from Mostafa's complete absence of symptoms that he had not suffered an embolism — it was more likely that some fine blood vessels in Mostafa's nose had burst and bled. Some people are prone to nose bleeds, which are quite common amongst divers — even experienced ones — and a little blood in the water that invariably gets into a facemask looks much worse than it really is. Having heard what tests the doctor had performed I was satisfied that this is what had happened.

Even so Barry decided to take a second doctor's opinion and was adamant that Mostafa would not dive again on that day at least, despite the cameraman's protests. With great reluctance Mostafa agreed that the filming sessions planned for the end of the afternoon should be exclusively from the surface. Barry said he wanted a long shot of the sunset with the *Aquanaut* in the bay. By discussing this at length he gradually took our cameraman's mind off the unacceptable prospect that he would do no more underwater photography.

In view of the chain of events that followed I can only

comment that had it not been for Mostafa's nose bleed we might never have got some of the most exciting sequences in the film.

It was 5.30 pm before we could get the *Aquanaut* out of the harbour, and again after a slightly blustery day the wind dropped away in the evening to become a zephyr. As the *Aquanaut* moved out into the bay we caught occasional glimpses of Donald playing around a buoy with two buzz boats. He swam over when we left the entrance to the harbour, but disappeared again in a few minutes. Maura and I kitted up and jumped into the water. As we had agreed to concentrate exclusively on above shots I did not wear an aqualung and did not take any cameras into the sea with me. We tried to get Donald to join us, but no amount of calling or rattling of our tin of stones would cause him to leave the boat with which he was playing.

I had taken on board the *Aquanaut* a small aquaplane, which consists of a board with handles, that is towed behind a boat on a long length of line. The diver holds on to the handles as he is pulled through the water, and by deflecting the plane of the board he can adjust his course above or below the surface. An aquaplane is usually used by divers to survey large areas of the seabed at speed with the minimum consumption of air. I suggested that I be towed near Donald in the hope that he would find my new mode of transport interesting. Barry agreed.

I took hold of the handles of the aquaplane, and raised one hand in the air, making the circular movement which is the agreed signal for the helmsman to put the engine into gear and slowly increase the revolutions of the propeller. I felt the sudden tug on my arms as the rope went taut, and then holding the board so that I would stay on the surface I felt the water surging past my body in a flurry of bubbles. The boat settled to a comfortable speed, at which the rush of water past my head would not sweep off my mask, and I was adjusting to the exhilaration of being towed when I felt a presence. I looked to my right and could see Donald's head cutting through the water at exactly the same pace as me. I could also see that he was watching me intently. In the stern of the *Aquanaut* Mostafa was pointing his camera at us.

Taking a quick breath I dipped the blade of the aquaplane, downwards, like an aerofoil I immediately went into a dive. At a depth of about five feet I levelled out for a few seconds and then deflected the aquaplane upwards. This caused me to rise to the surface very rapidly and I was immediately breasting the waves again. I began to feel I was capturing some of the joy of being a dolphin. I took a quick breath and pointed the handles down again.

When I was under the water I looked to my right and could see Donald keeping pace with me — this time completely submerged. So again I pointed the board towards the surface and we both rushed upwards and surfaced .in unison. It was a superb sensation. I felt I was a dolphin and the feeling was good. After several more thrilling minutes the boat slowed. Mostafa had run out of film.

Whilst the camera was reloaded the sound crew and Mostafa moved into a small boat with a powerful outboard engine. The outboard motor was started, and Mostafa was ready to photograph the aquaplane sequence from a new angle — alongside me.

As the *Aquanaut* set off I again experienced the thrill of riding the waves like a dolphin. However my joy-ride was short-lived. As I moved through the water I felt a gentle nudge on my right hand side. I looked to see what was happening and Donald was prodding my arm with his jaws as we sped through the water. At first I took no notice. Then he swam up to my elbow and bit it. I let go of one handle and managed to steer the aquaplane with the other as I yelled an account of what was happening to those in the inflatable. As I did so Donald came up underneath me and tried to push me off the aquaplane. I did not wish to appear unfriendly to my dolphin friend, but I was determined to enjoy my ride and again grabbed both handles. Donald, however, was equally determined to get me out of the driver's seat and nipped my right elbow painfully hard.

I knew then that Donald was not going to give up until I let go completely, so not wishing to lose my arm I released my hold on both handles of the aquaplane, which skimmed away from me bouncing over the surface. It was followed immediately by Donald who grabbed the board in his teeth and had a free ride across the sea behind the *Aquanaut*. I could not help laughing into my snorkel tube as I saw him disappearing in the distance.

Mostafa was again out of film so the boat slowed and circled back to me while the aquaplane was pulled inboard.

Donald was delighted with this new turn of events and played around the boat waiting to see what action would take place next. If he was working out some way in which he could recompense me for his free ride it did not take him long to think up a solution. He swam underneath me and his dorsal fin broke surface just in front of my face. I put both of my hands gently round it and held on. Donald moved off, slowly at first. I gripped tighter and then tighter still as he increased speed. His dorsal fin rose and fell slightly, to counterbalance the action of his tail. Faster and faster we went. Soon he was going full speed, and I was still clinging to his dorsal fin, the sea swirling up in white foam round my facemask and shoulders. On and on we went in a huge loop. Then Donald decided it was time to stop. He spun round in a very tight circle and barrel rolled at the same time, churning up the water like a powerful ship turning its propellers at top speed. I had no option but to let go as his fin was wrenched from my hand by the roll.

I looked down at Donald through the swirl of bubbles that were rapidly dispersing. It was the end of an express ride to end all express rides.

Later we were joined by Maura in the water and Donald gave both of us rides, with me hanging on to the fin and Maura clinging to me, then vice versa with Maura on the steering end. He then towed Maura in short bursts of great acceleration round the inflatable, turning sharply, Maura being flung out like a bucket on a string.

During the evening the sky had cleared and the sun started to sink, painting an orange-red line across the still sea. So Mostafa got his sunset shots. Not from high on the land as he had planned — but shots packed with action close to the sea. I commented on this to Barry as we made our way back to St Ives.

"When there is action," he said "forget the pretty-pretty stuff, and film the action."

In Barry's case he had achieved both the action and the pretty-pretty stuff, as he called it. What was more it had all happened almost by accident. It seemed his record for luck was holding out. I liked him. I was even coming to like Mostafa Hammuri more and more. There was something about the man's spirit that was hard to resist, and Maura too was clearly enjoying his irrepressible vitality.

17: Donald Shatters his own Image

After my exhilarating ride on Donald it seemed that everything came together to make the film a success. When we wanted Donald we would send out the inflatable and ask the appointed dolphin organiser to bring Donald to the boat or entertain him until the *Aquanaut* arrived. Somehow we never failed to find him. It was almost as if Barry Cockcroft had only to say "Cue dolphin" and up Donald would pop. After our first two days we were aided in this respect by one of the experiments we carried out in front of the cameras.

We were absolutely convinced that Donald had never been in a dolphinarium, or associated with man in any way before his arrival on the Isle of Man. Our major reason for this conclusion was that when we had first encountered him, although he was not timid, he would not allow himself to be touched with a bare hand. As the years had passed he had developed closer and closer associations with Maura and myself, and his unwillingness to be touched in this way disappeared. However, we felt we would like to test on film his reactions to the kind of playthings that dolphins in dolphinariums are presented with.

Most dolphin trainers admit that dolphins learn to play games very rapidly, and some trainers, aware of the extraordinary intelligence of the animals in their care, have suggested that it is the dolphins who programme their trainers, not the trainers the dolphins, to respond to certain signals. It is also widely accepted that dolphins have very good memories, and there are a number of cases on record, reported by well-known scientists, to support this conclusion.

So to investigate our hypothesis that Donald had never been in captivity we decided to present him with some of the toys he would be most likely to have encountered in captivity. To start with Maura and I threw a ball, in the form of a plastic buoy, one to another. Donald followed the ball, swimming to each of us in turn and watching our movements from under the water with his usual curiosity. However, after five minutes' play, even when we presented the ball directly to him, he did not take an active part in our game. He just watched.

We then threw the buoy back into the boat and started to play with a small rubber quoit which quite by chance was attached to a length of rope. We splashed it in the water and then tossed it to one another, again watched by Donald, who swam back and forth towards which-ever of us was holding it. Then I waved it underwater at Donald and called to him. As he came up to take it in his beak I raised it out of the water and he raised his head well clear of the surface to grab it. I tossed it to Maura, who did likewise. At last we allowed him to take it, then pulled it away from him and continued our game. Donald became more and more excited and was clearly getting the idea of the game. He began to take the ring from us and to hang on to it tighter and tighter. Then, when Maura held up the ring with both hands, he poked his beak into it and accelerated away with Maura desperately trying to hold on. She yelled to me and I too grabbed the rope. But so powerful was his pull that our combined efforts could not restrain him and we had to let go. For a brief moment we thought that we would be entangled in the rope and dragged after him.

I am sure from the way in which he behaved that he had

never played with a quoit before.

The next time he took the ring in his mouth, instead of swimming on the surface, he sounded and pulled the rope through my hands so rapidly I let it go because it burned. We thought that was the last we would see of the quoit. But a few minutes later he re-appeared with it still in his mouth, and after two more high-speed tows he left us, the inflatable with the camera crew on board chasing after him. Then someone on board managed to grab the trailing line and, much to the delight of everyone, he towed the inflatable with two of the camera crew at breakneck speed across the bay. Eventually the rubber ring could stand the strain no more and broke. Mostafa had loved every second of his ride.

Thereafter, if we wished to attract Donald's attention and he did not respond to our calls, one of the techniques we used to attract him was to trail a rubber quoit through the water from the inflatable.

Once Donald had been located and his interest engaged with the quoit, it was necessary to entice him to the area where we could film him. However, one of the disadvantages of the quoit technique was that if Donald was in a boisterous mood he was likely to tow the inflatable away from the *Aquanaut*, which was our floating base for filming operations. In this event we used our trump card in our deck of dolphin baits. That card took the form of the bare legs of an ex-rugby player named Jack Rogers, who was the chief electrician in the camera crew. We discovered Donald's predeliction for Jack's legs one day when he was swimming with the dolphin after a filming session. Jack was wearing a bright blue "shortie" wetsuit jacket. Several of the crew were swimming in the water enjoying the experience of being with the dolphin, but it was Jack whom Donald singled out for particular attention. Donald's penis became erect and he used it to stroke Jack's legs. It was as if the act gave the dolphin sensual pleasure — although as I have indicated before I do not regard this as having an exclusively sexual meaning, and I think that Donald simply liked the smooth soft warmth of Jack's legs and used his most sensitive tactile organ to experience it.

However, regardless of the reasons why Donald liked Jack's legs, we established the fact, and Barry used his electrician as human dolphin bait when appropriate. Jack was a little apprehensive when Donald made his first approach, as anyone would be in the circumstances, but he soon came to enjoy his new role in the film.

Here again, Donald was having his mysterious effect on human relationships. Crews in commercial television are often staunch union members and closely observe job demarcations. Yet I was intrigued to observe how often these demarcations were ignored when Donald was present. Barry Cockcroft's adroit diplomacy, coupled with Donald's magic, imbued the entire crew with a remarkable enthusiasm for the film, which overrode all of the barriers which could so easily have disrupted progress. And if ever Jack is asked to account for his role as "dolphin bait" to his union, I only hope that his colleagues too will take the view that one hour when work is fun is worth ten hours when it is a burdensome duty.

Having aroused Donald's interest in quoits, we thought we could use it to discover whether or not he had a preference for colour. Cathy Rooney, one of the production assistants, bought a set of hollow, smooth plastic quoits coloured respectively, red, blue, yellow, green and white, and a sixth quoit made from a yellow corrugated tube. I passed them one by one to Maura who presented each of them in turn to Donald during one underwater session, and he playfully bit them all. When I held them up to him in my hands, he showed no preference for any single one. He did however seem to have a preference for the first ring we had played with, which was made of sponge rubber not hollow plastic, and I got the impression he preferred it because of its texture. The colour appeared to be irrelevant.

We also tried feeding Donald with freshly caught mackerel. Although he would take them from our hands when we held the fish in the air, he treated them in exactly the same way as he had the rings when we offered them to him from the surface. He took them from us in his mouth, went underwater and then let them go. This episode cast doubts on the reports we had had earlier from the fishermen who thought he had eaten the fish they offered him. They would not have seen him releasing them from his mouth underwater, of course. This was also another small pointer to the fact that he had never been in captivity.

I was still puzzled by his reaction to the mirror. I asked Maura if she would take it down again, but she refused point blank, saying that it antagonised him. So I decided to show it to him again myself. I took the mirror, mounted in its strong wooden frame to the seabed, and pointed the reflecting surface towards the dolphin. Donald immediately attacked it, knocking it out of my hand. It zig-zagged to the bottom where it remained facing upwards. I went down to recover it, but every time I approached Donald swam over and pushed me aside with his head. I hung on the anchor line until he had gone out of sight, but as soon as I made my way back to it he swam up and pushed me aside again.

On the next dive, accompanied by Maura, I took another mirror with a thin plastic frame, and as I descended I held it reflecting side towards my body. When I reached the bottom, which was only about twenty feet down, holding it above my head, I turned it round so that Donald could see his own image. He spun round and swam nose first at the mirror at full speed. It disintegrated with the impact and the water glistened with a shower of mirror fragments that spun in all directions as they settled towards the bottom. Afterwards Maura said "I will never forget the look on your face, eyes popping with surprise, surrounded by glittering confetti."

When I had been able to recover from the shock of that very disturbing moment, we discussed this episode at considerable length. It was probably the only moment when I had ever been fearful of Donald in the water. Yet I do not think his gesture had been meant as an act of aggression against me. We tried to look at the situation from his point of view.

First, we considered that vision plays a small part in the dolphin's perception of objects around him. His most important sense is his "sound vision", and this would have told him that the object was a simple solid sheet. Yet he was being confronted at the same time with a visual image which indicated (part of) a dolphin-shaped object. This information clearly conflicted with that of the "sound image". This confusion could indeed have accounted for Donald's agitation. When he was unable to account for this new creature he was seeing his eyes but could not perceive with his sound, he no doubt became concerned for our safety and tried to keep us away from it. Finally, when we persisted in our apparent indifference to this potential source of danger he attacked it as he would have done a shark, by swimming straight at it snout first. It is well known that dolphins attack and kill sharks in this way, and the techniques could well be an instinctive defence mechanism. In the case of the mirror it certainly worked, for when he made his final attack it disintegrated into smithereens. He had destroyed the unknown threat.

In between our sessions with the mirror we also showed Donald a plain piece of Perspex. Maura was not wearing her hood at the time and she could hear him examining it with his "sound vision". She noticed he made a continuous sound, whereas when he was playing with us his sounds were intermittent. At no time did he show any agitation. He was simply interested. Maura placed the Perspex sheet over a crab on the seabed. Donald went down to examine it but made no attempt to move the Perspex. Maura then placed the crab on top of the Perspex and balanced it there as the crab attempted to crawl off. Donald immediately came down and nosed the crab, and the dolphin then shook his head in his usual gesture of amused curiosity. At no time did he display any of the hostility he had towards the mirror.

During our one week's filming, Mostafa's diving improved noticeably, and just as both Maura and I got to like him, Donald did also, and if ever Mostafa hung on the ladder Donald would hover just underneath biting at his fins and waiting for him to come into the water for the next round of high-jinks.

Barry Cockcroft's luck persisted for the entire week. On the final day, when he was taking some long shots of me calling Donald with my dolphin rattle from the very top of the cliffs, Donald astonished us all by appearing round the headland right on cue, leading the fleet of small boats going out to fish for mackerel.

As the television crew put the wraps on their mass of equipment and stowed it in the van, it started to rain for the first time and it became noticeably cooler. The heatwave had come to an end and so had the filming. I was sad to see the crew departing, for we got to know and like each other and we had all worked well together. How much of this was due to the personality of Barry himself I cannot say, but he was undoubtedly helped by Donald with whom everyone fell in love and whose friendly presence permeated boat and crew.

Maura and I stayed in Penzance for an extra couple of days, and we had one great pleasure left to us. We had dinner one night with Bob and Hazel Carswell, two of the television crew who had remained behind, and Geoff Bold and his wife Liz. The setting was the 'Lobster Pot' at Mousehole.

Geoff told us then that he had been visited by some members of the Whale Research Unit, with whom I too had exchanged much information on Donald. Whilst Donald was in Penzance, it seems, members of the team had managed to measure him and found his length to be 3.6 metres (eleven foot ten inches) from the tip of his beak to the end of his tail. From this and other measurements they had estimated his weight to be between 300 and 400kg (660-880lbs approximately). A full grown bottlenose dolphin reaches a maximum size of about twelve feet, though like humans not all animals grow to the same maximum size. Thus we could take it that by the time Donald reached Cornwall he had reached his maximum size.

That raised the question: *was Donald fully grown when he reached the Isle of Man in 1972?* Estimates of Donald's length when he was off the Isle of Man varied considerably, up to a maximum of fifteen feet. When one takes into account the fact that objects seen underwater appear one third larger than their real size, that made his length a maximum of about eleven feet. The difference between this estimated figure and the real length is probably insignificant, so it seemed reasonable to assume that if Donald was not fully grown when he reached the Isle of Man, then he was probably close to it.

This conclusion is interesting because it throws some light on the question that I am most frequently asked.

How old is Donald?

It is thought that bottlenose dolphins live to an age of about thirty years in the wild, and that they reach full size and maturity at about the age of seven. Thus we can deduce that in 1972 Donald was between six and twenty-six years old.

rtrait of a gentleman. Donald's benign nature is clearly expressed in his
e in this picture taken in Port St Mary.

Maura tries to sketch Donald in Port St Mary . . . but abandons the idea when Donald starts to bite her plastic pad.

Horace Dobbs

)onald has an intense curiosity for anything mechanical when it is work-
ng underwater. He came to inspect my cine camera the instant the motor
started to run. A chipped tooth in the middle of the top row provides one
of the many ways by which he can be identified.

)onald and Maura rendezvous under the keel of a fishing boat in Port
st Mary.

Horace Dobbs

Photo: Horace

My son Ashley (then thirteen years old) and Donald the dolphin (wh
is probably about the same age) in Port St Mary. A few minutes after thi
picture was taken Donald spontaneously lifted Ashley on his head an
gave the boy a ride round the harbour — an incident I shall never forge

I got a more accurate estimate of his age by doing some detecitve work on his teeth, in collaboration with Christina Lockyer of the Whale Research Unit. Unlike humans, the Odontoceti do not shed their first set of milk teeth. Their teeth have only a single root and the central pulp cavity is fairly small. After a time no further dental growth takes place and the pulp cavity gradually disappears. Like the teeth of most other mammals, man included, the bottlenose dolphin's teeth consist of dentine, surrounded with cement and covered with an enamel cap. In older animals the crown is often worn down, sometimes so far that the enamel disappears completely and leaves a row of dentine stumps. It is probable that a dolphin's teeth will show distinct signs of wear from the age of twenty onwards.

One of the photographs I took on the Isle of Man showed that one of Donald's teeth was broken, but the remainder looked to be in prime condition. In 1976 Donald's teeth were still in good condition, though they were perhaps showing the first signs of wear. So we concluded that in 1972 he was under sixteen years of age.

It has been found possible to estimate the age of a dolphin by removing one of the teeth and etching it — which reveals a series of annual rings. However as such a procedure would be unthinkable with Donald, we can only partially satisfy our curiosity and conclude that he was probably born somewhere between 1956 and 1965. If asked to pinpoint a specific year for Donald's birth I tend for no good scientific reason to plump for 1960 — which happens to be the year my son Ashley was born.

Among the other subjects we talked over that evening in The Lobster Pot were Donald's feeding habits, and his daily requirement of food. Here again we found our knowledge to be derisory. Nobody had actually seen him take fish in the wild.

In addition to pelagic fish, the stomachs of bottlenose dolphins have been found to contain cuttlefish,
and it is reported that when eating this food they spit
out the cuttlefish bone (known to all keepers of
budgerigars) and retain the edible portion. We know
too that dolphins use their teeth for capturing their
prey, not for chewing it, and that the fish they catch
are swallowed whole. A dolphin is able to swallow in
such a manner that very little sea water finds its way
into the stomach. Seaweed too has been found in the
stomachs of bottlenose dolphins. However, it is likely
that Donald feeds mainly on fish such as mackerel,
pollack and whiting, because these are common in the areas
he frequents.

Just how much he eats during the course of a day
we simply do not know. But we can make an informed
guess, based on some work carried out by Russian
scientists who measured the food requirements of the
Black Sea bottlenose dolphin and found that the intake was
5.6kg. fish (mackerel and mullet) per 100kg. of bodyweight.
Thus, if we estimate Donald's weight as being in the
region of 350kg., his daily consumption of food could be
about 20kg., that is 44lbs. per day.

Much of the food that Donald eats is required to keep his
internal body temperature higher than that of the sea
around him, for like all mammals he is warm blooded.
If we consider that still water conducts heat away
from our bodies about twenty-seven times faster than
still air, and that a normal human being loses consciousness
after three hours in water at 60°F, and after only fifteen
minutes in water at 32°F, we can appreciate what
problems the dolphin has overcome during the course
of his evolution into the marine environment. The
answer Nature has provided, for all of the whale family,
is a thick layer of insulating blubber under the skin.
This layer of blubber accounts for between thirty and

forty percent. of Donald's weight. The thickness of the blubber varies with different parts of the body, as does the human layer of subcutaneous fat. In a dolphin it is thin around the blowhole and the eyes, and this is almost certainly related to the need for flexible movement of the eyelids and the walls of the blowhole.

One of the characteristics of nearly all mature bottlenose dolphins found in the wild is that their skins are crisscrossed with scars. This was another of the many mysteries I sought to unravel. The skin of a dolphin is very thin and therefore easily scarred. But why should an animal like Donald, capable of very precise movements, become injured in this way? The question is compounded by the observation that numerous Cetaceans have been found to have signs of fractured ribs that have healed. In the Brussels Museum a skeleton of a bottlenose dolphin has indications that the third, fourth, fifth and sixth ribs have been broken and that the fractures have healed in the form of pseudo-arthroses.

In British Coastal waters, however, Donald should have few natural enemies apart from man. So it would seem unlikely that the scars are the results of encounters with species such as the giant squid which are thought to do battle with his larger cousins in the abysmal depths of the oceans. From my observations of Donald I knew that even deep wounds become pigmented to match the surrounding tissue once they have healed. I guessed, therefore, that Donald's criss-cross scars were only superficial and were the result of self-inflicted abrasions caused by over enthusiastic "buoy bashing" and similar activities when he was in his more exuberant moods.

As dinner progressed Geoff told us more about his relationship with Donald, and the special feeling he had for him. He confided that his great ambition was to dive with the dolphin, and that Bob and Hazel had already given him one lesson on snorkelling. Geoff had been very upset when Donald moved away from Penzance, because he felt the opportunity to get close to the dolphin he had been able to observe only from the surface was irrevocably lost. Maura and I had just one day left, so I suggested that the following morning might be a suitable time for Geoff to have an under-water introduction to his dolphin friend after all. Geoff was nervous and undecided so we left the invitation open. Next morning whilst we were having breakfast he appeared in our hotel. He had decided to join us, so we set out for St Ives.

We were greeted warmly by the car park attendant on the pier, who announced that Donald was just outside waiting for us. Geoff pulled on the jacket of a wetsuit he had borrowed and I loaned him one of my facemasks. He and Maura went into the water first and I followed some five minutes later. We rattled the tin full of stones but Donald did not appear. So we swam out to a buoy about four hundred yards offshore. Geoff was not a strong swimmer, it was his first snorkel dive in the sea, and he was apprehensive when he saw himself getting further and further out of his depth. We looked down into bright yellow sandy seabed that was peppered with spider crabs. There was no other visible forms of animal life. We clung to the buoy and rested. There was still no sign of Donald. As Geoff was getting cold we decided to swim back to the shore, still calling and shaking our rattle.

Throughout the return journey Geoff, who was not wearing a diving hood, could hear what he thought was the sound of a small outboard. My wife Wendy, who was watching our activities from the top of the pier, told us afterwards that Donald followed us all the way back, keeping about twenty yards behind us. The outboard noise that Geoff heard was obviously

Donald sounding us out. Then, when Geoff and Maura were just about to go ashore, the dolphin surfaced a few yards away. In a few seconds he cruised up to me. I called out to Maura and Geoff, who forgot the cold and came to join us in only about five feet of water. Donald kept swimming past so that I could stroke him and for ten minutes he stayed to play.

Geoff found the size of Donald awe-inspiring. Donald was not slender and his considerable length was matched by an equally impressive-looking girth. Geoff himself is a big, very strong man who keeps himself physically fit, and when he saw the dolphin glide past so effortlessly underwater he realised the immense power that was locked up inside the dolphin's body. He marvelled too at the feel of the silky texture of Donald's skin. Nervously and delicately he caressed Donald's head and the dolphin responded by brushing his belly against Geoff's bare legs. As the two made physical contact for the first time, and the environment gap between air and water that had separated them was closed at last, I found myself deeply moved by the great tenderness of the meeting. I could sense that for Geoff it was an overwhelming experience.

I was certain that Donald knew that Geoff was a little scared, for the dolphin made no moves that could frighten the novice snorkeller. Only when he switched his attention to Maura did his attitude change. He became more active and the two of them had a farewell cuddle and rolled around together, like two lovers in a haystack. Then when Donald swam to me I gently grasped his dorsal fin between both of my hands. It was as if I was a jockey who had just mounted a spirited horse. Donald accelerated out towards the sea. It was low water and I could see the dark green kelp and bright yellow sand passing in a blur underneath me as I set off on another switchback ride that set me tingling with pleasure and excitement. Faster and faster we went. Then came the inevitable barrel roll and turn which would send me into a flurry of waves and bubbles. It was the moment when Donald told me that he was the master.

I left the water delighted that we had been able to bring Donald and Geoff together in this way at last. I could see that the experience had made a deep impression on Geoff, and the obvious emotional bond between him and Donald set me to thinking again what a unique animal Donald was, and what a profound influence he had on people. In his odyssey round the coast of Britain he had already changed many lives, making them in some magic way richer and happier.

18: Flight into Fantasy

Shortly after I had finished filming with Donald in Penzance I left for a diving holiday in Sardinia with my entire family plus my daughter's boyfriend, Steve. We were Luciano's guests in a villa near Stintino at the rocky northern extremity of the island, which is an area renowned for exceptionally clear water — and therefore spectacular diving.

But upon our arrival in Sardinia it was apparent that Luciano was in the middle of a crisis. It seemed that only a few weeks before a reaction had got out of control at a chemical works in Northern Italy and spread a dangerous compound over the adjacent land and countryside. The accident was soon to be news all over the world as the 'Seveso affair'. And Luciano was concerned with the long-term effects the toxic substance might have on human beings. We discussed the implications of the disaster with intensity, and at length. Luciano was of the opinion that mankind had now reached a stage where there was no way forward without high technology. He maintained that in order for civilisation to survive, and to preserve aesthetic and human values, we had to accept this fact and evolve a new culture which would take into account the natural environment and the technology which threatens to destroy it. He called his philosophy "survival culture".

At first I thought it strange that his lines of thought should have been running parallel to some ideas in fantasy form, I had developed concerning the reason for Donald's association with man. On further consideration, however, I was less surprised because of certain sensitivities which were common to Luciano and myself.

Inevitably, we talked about Donald. On the basis of their

known behaviour, and the fact that dolphins, like men, have a large cerebral cortex (the part of the brain that in man is associated with the higher levels of mental activity, such as appreciation of music, for instance, creative thought, and deep emotion) we argued the possibility that dolphins have a level of consciousness on a par with, or even higher than, that of man. Although it is known that human brains have plenty of spare capacity, could we assume that the cerebral cortex of dolphins, which is roughly the same size as man's on a weight for weight basis, and bigger in terms of total mass, has a similar function? Exactly what role the cerebral cortex plays in dolphins is still very much open to speculation, but Carl Sagan has considered the possibility that the intelligence of Cetaceans is channelled into the dolphin equivalent of epic poetry, history and elaborate codes of social interaction . . . .

With these thoughts in mind I told Luciano that I had been trying to understand Donald's way of thinking. There were many aspects of his behaviour that I found intriguing. It is well known, for instance, that dolphins, like man, are gregarious animals. Why, therefore, was Donald always on his own? Why had he associated so closely with Maura and me? I told Luciano that in order to find the answers I had tried metaphorically to put my mind inside Donald's head. I had tried to perceive the world through the ears, eyes and frontal lobes of a dolphin. Before I told him about my flight of fantasy, however, I wanted to examine another mystery about Donald that was bothering me.

I knew that it is extremely rare for dolphins to become entangled in nets by accident. Indeed, it is extraordinarily difficult to capture any dolphin against its will. When dolphins were first put widely on exhibition in the United States in the 1950s, a number of methods of capturing them were tried. Deliberately netting them by conventional methods invariably failed, no matter how many ruses were used. With their sonic vision the dolphins were able to detect the nets from afar, to deduce what their would-be captors were about, and to take evasive action long before the nets were closed.

The technique eventually developed was to utilise the dolphins' delightful habit of swimming alongside and in front of boats. When the dolphins and the vessels were both moving at the same speed, the dolphin catchers plunged nets mounted on circular frames down into the water just ahead of the dolphins. Once they left the hands of the catchers the nets were virtually stationary in the water relative to the directional movement of the dolphins, and as the dolphins were making rapid forward progress they swam into them in a fraction of a second before evasive action could be taken.

Thus although I knew that during his stay in Wales Donald would be in a region where there were inshore fishing boats of various types I had little fear for his safety by accidental netting. However he was captured, not as it happens in a fishing net, but in a buoy line. It had happened in Wales, and I had heard about it afterwards. Quite how it happened was an enigma that I felt I had to unravel. But before I could answer this and the other questions I was posing myself, Luciano was called urgently back to his research institute in Milan.

The Seveso disaster was now an international scandal. Luciano appeared on the front pages of newspapers and on BBC Television. The dilemma of the authorities involved was one that raised moral, political and practical issues which might well arise in future in any of the advanced countries of the world. I could also see a remote analogy between this instance of the plight of man as the result of his own technology, and the continuing plight of the Cetaceans, not by their own doing, but by man's.

When Luciano returned he was keen both to know what had happened to Donald since their reunion in Wales, and to hear me expound the dolphin's-eye view I had promised him of the events that caused Donald's departure from the Isle of Man and followed his arrival off the Welsh coast. I suggested that Luciano should imagine that I was Donald himself, that my words were Donald's words, spoken from the dolphin's own mind.

Here is the story I told him.

> Since I left the seas where I first met the two-tailed mammals with the fast respiration, I have been fortunate. I have found another part of the sea which has made a good home for me, a place where there are many interesting sounds and movements. In many ways this new home I have found is like my previous one, and here too I have two places where I can rest and play.
>
> Nearby is an isolated land mass that causes the water to flow very rapidly between the tides. When the water is running fast the fish wait behind the rocks for their food to be swept by, and when they are gathered there I can easily feed myself. When the tide races through the water surface is rough. All of the other water beings take shelter behind the rocks and the two-tailed mammals who float on the top of my world with their noisy machines stay away. They are afraid. I am the master, the absolute master. When all the other animals are hiding I have my sea to myself.

(Port St Mary and Port Erin, two of Donald's favourite resorts on the Isle of Man, were separated by a distance of about seven miles by sea. The presence of an island — the Calf of Man, close to the land and between the two resorts — causes a dangerous tidal race which runs at its fastest between the periods of slack high water and slack low water. Likewise in Wales Donald "adopted" the two harbours of Dale Haven and Martin's Haven which are separated by about ten miles if a sea route is taken. The island of Skomer, just off the headland between the two havens also creates a dangerous tidal race through Jack Sound.)

> I can race through the water and I can dive up through the air. When I hit the air I feel the sensation of weight and gravity which I cannot feel when I am in my own

environment — the sea. The air feels much harder than the water.

When I leap into the air and I am pulled back down again into the soft welcoming water with a splash I realise how lucky I am to live in the sea. Feeling gravity for a few seconds is fun — but feeling gravity for all time must be dreadful as I remember when I was stranded on land two years ago. I consider myself fortunate to be an animal of the sea, where everything moves smoothly and freely. The two-tailed mammal comes from the land above the sea where the gravity forces make him extremely heavy. Moving fast with such enormous forces on his body must demand great strength and use up much energy. Perhaps that is why he needs to breathe so fast. I wonder what it feels like when he comes into the soft cushion of the sea where he has no weight? If he is so strong as to move on land why is he so slow in the sea?

Are the two-tailed mammals as slow in their own environment as they are in the sea? They are by far the most intelligent creatures I have encountered, but they are very slow in what they do and how they communicate.

There is however one feature of a two-tailed mammal that I do admire. It is his flippers with which he can catch things and move things better than I can with either my mouth or my flippers. In that one respect he is superior to me.

The two-tailed mammals appear to have little appreciation of the sounds of the sea. The sea is full of natural vibrations that I can hear and they cannot. Some of the sounds have distinct meanings, such as the scream of a wounded fish. Such vibrations are primitive, with a single meaning. The seals, who are warm-blooded mammals like me, make more meaningful sounds than the fish. They use some of their sounds for echo-location. I sometimes play with the seals in the water, and I enjoy that when they are not idling their time away on land. They are far less interesting than my first cousins the toothed whales and second cousins the whiskered whales. I can exchange complex information with my fellow Cetaceans by the use of sound. Each of our species has its own exclusive culture based on sound. Indeed, that is why I now lead this lonely life.

I remember when I was selected by the mentor dolphin of my school for my task. He told me that the sea, which had been ours for millions of years, was being invaded with so many new sounds that our survival was at stake. He told me that four dolphin generations ago our big cousins the whales made the loudest noises in the sea and that they could talk to one another over great distances. The sounds made by the two-tailed land mammals were very, very quiet — a few splashes near their own environment, the air and where the seabed met the air. When they travelled over our environment on floating wood blown by the wind the noise was local and no more obtrusive than that made by the sea foaming up a sandy beach.

Then the two-tailed mammals changed to vessels made of a material of high density to transport them across the sea. The new vehicles were pushed through the water with tiny tails that made unusual continuous rotational movements. They made a fascinating sound which penetrated deeper into our environment, and the noise continued for the entire time the transporters were moving on the surface of our undersea world. The two-tailed mammal must have a very great desire to move like us dolphins, because when the interface between our two worlds was ruffled many of their water transporters hit the hard seabed where it rose into the air, and their transporters sank into our world with the death of many of the two-tailed mammals.

Then two dolphin generations ago they started making many more sounds, not just interesting sounds but painful sounds that would kill our kind if they were nearby. Many of the hollow, high density transporters were broken by the powerful new sounds. Hundreds of the transporters came down into our sea with the loss of many of the lives of the two-tailed mammals. At first we could not understand what was happening. They appeared to be deliberately killing their own species, not just the old, infirm and deformed specimens, but many young fit specimens in the prime of their lives. They were behaving in a manner we had not before experienced even among the lowest orders of sea life — the sharks.

The sounds the mammals made, however, were only a small part of the world of sound in which we live. A very few dolphins were also killed. We were puzzled. But the sounds did not disturb us too much and we took no action. However, worse things were to come.

A much bigger invasion of our sound world came during the course of the last dolphin generation, and since then the situation has progressively deteriorated. The sounds they now make are very much more penetrating. When their transporters are on the surface they send out sound beams that penetrate deep into the sea. In addition they have built stationary objects that emit a continuous noise. The noises they make are now reaching a level where in some places they are interfering with our own communications.

In addition to sounds my sea is full of tastes. When a shoal of mackerel have passed nearby I can taste their presence in the water. But in many parts of the undersea world the natural tastes have now changed. In some areas where fresh water flows into the sea the taste has become bitter and noxious. We dolphins suspect that the two-tailed mammals have brought about this change. So now we have two types of pollution in our world, sound pollution and taste pollution. That is why I volunteered to isolate myself from the school to learn something about the two-tailed mammals who are threatening our present existence.

The mentor dolphin was wise, and told me that the dolphins must evolve and develop a new survival culture which will take into account the two-tailed mammals' culture of kill, destroy and pollute. To evolve our survival culture we must find out more about the two-tailed mammals. We had already learned a lot about the ingenious devices they manipulate with their remarkable flippers. Now we need to know something about what motivates their trend towards apparent self-destruction. In other words we need to know about the vibrations of their minds. To do that I was to attempt to let my own mental vibrations overlap with theirs.

My mentor warned me that my mission would be dangerous, because the one thing that characterised all information so far about the behaviour of the two-tailed mammal was that it is a very unpredictable species. He told me that I must always be on my guard. When he sent me on my mission he knew I would be gone for a long time, for in order to accomplish it I would have to isolate myself completely from close contact with dolphin vibrations. Only by doing so would I become sensitive to the sound vibrations of the two-tailed mammals, and the information that would be contained in their complex interference patterns. Occasionally a messenger dolphin would be sent from the school to find out news of my progress. I was to communicate with the messenger only briefly.

After my first encounter with the two-tailed mammals I felt that I was doing very well. First I sensed fear — acute fear — then that vibration gradually diminished and I sensed friendship. Then came the female with whom I had the maximum overlap. Not only did I receive her vibrations, she received some of mine and I was lulled into a sense of security. False security as it turned out. I thought all of the two-tailed mammals were basically friendly once they had overcome their fear. But my mentor proved to be correct. The next male mammal I tried to communicate with and help when he was catching salmon emitted first fear and then the new vibration I had never before experienced, but what the land mammals call hatred. I felt that mind vibration reach a maximum the moment before the explosive sound that tore into my flesh and sent me crazy with pain. For that brief moment I knew both the mind vibration and the sound vibration that is used by the two-tailed mammals on their course of self-destruction. My cries went unheard because the dolphin school was far away. So I kept clear of the two-tailed mammals until I had recovered. When the messenger came and I told him of my experience he told me to carry on my work and that he would carry my information to the mentor dolphin. So the next time I encountered the two-tailed mammals I sought out only those with friendly vibrations. With their help I gradually built up the courage I needed to fulfil my mission.

The complexity of the problem I had been sent to help resolve was brought home to me with startling clarity when I was stranded. With no water surrounding me, my full weight pressed me with increasing pressure harder and harder into the newly uncovered seabed. I was becoming hot and finding it almost impossible to expand my chest to breathe. I knew I would die if I could not get back into the water and again sent out my dolphin distress signal. Fortunately one of the two-tailed mammals who was nearby received my vibrations and immediately I sensed faint but familiar dolphin-like response vibrations. The mammal called upon the small school of other two-tailed mammals for help as he would if he were a dolphin, and I was saved as I would have been if I had been drowning and was near a school of dolphins in the sea. The next time the messenger dolphin came I gave him the new information and he said he would pass the good news to the mentor. He also informed me that I was to continue with my mission.

As I reported my experiences to the messenger dolphin I realised that the two-tailed mammals can be both cruel and kind. This I still cannot understand. First they tried to kill me, not just for food but for another reason which does not enter our culture. Then when I was stranded they behaved in a dolphin-like manner and rescued me.

I was pleased to report to the dolphin messenger my relationship with the two-tailed mammal who has visited me frequently. She is the one I have come closest to understanding and she seems to be the best of the two-tailed mammals at entering my world. I like it best when she is on the interface between our two worlds because there she can be most active and controlled. When she communicates with me in her own sound pictures they are limited to the long-sound part of my sound vision, which does not give me information on shape and density. Her sound is very deep as if a dolphin voice has been slowed down many times and the information it contains comes to me equally slowly. Sometimes I feel so good when I am with her I wish she could speak delphinese and then we could exchange much more information. As it is I rely mainly on mind vibrations, which we both have poorly developed, and with which we understand the ideas as they develop in our minds before we put them into sound vision to communicate for all to understand.

I liked her visits so much that I would have stayed in one place near her for a long time.

Then I heard a strange, very loud noise that I had not encountered before. It came suddenly, without warning, and stopped. I was frightened, and did not know what to do. For tide phase after tide phase* I swam, not knowing what to do and where to go. Then there was

*The time between one high tide and the next — about 12½ hours.

another single very loud noise — the same as before. The noises continued for several moonphases* and I became more and more distressed. Then one day when I was close by my favourite place, I was hit by an explosion.

The gigantic vibrations thumped into my body as if I were being beaten on all sides but with a single blow. I was so dazed I screamed for help but my two-tailed mammal friends did not come. My distress call was not heard by my own school of dolphins. Or if it was they did not respond as they would normally have done. Then there was another enormous sound and a crushing vibration. I cried as loud as I could but again my distress call went unheard. I sank on to the seabed and could barely remember that I must surface to breathe. Again and again I sent out my distress call but neither dolphin nor the two-tailed mammals came to assist me as I expected.

Then I remembered why I had been sent on my mission, to try to understand why the two-tailed mammals were polluting our environment with sound. Now I understood fully what my mentor dolphin had told me about the sound that the two-tailed mammals used to kill one another, and I realised that I needed to gather much more information. I was not going to die, but still crazy with the shock, I left my familiar seabed territory and swam and swam all through the dark moon phase**. Over deep water which I had not crossed for many moon tides. On and on I went skimming through the water until the shock damage was healed by the vigorous movements of my body.

When the dawn came I found myself exhausted and close to a high seabed which stretched up into the air.

*The time between one full moon and the next, i.e. one lunar month — about four weeks.

**Night.

Near to this mass I found a hollow object floating on the surface. It was attached to the seabed by a rope and I was thankful to find a place to rest. Although my entire brain was exhausted I knew I could only rest half of it and that the other half must be kept alert for danger and to make me breathe. So with the buoy to protect my resting side I stayed quietly all day recovering, first resting one side of my brain and then changing position to rest the other side.

When the evening came I was feeling better, but my body was aching from the long unaccustomed exercise and I swam slowly around the seabed peninsular in which I found myself to record all of its details in my brain. Whether I stay or go I will always remember this place. There is just a single floating ball to which the two-tailed mammals attach their hollow transporters but there are none of the transporters here and none of the mammals have come. It is good here. It is peaceful. I can be alone quietly until I recover.

The two moon tides (a moon tide corresponds to a cycle of the moon's phase from new to full moon or from full back to new moon, that is fifteen days) have passed and I am completely recovered. I think I shall stay here. I have explored the isthmus of seabed nearby through which the water flows when the tide is set fast and there is plenty of food. Beyond that is a promontory of seabed with more buoys and I have found a sea transporter the same shape as the one I often used as a resting station in my previous island. It is comforting to stay with it over my head. When I am alongside the dense part that comes deepest into the water I feel protected and can rest one side of my brain.

As the moon tides have passed I have had encounters with more of the two-tailed mammals. Some have come to visit me in my own environment. One day when I was near my feeding isthmus I sensed a familiar two-tailed mammal on one of the transporters. The overhead world was thick with water vapour, which is dangerous for the transporters, so I escorted it to the sea island I have made my base. As soon as the transporter stopped the two-tailed mammal with the interesting box in his adapted flippers came into my environment.

I was delighted to see him and told him time and time again to take a message to the female two-tailed mammal who was often with him before. He does not understand me like the female, but I hope he got the information I tried to convey to him.

As the moon tides have come and gone and the water has become warmer the two-tailed mammals have become more active and have brought their transporters to my small peninsular of water. One of the arrivals has been a familiar shaped transporter with the symbol *Sharron* on it beyond the water line.

Each day after sunrise I hear a two-tailed mammal arrive. He moves awkwardly over the land above the water to the beach. Then he starts his interesting routine. I like routines. First there is a general clatter, and then he pulls a small wooden transporter down the land towards the water. It makes a lovely sound as it bounces over the rocks and mixes with the regular rhythm of the sea swell running back and forth joining his world to mine. He splashes into the sea and pushes his small transporter ahead of him. Then he climbs into his vessel and moves it over the water with a wooden fluke which he moves with his adapted flippers.

The sound picture now changes. I hear clicks and groans coming from the transporter as it is stressed by the push of the wooden fluke, which sweeps like a tail in a figure of eight movement over the stern. That sound is mixed with the subtle swish of water as it hurries past the rippled sides of the transporter. I swim to greet him. I cartwheel high out of the water as I take a breath. He talks to me as he stands in his transporter propelling it over the water. When he arrives at the larger transporter with the sign on the side, he climbs aboard and leaves the small one for me to play with when he goes on his journey. I push my head up into the heavy air and look at him with my sight vision. He talks to me again with his deep slow voice as he starts his next routine.

Next, after a vigorous movement, comes the sound I know that will eventually make the small fluke at the back of the transporter start to rotate. Once the sound commences it settles to a regular thud that comes through the water like a very powerful heartbeat. I dance through the water around the transporter when this happens because I know shortly will come the sound I like most of all. Then it happens. Clunk, clunk, click, click, clunk in quick succession; pause, then clickety clunk, clickety clickety click. I dive down to the seabed and watch the anchor chain bounce on the seabed before the hook which is partially buried eventually breaks. It is a delicious mixture of shapes and sounds and movement. I follow it up through the water as the chain links slide over the side of the transporter. Clickety, clunkety, click, pause.

Then it is taken out of my world and there is a final session of random sounds before the heart-throb increases and the transporter moves to the edge of the land to collect its load of the two-tailed mammals. They clamber awkwardly over the dry seabed and then the transporter sets off for the big pool of land above the sea that is the home for many birds. I escort the transporter half-way to the island and then swim back to base, to see what other activities are commencing.

As the sun climbs into the air over the water it is time for me to rest and lie gently beside the small transporter left by the two-tailed mammal who has gone to the bird island. There is little danger here but I must always be on the alert. I rest beside the transporter and close one eye, pretending the transporter is another dolphin protecting my sleeping side. My outer eye stays alert and that part of my brain tells me when I must gently surface to breathe.

If another interesting sound comes to my brain when I am resting I awake in an instant and go to investigate. Often there are two-tailed mammals who come and visit the underwater world. I always go and see what they are doing. At first I keep out of sight, as I have been trained, and examine them with my sound vision. Then if the vibrations are good I go and investigate them and let them see me. Some of them come regularly and emit good vibrations. When I see them I let them touch me and I enjoy that.

The two-tailed mammal who always has a box in his flippers took the message to the female and I was very pleased to hear his sounds again. I was delighted to have the female back in the sea with me and we exchanged many messages. I like her to touch me all over because she is so gentle. I was sad when she left the sea, but just over one tide later I heard the signal she and her partner make with stones in a tin on the high land above water. I rose out of the water and then they saw me. They waved their modified flippers and made mouth noises. I watched them come down the rocks towards the water where I was waiting to greet them. I am very happy when I am with them.

I am also happy when I am near the two-tailed mammal who goes to the bird island every sun phase. He does not come into my environment with me, but I get very close to him and can feel that he has a good presence. Perhaps I feel this way towards him because I like the routine he has. Perhaps it is because he is also present in my territory at the part of the cycle of the sun when I am in my most active mood and feel the need for fun. That is the time when the sun is falling to meet the water on the distant horizon, before my moon phase feeding period begins.

I know his evening routine well. I hear the heart-throb noise far off and I know then that he is going to journey back to my territory, near his small transporter. That far distant sound sparks the feeling of happiness inside me and I swim round my territory inspecting all of the chains, hollow spheres and transporters one by one. I dive into the air gently as I go past each one and re-imprint them on my mind. Then I turn my attention again to the heart-throb noise. It is closer now.

I know he will be even closer by the time I have swum out to him. So my brain tells me not to swim straight towards the noise but to allow for the distance he has travelled. It is time to go. Go. One beat, two beats, three beats, four beats, five beats, six beats, faster, faster, seven beats, up to breathe and down we go, the water is flowing past me so fast it caresses me. On and on. There is the transporter.

Let me show them I am here, up we go. A quick circuit round the transporter so all the two-tailed mammals can see me. Up to breathe. Now let's have another look at that rotating fin at the back of the transporter. Let me put my nose very close to it so that I can feel the vibrations running through my body. The water it is forcing back over my skin strokes me like a long soft brush. Then sideways, away, circle, up for air and accelerate to the front where I can feel the forward push. Now no effort is needed to swim. I just adjust my flippers and tail and the water pushed aside by the trans-porter carries me forward like I have seen the seagulls gliding effortlessly in the air. I know I can swim much faster than this vessel. So if I drop under the forward moving water in front of this transporter I can accelerate safely away without being hit like I was many moon tides ago in a place far away. That tiny misjudgement cost me a nasty injury that could have killed me if it had been to my blowhole. However, that transporter was smaller and much faster than this one. This one is safe. We are coming into my base territory now. So let's rush ahead and sweep round the bay.

The heart-throb noise has slowed right down. He will soon be putting ashore his passengers, then the fun will really begin.

There they go half falling over the dry seabed. How ungainly they look stuck up on their two fins with all that weight pulling them over if they go too far. I wonder why they don't stabilise themselves and use their flippers and their tails like some of the other mammals. The hairy mammals that make a sharp repetitive noise and sometimes swim into the sea to collect a stick in their jaws seem much more able to cope with the business of moving over the rocks close to the water than the two-tailed mammals. But I have never seen any of the land mammals move with the speed and grace of a school of dolphins. They seem far less well adapted to movement on the land than I am to movement in water.

Ah! the heart-throb sound is increasing, he will be moving towards the small transporter. Yes. He's there. Then splash! followed by the delicious rattle of chains on the seabed. It is a sound picture I never tire of seeing and hearing. The heart-throb sound has stopped. He is moving about in the big transporter, securing things with those marvellous adapted flippers so that they will not dislodge during the dark phase of the sky. He's pulling in the small transporter towards the large one and has climbed aboard. The next stage is for him to put the stick in the water and use it as a fin to propel it ashore. It travels in a figure of eight motion and he starts his final journey towards the shore. I do not think I will let him go just yet. I will position myself upside down under the small transporter, push with my belly against the keel and swim with my tail in the opposite direction to which he is pushing. It is very easy to make him go any way I wish. He has stopped pulling now and is trying to push me away with his wooden fin and the transporter is wobbling. I do not think he would be very happy with me in my environment. I have never seen him come into it. Perhaps I had better leave him alone.

He is off again, moving slowly towards the shore. I

think I will go for a quick swim round the old homestead with a few quick dives into the air to express my joy. Round we go. Up, splash. Down and round. He is near to the land now. All of the other two-tailed mammals have gone except him. I don't want him to go. Can't he see that I would like him to stay a little longer. Just a little longer. I will give him just one more push out. This time I will push him backwards with my snout. Then he can see what I am doing and I can watch him standing in the transporter trying to scull it against my push. And I can hear him making low throat sounds.

The game is over, he has gone to his home on the land above. All of the other two-tailed mammals have gone too and I am now all alone in the sea with the non-mammals. The sun has disappeared behind the far horizon and the undersea world is changing. Many of the creatures of my world that hide away during the sunlight period are coming out. The lobsters are moving out of their holes in search of food. The conger eels, which keep well hidden with just their snouts protruding from their lairs during the sun phase, are coming out to swim free. The wrasse which were hurrying everywhere over the rocks during the sun phase are now quiet and resting close to the rocks in the moon phase. The octopus thinks he slides silently out of his crevice but I can hear even his slithery sounds. His sound is quite unlike the crawfish or spiny lobster, whose clicks penetrate far into the dark water. All of these sounds combine in the new orchestra of sounds that commence with the moon phase. They are the music of my environment. But in the far distance I can hear the heart-beat sound of a huge transporter, it is hundreds of times bigger than the largest whale. Even at the height of the moon phase the sounds of the two-tailed mammals are present. Although the two-tailed mammals have all gone from my homestead their transporters far away remind me that some of them are always on the move. Sun phase and moon phase. If we dolphins are to evolve a new survival culture we must come to terms with these monster transporters and the two-tailed mammals who control them. We cannot drive them out of our environment. We must try to understand them.

As the tide phases have come and gone I have investigated this territory. I have made contact with many two-tailed mammals and have enjoyed playing with them. Their transporters give me much pleasure and I enjoy teasing them.

I think some of them enjoy my humour, specially when they are small. But I have noticed that older ones seem to be less inclined to play. That is another difference have noticed. We dolphins never lose our sense of fun and frivolity. I wonder why the two-tailed mammals do? Perhaps it is because they have surrounded themselves with machines which have no sense of fun at all.

During one sun phase, when I was feeling in a particularly mischievous mood I heard the delightful rattle as a small transporter came to rest and the two-tailed mammals prepared to secure it to the seabed. I knew what would happen next. As the hook came down towards the seabed I grabbed it in my beak and swam away with it. Slowly at first, then at full speed. I could feel the weight of the transporter on the end of the line and amidst the flurry of seawater I could just hear the deep throat sounds of the mammals coming down through the water from the bottom of the transporter. When I was out of breath I dropped the hook and swam up to the air. Close by the transporter I humped and blew and I could sense that the mammals were emitting both fear and excitement. When they knew it was I who had mysteriously moved their transporter they were happy and wanted me to play with them some more.

All the time I am learning more about the mammals and the things they have made and put in my environment. One of my most salutary experiences occurred after I had been here for almost one long sun cycle (a year). It was the time when the two-tailed mammals' activities in my environment are at a minimum level. Most of them had left the small haven I had made my base during the warm season. As the rough seas made it uncomfortable to rest, I started to spend more of my time in my second territory (Dale Roads) where there were always floating buoys attached to the seabed. Here I could rest in peace and the hollow spheres provided me with fixed points around which I could play, for without the company of other dolphins I need some familiar objects that float between my world of water and the lifegiving but alien world of air above.

It was during the late sun phase (evening) that it happened. I was beginning to feel hungry and I could sense the energy for the fun of the chase building up in my body.

I swim around my buoy in circles and hump and swim vigorously. When I am far from the buoy I spray the water with sound to find it again. The sound picture comes back loud and clear and nearby I see the sound pattern of a solitary fish. Feeling full of energy, I dart forward at full speed to take my hors d'oeuvre. Just as I am about to take the fish in my mouth it senses my presence and darts sideways. I change course. Half in annoyance and half in fun as I swim past the buoy I hit it with all my might with my tail and at the same time I leap out of the water.

As I dive I feel something grab my tail. I am startled and accelerate to full speed in three strokes. Still I can feel the thing holding my tail. I continue to thrust at full power when the thing that has grabbed my tail pulls me to an immediate and complete stop. With my body at full speed the force required to do this is enormous, and I feel the grip round my tail increase to a sudden crescendo of pain. I think for one moment it will rip my beautiful tail by its roots out of my body. Frantic with alarm I swing round and try to swim away in another direction. But the thing that has grabbed my tail hangs on and will not release me. I try swimming this way and that but the harder I swim the tighter is the grip around the base of my tail and all I succeed in doing is to swim in a circle. The harder I swim the stronger is the grip and the more is the pain. Suddenly I realise that I am not going to die immediately and the panic subsides a little. I realise that as I swim less vigorously the grip slackens to a more tolerable level. I slow down and then stop. The grip remains persistent but is no longer painful. I must stay still and try to resolve this problem.

First, I must find out what creature or thing is holding my tail. I will turn round and use my sound vision. Slowly round. I can still feel it, but it follows my tail so closely I can't focus my sound beam on it at all. With my light vision I can see partly backwards, but can see no monster capable of withstanding all my strength.

If I cannot find out what is holding me I had better establish where I am. I will swim very slowly round and pinpoint my position on the contour map imprinted on my memory. I spray the seabed and the surrounding water with sound and in a few moments I know exactly where I am. I will superimpose the new sound picture on the one I have recorded many times before. Everything fits, the far buoy, the bump in the seabed and the far off hull of the small transporter tied to its mooring buoy. But one thing is missing, it is the buoy I slapped with my tail just before I swam after that fish. I look behind me again with my eyes and I can just see it in my peripheral vision. If I swim slowly away it follows me through the water. It is followed by another one.

It had been a good season for Peter Pearson. Throughout the summer months his hotel on Thorne Island, Milford Haven, had been full of guests. As there was no direct contact with the mainland he had spent much of his time ferrying his guests to and from their temporary summer sanctuary in the sea.

Peter Pearson, an ex-squadron leader who distinguished himself in World War Two, was tall, very craggy and tough. He often went barefoot and could be seen hauling heavy loads up and down the steep, stone steps leading from the landing stage to the fortress that had been converted into an hotel. The Pearson family had owned Thorne Island for about forty years and Peter Pearson had managed the hotel for some twenty-five of them. The people who came there were looking for a holiday where they could enjoy isolation and sailing. Peter Pearson had a dislike of power boats and enjoyed life most when he was sailing his guests round the islands of Skockholm and Skomer. For him the wind and the sea were magic.

He knew every nuance of the tides in Milford Haven and the buoys, vessels and other objects that protruded from the sea in the vicinity of Thorne Island were as familiar to him as the houses are to a postman on his rounds. When the summer season finished at the end of September he usually closed his hotel and moved to the mainland. Every few days thereafter, either when the mood took him or necessity dictated, he would revisit his island to check that all was in order and to carry out essential maintenance and redecoration. When the season finished on 26th September 1975 however, Peter Pearson decided to remain on the island until Christmas in order to build an additional bar.

During the early winter months Peter observed that the wild dolphin he had encountered on a number of his summer sailing trips round the islands was to be seen more and more frequently in Milford Haven. Like almost everybody in the area Peter had had an "experience" with the dolphin. When rowing ashore on a very calm summer evening Donald had decided to have a game with his grey inflatable, pushing it and making steering very difficult. Finally, the dolphin whisked the dinghy round in a complete circle and thumped the side with his tail, drenching Peter and his passenger from head to foot. It was an encounter that made Peter slightly wary of the dolphin. Nonetheless he enjoyed Donald's presence in the Haven during the quiet months.

The bar extension job was nearing completion by early December and one evening after a hard day's work Peter Pearson and his son Simon, who was in his early twenties, decided to row ashore. It was a flat calm evening and they set off on their mile-long journey at about five o'clock. About a quarter of a mile from Thorne Island they passed a mooring buoy. It drifted downstream with the tide and had a second smaller buoy attached to the rope to keep it afloat and make it easy to pick up. As they neared the buoy they noticed Donald's grey hump in the water near the buoy. It was one of Donald's favourite haunts. Peter wondered if Donald (or Dai as he knew him) would repeat his earlier performance and push the dinghy off course. The dolphin did not move. Peter looked again at the hump in the water and realised that there was something unusual about it. Then it came to him. "That's strange" he remarked to his son "the dolphin is facing downstream not upstream as he usually does. I wonder why?"

Pondering on this question they passed on their way, thankful that Donald had not pursued them.

I have been here two moon phases now and not one of the two-tailed mammals has come out to help me despite all of my distress cries. My school of dolphins are miles away on their migration route and they cannot hear my cries for help. My only companions are moronic fish. They can hardly help themselves let alone me. Fortunately there are none of those big stupid sharks cruising in the area. Ah, what's that I hear. It is the transporter of the two-tailed mammal who passes these buoys regularly on his way to the seabed pool. I have escorted him many times. He must surely hear my pleas for help. Yes, he's coming closer. I can hear the quiet regular splosh, pause, splosh as he pulls his soft transporter through the water. Closer, closer. I can just hear him making throat noises. I can feel he is aware of my presence. Will he help me? I cannot make him hear my sound cries or feel my brainwave emissions calling for help. He is still aware of my presence but he is not responding. He must hear me. He must stop. He is passing by. He is not going to stop. There he goes, still making voice sounds and pulling on the sticks that move him through the water. I wish I could move away from this place, even at his slow speed. I have tried many times, but each time I do I feel the grip tighten on my tail which is painful and sore. I will just have to stay here. But how much longer can I stay, anchored to this place with no food?

I could probably stay alive for many tides and probably even moon phases too, slowly using the reserves inside my body. But when these are gone and I start to utilise my blubber I will lose heat more quickly and then I will die. The prospect of being stuck here, unable to dive into the air and swim fast and deep, fills me with a sensation I have never felt before. I have sensed it sometimes in the two-tailed mammals, who call it despair. Now I am beginning to understand them more and more. What shall I do? Shall I sink, open my blowhole, and let the water that has supported me and given me so much pleasure seep into my body. If it does I know it will take me back into itself, but when it does so my dolphin spirit will be gone forever. If I were with my school of dolphins I know they would try to stop me giving my body back to the sea. They would support me and take me to the surface so that my blowhole could take in the air.

Perhaps for their sakes I should remain on the surface as long as possible. The moon phase is coming. It is getting dark. It is the time I would normally start to feed. I am hungry.

On the day following his observations that for some strange reason the dolphin was facing downstream of the tide, Peter

Pearson was again working at the extension to the bar with his son. From this high vantage point he looked out at the familiar scene of the haven. His hotel had once been a fortress, one of the many built when invasion was threatening Britain. The view from the gun emplacements was magnificent. The air was still, it was very peaceful. As he scanned the scene and looked down on the row of mooring buoys that rested on the sea as immobile as mushrooms, he noticed that the black hump of the dolphin's back was resting quietly beside one of the buoys. The hump sank slowly and then rose again. "There is something strange about that dolphin," he said to himself. "I don't know what it is."

He called Simon and both of them looked at the black hump that floated on the sea below.

"Come on, Simon, let's row out to him."

The two men clambered down the long flight of stone steps and launched the inflatable dinghy. The grey hump had sunk again.

"He'll probably swim over to us," said Simon, expecting Donald to leave the buoy. He looked into the water beside the inflatable, anticipating the sight of the familiar grey whale shape that turned white as Donald rolled on to his back and exposed his white belly, at the same time looking up towards the boat with that comical quizzical expression of his. But the grey streak did not appear. He looked ahead at the buoy and saw the hump again rise slowly in the water and sink.

"You're right. There is something wrong. He's not coming towards us."

In a few minutes they reached the buoy. As they came alongside the dolphin lifted its tail fluke clear of the water.

"No wonder the poor devil can't swim. He's got the mooring rope wrapped round his tail."

"Here, Simon, give me a hand."

The dolphin raised its tail out of the water and over the soft inflated wall of the dinghy. The two men unravelled the rope.

"How on earth did he manage to get into that mess?"

"I don't know, but he was intelligent enough to stay still."

"What is even more remarkable is that he showed us what was wrong by lifting his tail over the side of the boat."

In a few minutes the rope was untangled and the dolphin's tail was lowered over the side into the water.

"There you are, old boy. You're free."

Ah, freedom at last. One flip, two flips, three flips of my tail and I am away. How beautiful the water feels sliding past my body again. "I'm free. I'm free!" I shout into the water. But nobody can hear. The two-tailed mammals who rescued me are gone and none of my fellow dolphins are near. But it does not matter one periwinkle. I am free once again. And I am free because I have assimilated a new feeling from the two-tailed mammals. They call it hope.

Hope and despair are two of the vibrations I must report to the mentor. One instinctive vibration still beats strongly within me — survival. If I am to survive I must learn from my experiences, and experience teaches me that this place is dangerous. It is time I moved on. After being still for so long I must move on. Out of the haven where the life was soft and easy and where the two-tailed mammals have their machines and buoys and ropes — out, out into the open sea — where the wind blows, and the ceiling of my world rises and falls, and where it rises into peaks as the air rakes through it, splitting it into a shining white foaming mass.

I don't know where I am going. I care not where I am going. I am just thankful to be free again.

"Donald's run for freedom took him to Cornwall," I said to Luciano, having completed my flight of fantasy and speculated whether the dolphin's mission might take him yet further afield.

19: The Meaning Of It All?

In the village of North Ferriby where I live the beginning of the end of that amazing summer of 1976 came in the last days of August. The temperature suddenly dropped, and the rain lashed down bringing with it some of the prematurely parched leaves from the trees. Overnight we were back in a typically capricious English summer.

Two days before we thought the heatwave would never end, Barry Cockcroft had telephoned to ask me to go to St Ives to get some additional material. He wanted some POV shots (point of view shots, as if seen by the dolphin) to round off the film. He said he would take David Aspinall, the man who was to edit the film, with him, so that he could savour the atmosphere of St Ives and get some feel of the effect that Donald had upon people.

With Ashley, now sixteen, chatting happily beside me I drove to Manchester Airport to collect Maura before driving on to Cornwall.

At 9.30 a.m. on Wednesday 1 September, Maura and I were again making our way along the now familiar jetty at St Ives. The *Aquanaut* had been brought round Lands End from Mousehole, and was moored alongside the harbour wall. The air was still and the morning was grey. As I looked over the side of the harbour wall I was dismayed to see that the water, previously light-blue and transparent, was a yellowy-brown. Underwater visibility would be dreadful. The wind, rain and bad weather of the prevous few days had filled the sea with suspended sediment, and I could tell by looking at it that high quality underwater photography would be impossible. I reported the situation to Barry and Mostafa. But despite our disappointment we enjoyed our reunion with

Bob and Hazel, and passed our heavy diving and camera equipment down to them on the *Aquanaut*.

We soon cast off and cruised slowly out of the harbour. The sea was flat calm. The small hire-craft, the buzz boats, swarmed over the surface like ants on a discarded sandwich. I had lost my dolphin rattle, the tin with stones in it, and Bob suggested I should use his technique instead, blowing into his small foghorn, which was like a straight brass car hooter, with the bell of the horn submerged.

I jumped overboard and blew. In a few minutes Donald appeared. But by the time we had the camera in the sea he had gone off to play with the buzz boats. We tried again but there were so many alternative attractions in the water that we could claim his attention for only a few minutes at a time. We spent over an hour in the water, but at the end had only a few useful feet of film "in the can". So we abandoned the filming session and made our way back to The Sloop for lunch.

When we were at the bar, one of Barry's many fishermen friends told me that he had seen Donald killing a sea bird. I could not believe that Donald would wantonly destroy any form of life, but the fisherman was adamant.

On the basis of our previous filming experience I was hopeful that we would have better luck with our filming in the late afternoon. When accordingly we set out again into the bay we saw a young guillemot skittering across the water. The bird was running at full speed and beating its wings as fast as it could, but it had obviously not yet learned to fly. Just in the rear of the mottled wake it left in the sea a triangular dorsal fin humped momentarily out of the water and disappeared again. The reason for the flight of the young guillemot was apparent. Donald was in pursuit. A few seconds later his head appeared and the guillemot was flung into the air, dropped back into the water and disappeared.

So the fisherman was right. Donald was killing birds. I was still finding it hard to believe the evidence of my own eyes when the guillemot surfaced some way from where I had last seen it. I snorkelled over in the direction of the bird, which was floating nervously on the surface. Then it dived of its own volition and I saw it swimming directly underneath me with streams of silver bubbles flowing back from its wingtips. It looked more at home swimming under the sea than trying to fly on top of it. Around us were a host of sand eels that were being caught by terns that were dive-bombing them like Kamakazi pilots. However, Donald took no notice of the terns. He was having fun with the poor guillemot that a few seconds later was again skittering flat out across the calm sea with Donald in easy pursuit. The match was as uneven as that between a cat and a mouse. But it did not end in the usual tragic manner for the mouse. Some time later we saw the young guillemot sitting on the sea shaking its feathers and regaining its composure like a genteel lady in a coffee shop, who has been insulted by an insolent waiter. My faith in Donald was restored. He was mischievous to the point of distraction by the recipient of his unwanted attentions — but he was not a bird killer. I could also understand how easy it would be for the fisherman to be mistaken.

Maura regained Donald's attention by trailing her yellow fin over the side of the inflatable, and we persuaded him to follow us to a place where there was a good outcrop of kelp on the seabed, as we wanted film of him in this type of terrain. But conditions underwater were so bad for photography that we abandoned the idea. I suggested that we should concentrate on surface shots and attempt, once again, to get Donald interested in a ball.

Maura and I tossed a plastic football between us with Donald playing pig-in-the-middle. First he swam back and forth between us, towards whichever of us had the ball. Then suddenly he managed to get it away from us. In a matter of seconds he had pushed it a hundred yards and was in a frenzy of delight. He threw the ball high in the air and when it landed he leapt over it. His game continued for one or two minutes, non-stop. I started to snorkel towards him, and looked up to see the ball quite still on the surface, with

Donald, his head down and his tail out of the water, arched over it, and so he appeared to remain for a considerable time. It was a most unusual posture to say the least, and I took it to signify that it was his ball. I continued to swim towards him and the ball. When I was about twenty yards away he accelerated across the surface of the sea and bore down on me like a speedboat under full power. For one panic-stricken fraction of a second I thought he was going to ram me. Then at the very last instant he veered away.

I got his message very loud and clear. He was playing with the ball and did not want me to interfere. He was again demonstrating that he was the master of the sea and I was a powerless intruder. Not wishing to suffer the same indignity as the young guillemot I conceded defeat and withdrew.

The following day the sea was so rough that all hopes of filming and diving were abandoned. The lifeboat went out to a catamaran that was dragging its moorings. The two boats bumped heavily when the lifeboat went alongside, and when the catamaran was safely tied up to the jetty the skipper donned a wetsuit and went over the side to inspect the damage. It was ironic that he should have sailed the boat safely all the way from the West Indies and then suffered damage in St Ives. However, he was certainly not the first man to experience disaster in the perfidious seas off Cornwall.

With filming out of the question we adjourned to our favourite coffee shop and chatted with the proprietor, Zena Christmas, who had become a friend as well as provider of endless cups of coffee and cakes for the television crew. Zena told me that Donald had become progressively more friendly during the summer. On the day before our visit, he had come right up to the steps outside her window at high water and allowed the children paddling there to stroke him, and even given some of them a gentle tow. I gave her a notebook and her young daughter agreed to keep a day to day log of Donald's activities.

I did not know at the time that she would never write a

word in the book. The weather was not improving and we agreed to abandon further filming and went home.

It was not a happy journey. Maura had an important meeting at the sub-aqua club the following evening, and although I stretched my driving ability and the performance of my car to the limit, we were held up by endless traffic jams and she missed her 'plane at Manchester for the Isle of Man. We were all fraught after the long hours of racing against the clock in the heavy holiday traffic. Maura broke down and wept.

We eventually transferred her flight to one from Liverpool the following morning. Silent and miserable we drove towards Liverpool and found a suitable hotel in Warrington. It was very late when we left Maura, and Ashley and I set a course for home.

My luck was running out.

On Saturday, 11 September 1976, the longest, hottest, driest summer in living memory eventually smashed like a bottle dropped from great height on to concrete. The sixty-foot-high trees outside my house waved like saplings. As the wind rose to gale force water sheeted out of the heavens. It was a storm that produced floods of biblical proportions. On the morning after the storm the lawn in front of my house was strewn with branches ripped off the trees. Although the rain had ceased, parts of the countryside which earlier had been parched and cracked were hidden under inches of water.

The reason I can remember the day so well is that it was our wedding anniversary, and to celebrate I took my wife, my mother and my son out for lunch to the Corn Mill at Stamford Bridge. The low-level rose gardens adjacent to the converted water mill were under two feet of water. I looked at the river where I had dived when searching for old bottles. The water, instead of cascading down the weir as I had seen it previously, came over the top in a solid unbroken arch of brown. It crashed on to the river below and raced forward like a big dipper at a fairground.

I watched, mesmerised by its strength and brutality. A

branch, caught in a whirlpool beside the fall, was beaten back into the depths every time it surfaced. Sometimes the end of the branch rose out of the water like the shining head of a monster in its death throes, only to be smashed back into the depths and pummelled by the river bed. I remember feeling how equally cruel the sea can be.

A few days later I received a cutting from a West Country newspaper which reported that St Ives had suffered its worst northerly gale for many years. It gave an account of the valiant attempts of the lifeboatmen to save the ships in St Ives harbour. One of the St Ives fishing boats, which I could remember, the *Compass Rose*, had sunk after being holed. Many other vessels were damaged and a number of small boats filled with water and sank at their moorings.

I telephoned Zena Christmas and she told me that Donald had disappeared.

Was his luck also running low, I asked myself? I had for some time been reflecting on the increasing risks to Donald's safety as his presence became known to more and more people, some of whom showed the grossest insensitivity to his vulnerability. The trippers in their buzz boats in Cornwall were only one such hazard, and there was always the chance that he would encounter an unfriendly fisherman. It almost seemed as if Donald was himself deliberately compounding the risks — from the remoteness of the Isle of Man he had moved to Wales, and then to Cornwall, each move being to a more heavily populated area. In Cornwall, because it is a holiday centre attracting visitors from all over the country, he had become the centre of national publicity. And I of course had played a part in this, by helping to make Barry Cockcroft's film. I reasoned that if Donald was to become known, it was important that he become *well* known, that public sympathy and understanding be aroused on his behalf so that he would have friends among human beings who would keep an eye on his wellbeing. But I was not altogether certain I had done the right thing.

As if to confirm my fears, a few weeks later my wife

returned home from work to warn me that she had sad news — she had heard that Donald was dead.

I was stunned. By a series of the kind of coincidences that already haunted my relationship with the dolphin, it seemed that Wendy had heard the news from one of my ex-scientific colleagues, Dr Mike Rance. Mike's parents had recently returned from a holiday in St Ives in Cornwall, where one day after the storm they had found a dead dolphin washed up on the beach. The sight of the dead dolphin was such a distressing sight for Mike's sister that the entire family had set to and buried it, spontaneously conducting a little funeral ceremony that moved Mike's sister to tears. It was reported in a local West Country paper that the dolphin which had befriended divers and had become the playmate of children in St Ives was dead. Mike's parents had no idea of my interest in that particular dolphin, but Mike did.

I could not believe that Donald would no longer be part of my life. Were a few photographs and an unfinished film all that remained of him? I felt as empty and bereft as if I had lost a close personal friend.

When the news had sunk in I telephoned Zena Christmas for confirmation of the story. To my surprise she had not heard of the dolphin's death and burial. I thought it strange that in a place as small as St Ives she would not get to know of such an occurrence, so a tiny ember of hope started to glow in the ashes of my grief.

I telephoned Mike and asked him to repeat the story, to make sure that I had got the facts absolutely right. I asked Mike if there were any identifying marks on the body and roughly how big was the dolphin? He could not answer my question and gave me his father's telephone number.

I hurried through the formalities of self-introduction and put the same questions to the older man. And when he said the animal they had buried was five to six feet long, I could have shouted for the sheer relief of it. When he had answered a few more questions there was not a shadow of doubt in my mind: the dolphin his family had buried with such touching ceremony was not Donald. From his description I deduced it was a common porpoise.

Each time Donald moved, as I realised in retrospect, he appeared to have a very good reason for doing so. The underwater blasting in Port St Mary on the Isle of Man must have made his stay there uncomfortable, to say the least, and was potentially very dangerous. Hence his emigration to Wales. Then at Dale Haven he suffered the trauma of being caught up for days in a buoy line, and after his remarkable release very reasonably beat a retreat from that area too.

And Geoff Bold had no doubts as to why Donald abandoned his next adopted territory, around the Penlee Lifeboat Station. He said a group of servicemen who were camped nearby drove the dolphin nearly to distraction by buzzing him and trying to run him down in their inflatables, which were fitted with powerful outboard engines. Geoff protested, but the servicemen ignored him.

Then the fearful storm in St Ives would have indicated to the dolphin that although St Ives was a comfortable place in the summer months, in the winter he could expect a little rest. He needed to find a sheltered location where boats were moored. Only in such a situation could he relax sufficiently for part of his brain to sleep. Where, I asked myself, would he find such a place? A look at the map showed several possibilities, depending upon how far Donald was prepared to travel for a winter resting place.

A short time later I heard that a wild dolphin had appeared in Falmouth. And once more, the information involved a curious coincidence. Some neighbours, Jimmy and Isobel Simpson, with whom we enjoyed considerable friendship, had moved to Cornwall — Jimmy was a maritime engineer with Lloyds Register of Shipping, who spent much of his time on boats in and out of Falmouth, and from his office window he could look out over the harbour. He had observed what some of the local residents had already commented upon — some of the small boats were moving back and forth on their moorings for no apparent reason. Donald had found a new home. He had also discovered one dinghy which was particularly to his liking and would spend hours playing round it, just as he had done in Port St Mary, at Martin's Haven and St Ives.

As the spring daffodils came into bloom in 1977 Donald was already winning hearts in Falmouth and the inhabitants of St Ives were mourning their loss. A news item from the West Country announced that a man who had fallen overboard had been helped to the surface and saved from drowning by a dolphin in Falmouth harbour.

History was repeating itself. As it did so the questions that I had asked myself many times before again raised themselves. Do dolphins really have a special mysterious sensitivity to their environment — including some kind of unknown understanding of man himself? Were for instance the two occasions on which Donald had been reported to have saved human lives, evidence of this understanding — and not only understanding, but a peculiar dolphin benevolence? Were they also proofs of dolphin intelligence?

The subject of dolphin intelligence is a very controversial one amongst scientists. The fact that some of the best brains in the world are seriously debating the issue lends a certain credibility to the hypothesis that dolphins are in some way unique as a species. Professor Teizo Ogawa of the University of Tokyo describes the intelligence of whales and dolphins as follows: "In the world of mammals there are two mountain peaks, one is Mount Homo Sapiens, and the other is Mount Cetacea". But a major difficulty in comparing the intelligence of man with that of dolphins is the fact that we have evolved in two such different environments. The so-called "environmental factor", which makes comparisons of intelligence even between different ethnic groups of men extremely difficult, becomes an almost impenetrable barrier when comparing men and dolphins.

On 20 February 1976, Sidney J. Holt, who is a Fisheries and Environment Adviser to the Food and Health Organisation of the United Nations, produced a memorandum. It was addressed to Members of the Advisory Committee on Marine Resources Research, and reviewed the

Committee on Marine Resources Research, and reviewed the published literature by various authorities on Cetaceans. He pointed out that only in recent years have scientists come to abandoning the idea that race or colour can determine intelligence among human beings. Was it time, he suggested, that the Committee widen its perspective still further and concede that intelligence is not to be confined to the human race, but recognised in other animals? Should in particular Cetaceans be accorded a special status different from that of other marine animals or indeed any other animals than man?

I do not know how the recipients of that memorandum reacted when they read it, but its existence does indicate that members of the United Nations are at least giving serious consideration to the possibility that there is something special about the whale family.

Whales in the past have been treated simply as a resource to be husbanded and exploited for our benefit. Should we now establish a new category of animals, completely separate from man, but which are accorded intelligence, social structure and a consciousness on a par with that of man? If we can humble ourselves enough to accept this possibility, we may find that we are at the dawn of a new era of understanding of what life is about.

Man through his history has devoted most of his energies to the provision of food, shelter and transport for himself and his family. Today, for instance, motor car assembly workers labour at producing the means of transport and are paid in money, which in turn enables them to buy food produced by farmers and fuel hacked out of the ground by coalminers. Man in other words has devoted his intelligence to adapting the environment to suit his needs. The majority have little time to play and enjoy themselves.

Cetaceans, on the other hand, instead of attempting to control their immediate surroundings, have themselves adapted through the process of evolution to harmonise with their environment. A dolphin lives in an ecosystem in which food is abundant. He has no need to construct a shelter.

Donald could travel with ease, speed and grace, leaving no trail of toxic exhaust. Unburdened by possessions, avarice would be unknown to him. With the open sea as a common heritage Cetaceans do not suffer the tensions of living in high rise blocks of flats, the resentments of the squalor in shanty towns, or the burning hatred of suppression in ghettos. Having no money with which one dolphin can exploit another, they have no problem with the corrupting influence of power. No one dolphin has a fortune whilst another suffers the misery of poverty, and no starving dolphin swims alongside a bloated glutton. Unspurred by the greed for land, no dolphin technology has needed to develop mustard gas, flame throwers, defoliants or any of the other hideous instruments of human warfare.

At least until man dropped the atomic bomb of his technology into the undersea world of the Cetaceans, one might almost have said that dolphins lived the ideal of that socialism that has long been a human ideal but which man himself has so far failed to achieve because of his own greed.

With no technology, no art, no scientific achievements, one might ask, for what purpose did the Cetaceans evolve their large cerebral cortex through the past ten million years?

One answer to that question might be that the dolphins have evolved in order to enjoy and revel in the pleasure of simply being alive, of being dolphins.

And when the day comes that we can communicate intelligently with dolphins, they may introduce us to the concept of survival without aggression, and the true joy of living, which at present eludes us. In that circumstance what they have to teach us would be infinitely more valuable than anything we could offer them in exchange.

It is in that context that I had evolved my fantasy of Donald's mission to man.

To some readers such a hypothesis may sound outrageous. My reply to them is that it is no more improbable than, for instance, the concept of a divine God, to which, in some form or another, most human cultures subscribe.

And there are many other experiences in life that cannot be explained in terms of the current state of our scientific knowledge — among them a whole series of happenings generally known under the unwieldy title 'paranormal phenomena'. There are now scientists all over the world who are willing to concede the fact that although we have no explanation for them at present we should not brush them under a carpet of scepticism.

Less open to speculation is the effect Donald had on the various people he encountered. Each person who came into contact with Donald established a relationship with the dolphin which was as unique as the personality of the man or woman concerned. This was something both observed and experienced — it was real to me, to Maura and many others.

To Maura, for instance, Donald was 'a person' — she has often told me so. She loved him like a person, and that love actually seemed to break down some of the gigantic barriers that inevitably exist between species. Her relationship with Donald was such that she could understand and interpret his moods and behaviour in almost the same way as she expects to do with another human being with whom she has lived through good times and bad times.

To Mostafa, Donald was an extension of his extrovert self — excitable and generous. Like Mostafa, Donald was a law unto himself.

To Geoff Bold, the relationship with Donald was almost some kind of therapy. Donald interacted with Geoff in such a way that the lifeboat mechanic's preoccupations were directed away from an area that caused him stress, into a realm where contentment could at last be found.

And to me Donald symbolised freedom. Knowing him caused me to rethink my life and the values I placed on different aspects of it. He caused me to ask myself what was important and what was trivial. But above all else he made me realise that the thing I cherished way above all others was freedom. And indirectly, at least as far as my work is concerned, he even gave me that freedom, for had it not been for Donald I would almost certainly have taken another full-time job.

Not for one single moment have I ever regretted my moment of decision when he turned up, literally out of the blue, off the Welsh Coast and I decided to attempt to make a new living from freelance work.

To me, Donald achieved the ultimate. Like King Solomon's lilies of the field, he sowed not neither did he reap. He was free to associate with humans and things human when he wanted, and he was also free to take to the wild and wide open sea. And I felt his ability to do this must remain sacrosanct — for to me freedom is a dolphin.

Both Maura and I agree that Donald had a spirit of complete happiness that goes with complete freedom. We witnessed it on many occasions. It affected us personally, the television crew and everyone else we know who came closely into contact with him.

Scientists will be sceptical, and rightly so, about this joy that people said they felt when in Donald's presence, until some more tangible evidence can be produced. But until someone invents an instrument to quantify it and measure it — a dolphin happiness meter, perhaps, we shall have to be content with the evidence of our own subjective experience.

Who knows, maybe one day we shall be able to identify and isolate the spirit of the dolphin, as we have been able to capture the fragrance of flowers and concentrate them into perfumes, or to extract from foxgloves a component that has kept men's hearts functioning when they might otherwise have stopped. I like to think that if we ever do discover the essence of the unique power of the dolphins, they will let us use it one day to treat broken human minds.

But until that time arrives, the dolphins may at least lead us, by example, to learn to enjoy today, instead of constantly battling for the good life of a tomorrow which may never come.

20: Marriage of Minds

One of the topics I discussed with Barry Cockcroft when we were making the film *Ride a Wild Dolphin* was that of dolphins in captivity. To me the idea of confining such a joyous, free-ranging, beautiful maverick in a concrete cell was unthinkable. 'Putting Donald in a dolphinarium would imprison his mind as well as his body,' was how I expressed my view when I was being interviewed for the film.

Even when Donald eventually vanished from Cornwall in 1978,* the capture and use of dolphins as acrobatic clowns continued to trouble me. I felt we were abusing their spontaneous friendship towards humans, and I openly opposed such places as Marineland at Morecambe near Blackpool, where a dolphin called Rockie was kept in solitary confinement in a tiny concrete tank, just a few metres away from the open sea.

What was life like for Rockie?

To answer that question, I tried to put my mind inside Donald's head, as I had so often done before, and went charging through the water, leaping into the air for no better reason than the sheer, uninhibited, uncomplicated joy of being a free spirit. I then switched to being Rockie, swimming in endless circles in a cramped box of chlorinated water laden with my own excrement.

Never again would I feel the run of the tide, hear the rumble of pebbles on a distant beach, or watch a gannet arrowing through the water; never again would I chase a

---

* The story of Donald's life until his mysterious disappearance, without trace, is told in my book *Save the Dolphins* (Souvenir Press).

live fish, cavort with a seal, see the sun dapple the seabed and the seaweeds wave back and forth in the swell, or listen to the gurgle of water as it was funnelled between the rocks; I would never again frolic in glistening white foam, rush through the sea on a dark, moonless night using my inbuilt sonar like a giant sonic searchlight to illuminate the way ahead, or enjoy a rumbustious rough-and-tumble with my fellow dolphins.

With my face fixed in what humans interpret as a permanent smile, my jailors inform everyone I am happy. They feed me dead fish loaded with the vitamin pills essential to keep me alive, and tell the world how fortunate I am not to have to forage for my own food or face the dangers of the open sea. It is the life of beer and skittles they all dream of. They have to come to 'work' to teach me how to 'play'. They know I have a brain that is physically as large and complex as their own. They appear to overlook, however, that it endows me with a potential for intelligent and intellectual thought processes equal to theirs, and that, if their scientific understanding of the role of the silent layers of the brain is correct, I am as capable as they are of enjoying aesthetic experiences — which many of them regard as the ultimate human achievement.

It was thoughts like this that fuelled my quest to find out more about dolphin psyche. My fellow scientists claimed that to achieve meaningful results it was essential to work with captive animals, but I argued that to find out how a dolphin thinks and to identify the source of its joyous spirit, it was essential to meet dolphins on their own terms in their own environment. As a result of my experiences with Donald, I knew that this could be done. Eventually I hoped that it would be achieved by humans being accepted into schools — or tribes, as I preferred to think of them — of free-ranging dolphins, and then following them, night and day, from spring to winter, on their nomadic odysseys. But we had a long way to go before that could happen.

Firstly we had to gain their trust. We couldn't do that if

we swooped into their communities, which were socially highly organised, and plucked out youngsters to imprison in pools for our entertainment, quite apart from the damage we were doing to their environment with fishing and pollution. From the dolphin's point of view, it seemed to me that the very last creature any sensible dolphin would want to associate with would be man. However, as we have already seen, Donald had chosen to do just that. By doing so he had pointed a way ahead, for me at least, but it involved a lengthy learning process.

As the years went by, it gradually became apparent to me that if I were to succeed in my quest there would have to be a two-way input, with the dolphins being given every encouragement to make their own contribution, instead of simply co-operating with me in my scientific experiments. Firstly I needed to find one or more dolphins who demonstrated by their behaviour that they wanted human company. I would then have to build up trust and friendship with them to a level where we could associate freely and easily with one another. So when Donald disappeared in 1978 I had to face up to the problem of finding another candidate to help me fulfil my dreams.*

One dolphin I became particularly friendly with was dubbed Percy, and I spent three wonderful summers frolicking with him off Portreath in Cornwall, very close to St Ives where I had had such memorable times with Donald. I worked with a freelance film-maker, Laurie Emberson, on a film about Percy, which was called *Eye of a Dolphin* because it set out to show a dolphin's eye-view of the world. After it was shown on BBC TV an unprecedented number of viewers, suffering from various forms of depression, wrote in, saying how uplifted they had been after watching Percy's antics in the open sea.

There was one particularly moving experience which I

* How I set about it is described in my books *Save the Dolphins* (Souvenir Press) and *Tale of Two Dolphins* (Jonathan Cape).

recorded with my stills camera but which was not filmed. Tricia Kirkman, a mother who could not swim, overcame her intense fear of open water and got into the sea with Percy, who came up to her and gave her a gentle tow. Afterwards she expressed the emotion she felt coming from him as 'pure love'. The response to the film, combined with Tricia's hypersensitivity to the magical quality of the dolphin, led me to set up a project called *Operation Sunflower*, to discover whether dolphins could help people suffering from depression. In 1987, once the scheme was really under way, I took three patients suffering from depression to swim with a wild dolphin off the coast of Ireland. The long-term effects of the extraordinary events that took place in Dingle were filmed and are still unfolding.*

One consequence of *Operation Sunflower* was that in 1988 I met Dr Betsy Smith, at the first Whale and Dolphin Conference at Nambucca Heads, about 300 miles north of Sydney in Australia. To my knowledge she was the only other person in the world who had been conducting serious research in an area related to *Operation Sunflower*: she was investigating ways in which autistic children might benefit from contact with dolphins. Knowing how committed most of those at the conference were to preserving the freedom of dolphins, Dr Smith explained that the dolphins she worked with were in what is called 'elective captivity' — that is, they had been captured but had access to the open sea if they chose to take it. This, I felt, was a major step forward by a fellow scientist, particularly an American from Miami, which was where the first dolphin circus had started in 1938. By the 1980s dolphin shows had become big business, and the Florida Keys had the highest concentration of captive dolphins anywhere in the world.

However, attitudes to keeping animals, especially cetaceans, in captivity were changing. Indeed, a new business

* They form the subject of my book *Dance to Dolphin's Song* (Jonathan Cape).

had sprung up in the United States — Whale Watching — in which more money was being made by watching whales than in the heyday of an erstwhile industry whose aim was to slaughter as many whales as possible. I knew dolphin watching could also work financially because I had a friend in Gibraltar, Mike Lawrence, who made a living at it.* I was pleased to hear that the idea had spread to the Florida Keys and that a Captain Ron Canning was taking paying customers out to see wild dolphins. Early in 1989 I decided to visit the Keys with my wife Wendy, to see for myself the new age dolphin centres where the dolphins were in 'elective captivity', and to visit Ron Canning at Key West, on the southernmost tip of the Keys.

In May, just before we departed, I was contacted by a diver in York, Les Halliday, who strongly recommended that I visit the island of Providenciales in the Turks and Caicos group. There, he told me, I might encounter a friendly wild dolphin by the name of JoJo. I already had a note about JoJo in my file of friendly solitary dolphins, so after a phone call to establish that the dolphin was still receiving visitors, our plans were quickly modified to include a short visit to the British West Indies.

One of the more memorable events in the life of my son Ashley, apart from riding on Donald in 1972, was his marriage ten years later to Roxanna Steele, a stunningly beautiful girl from Miami. An unforseeable outcome of these nuptials was that Wendy and I were given a warm welcome by Roxanna's mother, Nancy, when we arrived at Miami airport *en route* for the Florida Keys in 1989. Nancy was of Cuban origin and had an enormous number of relatives, so that Wendy and I found we were related by marriage to half the population of Miami. This band of American Cubans was always on the look-out for an excuse to assemble for an enormous knees-up, so to avoid starting a mini carnival, our presence in Miami was kept under som-

---

* See my book *The Magic of Dolphins* (Lutterworth Press).

breros and stetsons (Roxanna's father was from Texas) until we slipped our moorings and headed south.

On the way to the Keys we stopped overnight with Betsy Smith and her family in their rambling house on the rural outskirts of the vast, sprawling metropolis of Miami. We departed early the next morning and by 8.30 am I was fully kitted up in aqualung diving equipment and sitting on a platform beside a pool at Dolphins Plus in Key Largo. This was where Betsy had carried out her studies with autistic children. Two of the dolphins involved in that project were swimming around below me, obviously aware of my presence and waiting for me to go into the water. It was already baking hot, and I launched myself into the tepid water accompanied by one of the staff. The dolphins were excited by their first aquatic visitors of the day and circled round us, coming into and out of view in the hazy green water. They were confined to an area about the size of the average municipal swimming pool by an open mesh fence through which the water and small fish could freely pass. After our introduction, we swam out through an opening, like a gate in a tennis court, into a narrow channel which connected with the open sea at both ends. There was a slight current here, providing a continuous supply of sea water which slowly flushed the pools and rendered chemical treatment unnecessary.

In some ways the strange atmosphere in the canal was not unlike that in the upper reaches of the River Thames in which I had dived many times. The bottom was scattered with bits of junk of the kind that invariably litters the bed of any river close to human habitation. It was a strange, alien underwater landscape — like the earth might be after the Bomb. Slowly rusting cans were covered with fine silt which swirled up like clouds of smoke if they were disturbed. Sergeant major fish, not unlike perch, constantly rushed in and pecked at anything that looked remotely like food. Some areas were covered with light green weed. However, it was the yellow-green luminescent glow created by the sunlight interacting with algae suspended in the water, which was most reminiscent of a freshwater, not a seawater, dive. Into the beams of light that shone down into this fog-filled dance hall zoomed the two dolphins, never staying still for a moment. Like day-time disco dancers, they moved to music in their minds which I could not hear.

Above us a small boat gave us cover. My diving companion produced various items from the pocket of his buoyancy compensator and gave the dolphins positive hand signals which they appeared to respond to occasionally. The dolphins stayed with us in the channel; we never ventured under the bridge where the channel became narrower, nor did the dolphins.

On the far side of the channel from which we had entered the water, a couple of dolphins raced back and forth behind their mesh fence, intently watching what we were doing. At the same time they exhibited what appeared to me to be an eagerness to have more than a platonic friendship with their fellow dolphins free in the channel. I had the distinct feeling that if they had been allowed out with us, a lot of boisterous highjinks would have ensued. This might well have made it difficult to entice them back into their respective pens when our session was over. After zooming around whilst clinging to an underwater scooter, which interested my dolphin companions only briefly because of the counter-attraction on the other side of the fence, my partner signalled that it was time to return to the platform. So we swam back through the gate into the pen to join the dolphins who had rushed ahead of us.

By the time we left the water, the first group booked for a swimming session with the dolphins had already assembled and was being briefed. They were given an intensive talk on dolphin biology before being allowed in the water with the dolphins for 25 minutes, which was what they had paid for. Emphasis was laid on the fact that the dolphins they were about to swim with were fed regularly but definitely not as a reward for performing tricks. Thus any interaction that took place between them was decided upon by the dolphins themselves, and if they chose to ignore the fee-paying customers, it was 'hard cheese', as they say in York-shire. This approach was in keeping with the fact that all public swims with the dolphins had to be booked in advance, there was no advertising and the unassuming entrance was through a gate in the fence. The secret of finding Dolphins Plus, we were told by Betsy Smith, was 'to turn off at the stop light at mile marker 100 on US Highway 1'.

Dolphins Plus was a family-run enterprise, launched by Richard Borgess in 1984 after he became disillusioned with his job as provider and trainer of animals for shows in which dolphins jumped through hoops and performed repetitive tricks. I was told that he eventually hoped to reach a stage where the dolphin swims would take place in the open sea. The frontman and chief administrator was Richard's father, Lloyd, whose grey swept-back hair, good looks and raffish personality would not have been out of place in a George Raft movie. I had corresponded with him in 1987 when I started studying the effect wild dolphins had on humans suffering clinical depression. In his reply he mentioned that since 1982:

> we have had in-water interactions with such handicaps as autistic, blind, paraplegic, quadriplegic, muscular dys-trophy, Down's Syndrome, and have recently begun ses-sions with Hospice Program which deals with terminally ill individuals and their families and as a form of bereave-ment counselling for individuals who have had a difficult time coping with a loss.

> With all these sessions we have had degrees of positive-ness and, as Dr Smith is fond of putting it . . . the bottom line is that the individual will at LEAST have had a good time and that an occasional good time is lacking for these people.

Our next port of call on our journey south was the Dolphin Research Center at Grassy Key. Before our departure for the States I met Paula Barnett in York. She had worked as a volunteer trainer and had shown me the manual of instructions she had used during her stay at the Dolphin Research Center.

Quite by chance, Wendy and I arrived at a time when the centre was closed to the public because the day was allocated for the research of Dr David Nathanson, a psychologist from Miami. We watched as he conducted his unique clinic with a succession of individual patients, each suffering from a severe learning disability. He sat on a platform beside the dolphin pool with a trainer who was armed with a bucket of fish. Here he conducted what amounted to school lessons in the company of one or more dolphins anxiously awaiting a signal and then a reward. He gave his young pupil patients great encouragement to master what was asked of them and then warmly applauded the result if they were successful. It was a reward system. Towards the end of their sessions the patients went into the water with the dolphins and were given a tow. Sometimes they acted the role of trainer, giving hand signals to get the dolphins to perform their tricks.

One of the patients we watched was a delightful boy of nearly three years, with Down's Syndrome. The scars on his chest bore witness to the two open-heart surgery operations he had endured. David Nathanson was teaching him to speak using wooden picture boards which were tossed into the water, retrieved by a dolphin and shown to the boy by Dr Nathanson who also spent some of his time in the water. The semi-aquatic teacher told the boy the name of the object depicted and then asked his young pupil to repeat it. At the completion of the lesson the boy joined his mother in the water, and she supported him while they played together with the dolphins.

The trainers were dedicated to their work and obviously loved the dolphins, treating them like children. Their role was to direct them and reward them with fish and lots of vocal encouragement after they had responded correctly to the hand signals. For their part, the dolphins seemed to have no learning difficulties whatsoever. They performed their tricks with the energy, precision, speed and apparent enthusiasm of a platoon of soldiers competing to assemble a field gun in the shortest time, then hurtled back to the platform to claim their fish reward.

The Dolphin Research Center was situated beside a shallow lagoon, and the dolphins were confined in pens composed of open-link wire fences that were only slightly higher than the surface of the sea. I was told that although the dolphins could easily have jumped over them they seldom did, and always came back when offered food. They were highly trained and often used in films. When I left I had the uneasy feeling that the dolphins at the DRC were being exploited because they were so goodnatured. Furthermore, I was concerned that the success of Dr Nathanson's method might be used to justify training even more dolphins to do tricks in situations where they would not have the choice of a free life in the open sea.

With a ten-metre high concrete dolphin outside announcing its existence, there was no mistaking the location of the Dolphin Research Center. I deduced that mile marker 59 nearby indicated that a further 59 miles down the road would bring us to our next destination, Key West.

The following day, we left the stultifying heat of the land to sail over the sea with Ron Canning and his attractive girlfriend Melinda. There were four other visitors on board his catamaran *Patty C* and we were all there with one purpose — to meet and swim with dolphins not confined in any way. We sailed out to a shallow reef which Ron knew was frequented by a school of dolphins, and we spotted them just a few moments after we arrived on site. Ron had been trying to build up a friendly rapport with this school and immediately throttled back so that they could make contact with us — rather than we chase after them.

It was not long before I was in the water. Snorkelling down to the seabed I built a little underwater sandcastle to arouse the curiosity of the dolphins, which it did. As I held my breath and worked at my mini masterpiece, which I decorated with the empty tests of local sea urchins, called sand dollars, I saw the grey shapes of the dolphins looming in and out of the limited visibility of the milky water. As I expected, however, my building operations provided only a temporary diversion from the business they had in hand — which was that of an early lunch.

From the behaviour of the school, I could see that they were herding fish and then rushing in quickly to catch their snacks. Then we lost them. Being an ex-fisherman, Ron did what lots of fishermen do when wondering where to fish: he looked to the heavens. In the distance he could see some frigate birds dropping out of the sky and diving into the sea. So we cruised gently in their direction and, sure enough, we found a group of dolphins feeding on the same shoal of fish as the birds. Frigate birds are so called because of their piratical behaviour, sometimes harassing other seabirds until they disgorge the food they are carrying back to shore to feed their young. Ron told me he had seen frigates swoop down and take fish from dolphins.

One activity all the visitors on board enjoyed was being towed behind the boat on a line. The dolphins swam around, not making physical contact, but obviously appreciating the presence of the humans in the water as another diversion in their daily lives, which allowed plenty of time for play. Indeed, on the last contact we made, the dolphins were engaged in a very special type of play. Through my binoculars I saw a small group rolling over, their bodies flashing in the brilliant sunshine. A pale pink belly, with a red phallus extended, appeared briefly in my field of view as one of the dolphins rolled like a log on the flat-calm surface of the sea.

I had seen similar behaviour before amongst Humpback dolphins in the Indian Ocean, off Karachi in Pakistan. On that occasion the wise and gentle old fisherman who was my guide and had taken me out into the mangroves in his boat, told me I was very lucky because I had been privileged to be there during what he coyly described as a 'dolphin wedding' — a sight he himself had seldom seen. However, such was the uninhibited nature of the Bottlenose dolphins off the Florida Keys that their courtship play was something for everyone to see and enjoy. Tumbling through the water like a troup of strolling players in a carnival procession, they even came and frolicked with the people hanging on the tow line.

An ironic twist to this display of joy and friendship was that it took place near the US Naval Base, where humans were attempting to pervert the gentle and peaceful nature of dolphins in order to embroil them in the senseless conflict of war. Ron insisted that I should meet Ric O'Barry, the man who had trained Flipper for the famous TV series of the same name, which indeed I did just before we left Miami. At the airport Ric told me how he had been approached by the CIA to help train dolphins for warfare — an offer he had flatly refused. It was one of the factors that led him eventually to feel that the entire process of capturing dolphins, for any purpose whatsoever, was morally wrong. 'We are creating disposable dolphins for the amusement and defence of a disposable society,' was how he passionately expressed his new attitude. He openly voiced his view that putting dolphins to work in dolphinariums was ethically little different from Hitler putting Jews in concentration camps, and thought it possible that his open attacks on the US Navy and the CIA might lead to his own imprisonment.

Ron Canning, who had worked at the Dolphin Research Center, took a similar attitude towards the confinement of any cetaceans and was doing what he could to provide an alternative method to enable sensitive people to come close to dolphins. During our safari he immediately recognised many of the dolphins, most of whom he had names for. He was also slowly coming to identify their personalities and different behavioural traits. Taking out visitors to see the dolphins was his living, but his approach to the cetaceans was that of a polite visitor, which was a far cry from the gung-ho, go-out-there-and-make-it-all-happen attitude that seemed to dominate business attitudes on both sides of the Atlantic Ocean. Perhaps Ron had learnt something from the dolphins themselves.

Among those on board the *Patty C* was Carolyn Brooks-Kidd who lived in Key Largo and was one of the expanding groups of people who make a living from counselling. Carolyn used relaxation, meditation, breath control and visualisation of dolphins to help people overcome their psychological hang-ups. One of the premises of this therapy is that dolphins have very special, almost magical qualities which, when tuned into, can impart joy and peace to the human soul. She had conducted some of her sessions on board the *Patty C*. At first Ron, a pragmatic person with a no-nonsense attitude to life, had been very sceptical about the entire process; however, having become involved, he was beginning to succumb to the concept that when humans have reached a certain state of mind, dolphins may be able to play a significant role in helping them come to terms with stress and other psychological problems. Such an idea is not inconsistent with the legends of ancient Greece and some American Indian tribes, in which humans were transformed into dolphins by the gods, thus signifying the spiritual closeness of the two species.

Just how close — both spiritually and physically — a relationship between humans and dolphins could become, was vividly demonstrated to me a few days later, after Wendy and I landed on the island of Providenciales, in the Turks and Caicos Islands. I had never heard of Providenciales before, but the Turks and Caicos group stirred dusty images in the archives of my memory when, as a very young schoolboy, I had collected postage stamps. I recalled that Mozambique and the Turks and Caicos produced colourful stamps that caught my eye and my imagination far more than the penny black had ever done. However, before I departed from the Keys I found out that Providenciales was in the Windward Islands, about 575 miles south-east of Miami.

I later discovered that the Turks and Caicos Islands are still a British Protectorate, although you would never think so because of the strong American influence. The fact that you drive on the left-hand side of the road has nothing to do with Britain: the decision was made in 1962 when the only two vehicles on an adjacent island had a head-on collision. To avoid a similar fate befalling the two cars that had just arrived on Providenciales, the owners had to decide which way to pass one another. As the brakes on one of them pulled to the left, the commonsense judgement was made that it would be safer if both parties kept to the left-hand side of the road. Virtually all of the cars on the dusty island roads originate in the USA and therefore have left-hand drive; the ruling to drive on the left remains, however.

This delightful state of affairs is typical of the free-and-easy attitude that prevails on the island. When I first heard about it, it brought a flutter of hope to my heart that there are still a few oases left in the world where everyday life is not totally dominated by EEC-style regulations drafted by faceless bureaucrats.

Snippets of invaluable background information such as this I gathered before we arrived in Providenciales because, by one of those delightful quirks of fate that have ruled my life ever since I first encountered Donald, I met Chuck Hesse when I was checking in my Alamo hired car near Miami Airport. He was to be our host on Providenciales, but we had never met before. However, as one of my arms was longer than the other from the weight of films I was carrying, and Chuck was clutching a box containing a 16mm ciné projector, it was natural that we should gravitate towards one another. We reserved adjacent seats on the flight, and by the time we touched down I had a much better understanding of why Chuck Hesse, who headed an organisation called PRIDE (an acronym from Prevention of Reefs and Islands from Degration and Exploitation), was very keen for me to meet JoJo the dolphin, and a man named Dean Burnal.

Reports on the first appearance of the dolphin varied. According to Venetia Piper, JoJo first appeared in the company of two adults in 1983. The adults disappeared the following year and the young dolphin gradually built up a friendship with the swimmers outside the Island Princess Hotel and along the beach. When the Club Med opened a new hotel nearby there was an instant major increase in all forms of aquatic activity and JoJo started interacting with people on a much larger scale. With up to 600 visitors at any one time, most of whom came for beach-orientated sports, the dolphin had plenty of human playmates to choose from, but although he mingled freely with the visitors, he seemed to prefer the company of familiar friends. He was given several names, but the one that was eventually adopted most widely was JoJo — after one of the diving instructors at the Club Med.

Another instructor to whom the dolphin took a fancy was a young American, Dean Burnal. In 1988 Dean left Club Med to take the post of Marine Program Director with PRIDE. He was allocated an office in the geodesic, dome-shaped laboratory and administration centre at the world's first commercial conch farm, which was run by Chuck Hesse and situated on the beach in the heart of JoJo's territory. The conch (pronounced conk) is a giant sea snail that is eaten throughout the Caribbean and in Florida but is declining at an alarming rate through overfishing. Although Dean was employed on a pittance by PRIDE to help conserve the conch, his primary task was to extend his relationship with JoJo and do what he could to ensure the dolphin's future health and safety. To this end he was utterly dedicated, and financed his own trips to visit as many dolphin experts in the United States as he could afford.

Dean frequently went out to swim with JoJo, and only a few weeks before our arrival had used the increasingly close relationship that was developing between them to good effect, when JoJo had become very listless and shunned human contact. The dolphin's activities and state of health were of interest to everyone, including the children of all the islands, who had adopted him as a special pet. As a result, Dean wrote regular reports on JoJo for the Turks and Caicos newspaper, *The Islands' Sun Times*. In successive articles he told of his growing concern for the dolphin following the discovery of several severe abscesses. After consulting an expert in Miami Dean decided, with the aid of the local veterinary surgeon, Mark Woodring, to attempt to dose JoJo with antibiotics. It was feared that darting or injecting the dolphin would make him very wary of further human contact, so they thought they would try to feed him with an octopus loaded with antibiotics, which JoJo would find for himself.

On Wednesday, 19th April, Dean snorkelled down fifteen feet and planted his eight-legged pill package under the sand. He then signalled to JoJo to find it. The dolphin obliged immediately, shoving his beak into the sand and eventually pulling the octopus free. He then waved it around in triumph, showed no desire whatsoever to consume it, and promptly presented it to Dean. Several more attempts ended in the same game. It was back to the drawing board. Fortunately their relationship had reached the stage where Dean could open the dolphin's mouth and rub his tongue. He decided therefore to attempt to put the tablets directly into the dolphin's stomach by hand, a method which had been used with captive dolphins accustomed to taking dead fish, but was unheard of with a wild dolphin in the open sea.

At 9.00 am the next day Dean, using his own special calling device, summoned JoJo. When the dolphin arrived the young man kept saying in his mind, 'JoJo, you have to trust me on this one, and please forgive me.' Slowly he prised open the dolphin's mouth, hesitated for a split second, and then shoved his entire forearm down the dolphin's throat. The first dose of antibiotics was in. Not surprisingly, however, JoJo was not amused. He squeaked and squealed and shook his head and body, signifying to Dean that he had taken the bonds of friendship too far. He then appeared to forget all about it, at least until the afternoon, when Dean succeeded in repeating the dose. By the time the dolphin received his final dose, on the Saturday afternoon, administration had become distinctly difficult. Nonetheless, Dean succeeded, and by the following day JoJo was already looking and acting much better. The last dose was given exactly four weeks prior to my arrival. Long before we touched down, I was excitedly looking forward to meeting Dean and his aquatic buddy, JoJo the dolphin.

I met Dean shortly after my arrival but had to wait until the following day to meet JoJo. Both of them more than lived up to the not inconsiderable build-up they had been given by Chuck Hesse. Dean was bronzed, charming and, even to my heterosexual eyes, good-looking. My wife Wendy who, I might add, had produced our son, Ashley, who was a few years older than Dean, pronounced the young American 'devastatingly handsome'. However, eavesdropping on a conversation she was having with our daughter Melanie after we returned home, I had to elevate him a notch. He was up there alongside Robert Redford and made her 'feel all wobbly at the knees'!

From long experience with dolphins, I knew that JoJo would not be impressed in the slightest by the diving instructor's appearance: it was what was inside that mattered. When I left the island three days later I had absolutely no doubt in my mind that it was Dean's ultrasensitivity to the dolphin's needs, not his good looks, that had won JoJo's heart. It also reinforced my view that it was sensitivity, not sex, which had motivated the very special relationships Maura and Tricia had had with the male dolphins Donald and Percy respectively.

As for JoJo himself, he was one of several sub-species of Atlantic Bottlenose dolphins (*Tursiops truncatus*). Just as the various races of humans have different physical characteristics, ranging in Africa alone from tiny pygmies to the extremely tall Masai, so JoJo was distinctly different from Donald. The main difference was size, JoJo being approximately six feet (1.8 metres) in length compared with Donald's 12 feet (3.6 metres). His environment was different, too. JoJo's home was in the warm, clear, shallow waters of a tropical lagoon fringed by a reef, beyond which the sea immediately plummeted to immense depths — far in excess of those of the European Continental Shelf where Donald spent his time.

I only had two sessions with JoJo, but the quality of those encounters provided ample time for me to assess his personality and the strength of his relationship with Dean. The first meeting, by way of introduction, took place on Sunday, 21st May. With Andrew Dalton, the marine biologist from the Conch Farm, at the controls of a Boston Whaler, we skimmed out across the lagoon to one of JoJo's favourite feeding grounds.

Maura and I had used a tin of stones which we rattled underwater when we wanted to call up Donald. It was our signature tune. Dean, who knew nothing about this, had developed his own simple calling device which, judging by the speed with which JoJo appeared on the scene, was equally effective. I didn't get into the water immediately as I wanted to observe JoJo and Dean from the surface before interrupting their reunion, which was obviously a joyful event for both of them. I could see that there was a lot of physical contact, and several times Dean hurtled away from us, being towed along by the dolphin. Dean was very strongly built, broad shouldered, extremely fit and thoroughly at home in the sea — a young merman with whom the dolphin could engage in rough games with impunity, should they both decide to play underwater rugby.

But watching from the surface only gave a small part of the picture. It was not until I slipped over the side with my camera that I was fully able to appreciate what was going on in conditions absolutely perfect for photography. JoJo took little notice of me until Dean grasped me round the waist from behind. He then confronted JoJo with me, holding me like a shield between himself and the dolphin who was facing us. Dean made some hand signals which, combined with a hug, was his method of formally introducing people to JoJo. The dolphin wagged his head in acknowledgement and approval. We were friends.

No introductions were needed when Andy joined us in the water. JoJo obviously enjoyed the company of the young English biologist, who frequently snorkelled down to the seabed foraging for samples of marine life that might prove interesting to himself and JoJo. Dean and Andy were hoping to progress to the stage where the dolphin would search for specimens and bring them to the biologist. They were already making good progress in this direction. Dean told me the story of how he had planted a live lobster on the reef and sometime later signalled with a special hand signal to JoJo to go and fetch it. A visiting snorkeller happened to be passing as the dolphin returned with the flapping lobster between his teeth. When JoJo swam up to Dean and presented him with his prize the snorkeller gaped in amazement. They would never believe this story back in the Bronx.

Wendy and I were installed at the Island Princess Hotel, where we had a comfortable room with a balcony overlooking a beach of dazzling white coral sand, and the turquoise sea beyond. When we awoke next morning, a smart sailing catamaran named *Beluga* (which is a type of dolphin found in Arctic waters) was moored outside. Its owner and skipper, a Canadian engineer-cum-boat designer Tim Ainley, offered his vessel as a floating base for my next meeting with JoJo — assuming of course that the dolphin wanted to see me again. Tim and I had plenty in common — for instance we both knew the designer of his catamaran, James Wharram. James and I had had many dolphin adventures together, and I knew that dolphins liked frolicking with sailing catamarans; I could see no reason why JoJo should not do likewise.

After breakfast Tim sailed his boat up to the beach where it was quickly loaded with food, drink and a collection of guests. A few moments later we had backed off and set sail, propelled by warm trade winds. The dolphin joined us exactly where Dean predicted he would. We threw one of the guests, Beryl (pronounced Burl), over the side as human bait and towed him behind the boat at the end of the line. JoJo enjoyed the company of the man whizzing through the water, and at times the two of them dived and rose again in unison.

When we stopped and anchored, everyone jumped into the sea, including a young girl who had been clambering about the rigging like a monkey. She was one of the first to swim with the dolphin and was totally blasé about doing so. She was just as active in the sea as she was on board and performed somersaults in the water for her own amusement. She wiggled all over the place, like a supercharged tadpole, and not surprisingly engaged the attention of the dolphin much more than I, who must have appeared by comparison more like a geriatric frog. Even so, all members of the party enjoyed swimming and diving with the dolphin who showed no signs of wanting to move away from us while we were in the water. Indeed, JoJo was obviously so attached to Dean that I would have been surprised if he had swum away.

After a couple of hours we all climbed back on board for a rest, and when we felt like going back in again the dolphin had disappeared. We had a debate about going to find him, especially as I was keen to take more pictures, but Dean, ever concerned about the needs of the dolphin, said he thought JoJo would be feeding and that we should not disturb him. Despite the fact that we all knew Dean could distract the dolphin and entice him to play with us again, we deferred to his judgement and set sail for home. The following day Wendy and I returned to Miami and the next day completed our dolphin odyssey by flying back to Britain.

Nearly fifteen years had elapsed since that fateful day in August 1974 when we had sailed to the Isle of Man and I had had my first encounter with Donald. From that moment on, my life seemed to have been touched by magic. I had explored parts of the world I never thought I would see — even in my wildest dreams. I had written numerous books. I had gone into partnership, founded a film company, and had my own series of underwater films on television. It naturally included a film on dolphins.

Although I had been working in industry for 25 years before I met Donald, when I did so I felt as excited as if I had just left school and was starting my working life all over again. After meeting JoJo, I felt not that I was just about to make another new start, but that the whole world was hovering on the threshold of an exciting revelation. In the waters off the Caribbean Island of Providenciales, a quantum leap forward was being made in the *partnership* between man and dolphin. A marriage of minds was taking place.

No one can say what the outcome will be. The prospect of the two most complex brains on this planet coming together harmoniously, each accepting and respecting the needs of the other, neither seeking to dominate the other, in an environment that, like space, has no geographical boundaries, is the stuff of science fiction. But so was flying to the moon when I was a boy.